D1046975

THE WALL STREET JOURNAL.
GUIDE TO WINE

THE WALL STREET JOURNAL.
GUIDE TO WINE

DOROTHY J.
GAITER

JOHN
BRECHER

Broadway Books • New York

BROADWAY

THE WALL STREET JOURNAL GUIDE TO WINE. Copyright © 1999 by
Dorothy J. Gaiter and John Brecher. All rights reserved. Printed in the
United States of America. No part of this book may be reproduced or transmitted
in any form or by any means, electronic or mechanical, including photocopying,
recording, or by any information storage and retrieval system, without written
permission from the publisher. For information, address Broadway Books, a division of
Random House, Inc., 1540 Broadway, New York, NY 10036.

Broadway Books titles may be purchased for business or promotional use or for
special sales. For information, please write to: Special Markets Department,
Random House, Inc., 1540 Broadway, New York, NY 10036.

BROADWAY BOOKS and its logo, a letter B bisected on the diagonal,
are trademarks of Broadway Books, a division of Random House, Inc.

THE WALL STREET JOURNAL® is a trademark and service mark of
Dow Jones & Company, Inc.

Library of Congress Cataloging-in-Publication Data
Gaiter, Dorothy J.
    The Wall Street Journal guide to wine / Dorothy J. Gaiter
and John Brecher.
      p. cm.
    ISBN 0-7679-0389-7 (hc)
    1. Wine and winemaking.   I. Brecher, John.   II. Title.
TP548.G175 1999
641.2′2—dc21   99-26470
                                         CIP

FIRST EDITION

Designed by Fearn Cutler de Vicq

00 01 02 03 10 9 8 7 6 5 4

To Media and Zoë

CONTENTS

DESSERT WINE

INTRODUCTION

We met and fell in love on June 4, 1973, the day both of us began working as reporters at the *Miami Herald*. We had both just finished college—Dorothy at the University of Missouri, John at Columbia—and we were both twenty-one years old. We fell in love with wine soon after that. Neither of us grew up in families where wine was served at meals, so we started at the bottom, learning by drinking inexpensive wine and reading books. In the late 1970s, we began taking notes on our wines and saving labels, just so we could relive some of our experiences ("Oh, yeah, remember *that* Chardonnay?").

Wine, for us, has never been an end in itself. It is just one part of a good life. We remember good times—and bad—through the wines we were sharing at the time. Ask us about almost any moment in our lives—even just a restaurant meal—and we'll tell you how the wine was. We have been through twenty years of marriage, several jobs, two children, and one near-death experience together, and wine has always been part of it.

We had never written about wine, nor intended to, until early 1998, when the *Wall Street Journal* began its Weekend edition, which is published as part of the newspaper every Friday. John is the Page One editor of the *Wall Street Journal*, and Dorothy is a national reporter covering issues of race. Because the Weekend section's editor, Joanne Lipman, knew of our interest in wine, she asked us to write a weekly column called "Tastings." The column, we're happy to report, was an immediate success. We have received hundreds of warm, delightful, and instructive letters from readers all over the country. Wine merchants everywhere report that customers—many of them new customers—rush in to buy our recommendations every Friday morning. Most important to us, many people tell us they're enjoying wine more because our column helps make it more approachable.

This book is an outgrowth of those columns, and borrows liberally from them. In this book, as in our column, we aren't writing for aficionados. Although we hope aficionados enjoy our writing, there are many excellent books and magazines for them on the market. We're also not writing a book for dummies, because we don't believe anyone who wants to know more about wine is a dummy. Instead, we're writing for a frustrated majority: people who can afford more and better wine, who want to know more about wine, but who don't know where to begin.

Too often, those people are told they have to become wine experts before they can appreciate wine. We think that's backwards: We want you to enjoy wine, which might then prompt you to learn more about it. Our purpose is not to "educate" you, but rather to make you more interested in wine by sharing our passion. As your interest grows, you can read other books, some of which are listed on pages 275 to 278 and mentioned throughout this book. More important, you can educate yourself by trying new wines. That, in the end, is the only way you'll truly learn anything really worth knowing about wine.

We don't pretend to be experts. Sure, we know more about wine than most people, but we don't know nearly as much as some others. Wine, to us, is one of those things that the more you know, the more you realize you don't know. After all, there are thousands of different wines; new wineries, and promising new wine regions, appear all the time; there's a whole new vintage every year; and, most daunting, every wine from every previous vintage changes over the years. The fun isn't mastering all that—it's simply trying to keep up.

We consider ourselves to be on a lifelong journey of discovery about wine. What that means is we're not very different from you. We may be a few steps ahead of you, but there are so many miles to go on this journey that we have far to travel together. We're not explaining wine to you from the mountaintop. Instead, we're still on a trek toward that peak of wine knowledge. We'd like you to join us.

How to Use This Book

This book isn't a comprehensive look at the wine world. Instead, we've focused on thirty kinds of wine we like and think you'd like. We've also added additional information on topics such as chilling wine, choosing a wine store, and how to order wine in a restaurant, so you can enjoy the wines you choose even more.

At the end of each chapter, there are notes about the wines that emerged as winners from our blind tastings. We've rated the wines on a scale that, from worst to best, goes like this: Yech, OK, Good, Very Good, Delicious, and the rare Delicious! This has been our personal scorekeeping system since we began taking notes a quarter-century ago. This is just a guide. Don't get obsessed with these specific wines. We list them only to give you a point of reference—a kind of road map of what this particular type of wine should taste like.

In any event, several factors will conspire against your finding any specific wine. Most very good wines aren't made in huge quantities, they don't often stay in stores for very long, and wine distribution is so screwy that it's hard to say what wines are available in any state. Instead, focus on more general advice: For instance, we think Merlot around $20 is much better than Merlot that costs just a few dollars less; we think Muscadet and Beaujolais are two of the world's great wine bargains; and we think—and we were surprised to find this—that it's hard to go wrong with American Pinot Noir.

In the Wine Notes, we try to give some general guidance about wineries and shippers. For instance, you might not be able to find the Saintsbury Pinot Noir in the vintage we recommend, but Saintsbury is a reliable name in Pinot Noir, and you should look for that label in a different vintage. We don't even try to find the "best" of all the wines—there are far too many wines out there, from too many years, stored under too many different conditions, to ever declare a "best." Instead, we've listed a few wines that we enjoyed in our tastings, with descriptions that will give you an idea of why we liked these best among the many we tried. By imagining how these wines tasted, you can then get some idea of how this kind of wine should taste at its best.

The prices quoted in the Wine Notes are meant as a very general guide. This is what we paid in wineshops, usually in New York, Los Angeles, or Chicago, in some cases in early 1998. Prices fluctuate wildly all over the country. But if we say that one wine costs $7 and another costs $40, at least you will have a general idea what kind of money we're talking about.

We believe in value, but we believe value and price are very different. Some very expensive wines are great values, and some cheap wines are terrible values. That philosophy infuses this book. More broadly, our philosophy is that we cherish our independence. Almost all of the experiences recounted in this book occurred long before we were wine writers, so we received no special treatment. Nor do we want any now. We do not accept any free wine, free lunches, or free trips; we do not meet privately with winemakers when they visit New York; and we do not attend events that are not open to the public. Our wine is bought under the same circumstances in which you would buy it—at retail stores, except where noted otherwise. It's paid for either by us or by our employer, the *Wall Street Journal*. We do this because we believe the playing field should be level, and because we believe wines should speak for themselves.

That's not to say we are objective. We don't believe there is anything objective about wine. It's simply impossible, as we say again and again in this book, to separate the taste of a wine from the experience you're having when you drink it. The same exact wine will taste different depending on whether you're having it with the boss at lunch or with a loved one on a terrace overlooking a pond at sunset. It's pointless—and contrary to our whole approach to wine—to pretend otherwise. In other words, we don't believe in dogma. There is no right and no wrong in wine. If anyone disagrees with any of our conclusions, that's fine with us. Can you imagine anything more fun to debate than wine?

In short, wine is supposed to be fun. That's how to use this book: to have fun.

WHITE
WINE

CHARDONNAY
Forget the Conventional Wisdom

HOW POPULAR IS CHARDONNAY? Popular enough to have sparked a backlash, like the ABC Club—Anything But Chardonnay. Some folks think American Chardonnays are too big, too heavy, and too oaky. Well, maybe that's true, sometimes. But for the kind of white wine that makes you want to kneel and give thanks, you've got to turn to Chardonnay. It's the greatest white wine grape in the world, the grape of the famous Montrachet from France, as well as the suddenly hot Kistler Chardonnay from California. Of course, it's possible some meathead could ruin a good grape, but we—and, we'd wager, most wine lovers—have had more great wines made from Chardonnay than any other type of white grape.

With great wines, of course, come great experiences.

Back in 1980, there was a restaurant in New York's Greenwich Village called the Coach House that was famous for its black bean soup and corn bread. We walked down there from Gramercy Park on a mild June day to celebrate Dottie's being hired by the *New York Times*. We sat down and looked at the wine list. The people next to us were having something we'd never seen, a 1978 Chardonnay from Robert Keenan Winery in California, which wasn't on the list. So when our waiter came by, we asked if we could have a bottle of that. He squinted at us, hurried away—and came back with a bottle (for $18).

Here are our notes: "Spectacular! Huge! Much oak, obviously late-picked. Much character, complexity, even a hint of Riesling. Yet great butteriness combined with oak and bigness. Very wonderful."

We lost track of Robert Keenan Winery after that. It wasn't big or very famous. But more than a decade later, we came across Keenan again while eating lunch at another restaurant not far from the then-shuttered Coach House. This restaurant was called Capsouto Frères, and on its wine list was a Robert Keenan Cabernet Franc. Now everywhere you look you see "Cab Francs," but back then we knew it mostly as a blending grape. The Keenan was the first "varietal" Cabernet Franc we'd seen. It was excellent—so excellent, in fact, that when John returned to the office, still euphoric, he called Robert Keenan Winery to enthuse. The guy who answered the phone turned out to be the winemaker, who promised to send a catalogue so we could place an order. He did, we did—and we enclosed a note telling him about that fabulous Chardonnay at the Coach House.

Two weeks later, our order arrived—along with a gift bottle. It was the 1978 Chardonnay, the very same one we'd had at the Coach House. On it, in golden pen, was written: "Here's to the Memories. Robert Keenan."

We have had great Chardonnays from Idaho (Ste. Chapelle), Washington State (Chateau Ste. Michelle), and, of course, from all over California. What does a classic California Chardonnay taste like? It's big, rich, ripe, and buttery. It's mouthfilling, so you have to take small sips. It has a little bit of toastiness, vanilla, and some cream—those come from the wood—and it's almost chewy. Sometimes your nose can pick up hints of fruit—grapefruit or pineapple. The very best Chardonnays have all of this power going on in your mouth. But when you swallow, something miraculous happens. The "finish" is a clean, light one that lingers for several minutes, like the essence of plump, sweet grapes.

Now *that* is Chardonnay. Or at least that's the Chardonnay we grew up with in the '70s, and we make no apologies for being partial to it. If you don't like that style, which we call "big-ass Chardonnay" when the kids aren't listening, fine. If what you want is a more restrained Chardonnay style, buy a white Burgundy (see page 47). If you really want a crisp, great-with-food Chardonnay, buy a Chablis (see page 42). But unfortunately—for us, at least—starting in the '80s, critics began hammering American winemakers about their big, oaky Chardonnay. Ever sensitive to the market, some winemakers began to rein them in. Pretty soon, American winemakers were boasting about their "French-style" Chardonnay, meaning the wine had more restraint, a bit more lemon-acid taste, and less obvious flavors of wood. And to tell you the truth, we have to admit, sometimes those can be great, too.

When people talk about wood or oak, they're talking about barrels. Some wines, especially white wines meant to be fresh and fruity, never see the inside of a barrel. They're crisp, fragrant, and delightful. But most Chardonnay, like most good red wine, spends some time in oak barrels. Whether the wine is fermented in oak or just aged in oak matters. How long it's in oak matters. The size of the barrels matters. And so does the kind of oak itself. American oak imparts more dramatic flavors than French oak. New oak has more power than old oak, whose flavors have been depleted over the years and are mellower. "High-fire" barrels, which have been subject to more fire or charring in the barrel-making process, have more vanilla, toast, and caramel tastes than "low-fire" barrels. A winemaker once took us into his cellar and siphoned off two samples of a red wine, one from a new barrel and one from an old one. It was the same exact wine, but we never would have guessed it. While neither was ready to be bottled and sold, the wine from the older barrel was calmer, softer, while the wine from the newer barrel tasted so young and aggressive it was hard to swallow. Wood matters.

How much wood a wine gets—more generally, how a good wine is made—is a reflection of the character and vision of the winemaker. There's a lot of magic in the process, but there's a lot of method, too. Consider the winemaking notes about the 1997 Napa Valley Private Reserve Chardonnay made by Ed Sbragia, winemaker at Beringer Vineyards: "All of the juice went into small French Nevers oak barrels, most of them new, custom-toasted to caramelize the neutral sugars in the wood and contribute a sweet vanilla note to the wine. The wines were fermented and aged in these barrels, and the lees [spent yeast cells] were hand stirred back into the wine every week for about six months....We also put the wines through 100-percent malolactic fermentation to further enhance their dense, creamy mouthfeel. The wines were aged in barrels for over nine months before we made the final assemblage."

You don't need to understand all of that rigmarole. The point is simply that winemaking is an art, and a highly personal one at that. But you know what? In the long run, nothing matters more than the fruit. As Page One editor of the *Wall Street Journal,* John tells reporters: "No matter how good a writer you are, your story won't be great if you don't have great reporting"—the raw data, the facts that go into a story. It's the same way with wine: It all starts with the fruit. Even a great winemaker can't make great wine from so-so fruit. California produces great Chardonnay fruit—big, plump, and rich. Fruit that can stand up to, and even benefit from, some oak. But at the same time, big fruit and big oak can sometimes be too much. This is why California Chardonnay has gone back and forth over the years from big to restrained to uncertain—and why we have notes like this, about a Long Vineyards 1992 we drank on Christmas Day, 1994: "Delicious! A real WOW wine. Huge, oaky, chewy, and almost red in its intensity. Lots of oak and spice, with massive, vanilla-bean overtones. Long, overwhelming finish. Not at all '90s, but very much a '70s Chardonnay. Mouthcoating, warming, and rich."

So, how are Chardonnays now? We conducted two tastings to find out—one of Chardonnays under $20, and one of the high-priced stuff.

We tasted the inexpensive wines first. Quite a few of them were simple and inelegant, the kind of might-as-well-be-water stuff that too many people get at bars when they say, "I'd like a glass of Chardonnay, please." Think lemon water.

But there were many we really liked. We had never had a Sonoma-Loeb before, and this 1995 at $19.99 was a real California-style Chardonnay: bold, rich, round, powerful. In fact, even *we* found it just a bit too heavily "oaked." Whoa! Still, it was a fun, dramatic wine. The Byron 1996 ($15.99) also impressed us. This is a consistently fine label, and this offering was beautifully made, showing great restraint with plenty of fruit. A good food wine, this is what people are talking about when they discuss French-style California Chardonnay.

Nos. 2 and 3 were a toss-up, but the prices varied hugely. Both the Zaca Mesa 1996 and the Hahn Estates 1995 were remarkably good—plump, rich, mouthfilling—and easily $35 to $40 values. The Zaca Mesa was $15.99 and the Hahn, at $9.49, was the best value of the tasting. Like many good Chardonnays, it smelled and tasted of vanilla and nutmeg on a bed of rich, ripe fruit.

The best of the tasting was a monster of a wine. This wine was chewy, rich, complex, with the kind of finish that lingers in your mouth. It was risky: big at the front, crisp and clean at the end. As we said, without that restraint on the finish, a wine like this can be overly plump. Think of steak: A good bit of marbling makes a steak great; too much marbling and you just have a fatty steak. It's the same with wine.

This wine walked the line perfectly—and when we took it out of the bag, we laughed. It was from an old favorite, Estancia Estates, in this case the Private Reserve 1995. It sells for $19.99, but we feel it's worth more. Estancia's less expensive Chardonnay was our house white for years.

So the results of our first tasting weren't that surprising. The second tasting was another matter.

It's impossible to know why one winery suddenly gets "hot," but there's no question that Kistler Vineyards of California is hot. It's relatively new—founded in 1978—and for a time was simply one of many fine California wineries. Our first Kistler Chardonnay was a 1980 (Sonoma-Cutrer Vineyard—ABC Farms) that we bought for $18.75 in 1981 and drank in Central Park during a night of free opera in 1983. "Delicious," we wrote, "but shocking in its bigness. Massive and oaky, with a long, oak finish. Powerful, chewy, and very American." As years passed, Kistler became less of a wine than a phenomenon. People seemed to be willing to do just about anything to get it. And we wondered: Could this wine possibly be worth the trouble?

So this is what we did: We found three different Kistlers (Sonoma Coast '96, for $45; Durell '95, for $62; and McCrea '95, for $62). Then we bought a whole bunch more of America's best Chardonnays. During our blind tasting, this was clear right away: There's a reason some Chardonnays cost a lot of money. There's a combination of ripe fruit, elegant tastes, and self-confident winemaking that gives a great Chardonnay special character—serious and approachable at the same time. But when we ripped off the bags, unfortunately and surprisingly, none of the Kistlers were in our top ranks. We were shocked. What had made the cut?

The No. 4 wine was an old standard: the Beringer Private Reserve 1996. We also tasted the '95, which followed it in our rankings. Both cost $29. Beringer produces outstanding Chardonnays in surprisingly large quantities, and has become justly well known for this wine.

No. 3 also was familiar: a Silverado Reserve '95 ($39.95). We've always liked Silverado's wines, and we thought this one was classy, with huge amounts of lemon and cream. (If you ever find yourself at a Disney resort looking for a good wine, you can always find Silverado—it's owned by Walt Disney's family.)

The runner-up wine was big and rich, with lots of nutmeg and oak. It tasted really expensive, but it wasn't. We're always looking for something new. As we were stocking up for this tasting, we ran across something we'd never even heard of: Pezzi King 1995 Chardonnay from California, at $22 a bottle. It seemed a bit downscale for this tasting, and as a newcomer, we didn't expect much from it. So we were amazed this turned out to be the clear choice as the No. 2 best wine.

But we were even more amazed by No. 1. "Classy and elegant," we wrote. "Muscular and lean. Big, yet with real restraint." Among cases of wines that were expensive and hard to find, this turned out to be Sonoma-Cutrer Russian River Ranches 1995, which cost $23. This is why Sonoma-Cutrer is perennially one of the most popular wines ordered at restaurants. They need a few years, though, before they're ready, so keep that in mind when buying them.

On the whole, it was clear that the expensive Chardonnays had more depth, more fruit, and more class than the less expensive wines. But it was also clear that, at any price range, there's no reason to settle for so-so Chardonnay.

Wine Notes

Wines made from the Chardonnay grape are the standard by which white wines are judged, and that's not going to change, regardless of the current debate about "over-oaked" American Chardonnay. There are a lot of so-so Chardonnays under $20, so be careful. Big, rich California Chardonnays should be served at room temperature or, at most, lightly chilled in the refrigerator for a half-hour. A good Chardonnay shouldn't be just an OK beverage to have in your glass. If it doesn't insist you pay attention to it, you're drinking the wrong Chardonnay, at any price.

Under $20

Estancia Estates Private Reserve 1995   **$19.99**
VERY GOOD/DELICIOUS • *Best of tasting. Huge and ripe, with cream and lemon and a loooong, burnt-wood finish. Big, yet with some restraint. A bit risky. This wine demands attention.*

Hahn Estates 1995   **$9.49**
VERY GOOD/DELICIOUS • *Best value. Big, plump, and rich, with lots of nutmeg on the nose and in the mouth. Powerful and yummy, with a chewy, vanilla finish.*

Zaca Mesa Winery 1996 (Zaca Vineyards) $15.99

VERY GOOD/DELICIOUS • *Flinty and "sour" like Chablis. Lots of lemon, wood, and care, with a nice complexity of tastes.*

Sonoma-Loeb Wines 1995 $19.99

VERY GOOD • *Hold on to your hat! Massive oak-vanilla flavors, rich, a major mouthful of wine with a finish that lasts forever.*

Meridian Cellars 1996 $9.99

VERY GOOD • *Proof that a California Chardonnay doesn't have to be big or expensive to be a winner. Lovely nose, lovely taste, and just enough "sweet" fruit. Totally winning. Have it with dinner tonight.*

Byron Vineyard & Winery 1996 $15.99

VERY GOOD • *Flinty, classy, and restrained. This is what a good "French-style" American Chardonnay tastes like.*

Over $20

Sonoma-Cutrer Russian River Ranches 1995 $23.00

DELICIOUS • *Best of tasting. Classy and elegant. Not creamy, but instead muscular and lean. Big, yet with real restraint. The art of wine-making.*

Pezzi King Vineyards 1995 $22.00

DELICIOUS • *Best value. Big and chewy, with seductive smoky flavors. Tastes expensive, with a long, languorous, nutmeg finish.*

Silverado Vineyards Limited Reserve 1995 $39.95

VERY GOOD/DELICIOUS • *Another winner from a reliable winery. Lemon, cream, and class.*

Beringer Vineyards Private Reserve 1996 $29.00

VERY GOOD/DELICIOUS • *Loads of oak, butter, and nutmeg create a big wow in the mouth, but the finish is clean and cleansing.*

Beringer Vineyards Private Reserve 1995 $29.00

VERY GOOD • *Lots of taste and beautifully made, but the fruit just isn't quite ripe enough.*

To Chill or Not to Chill
Serving Wine at the Right Temperature

Sometimes Pinot Noir, a red wine, should be served slightly chilled. Sometimes Chardonnay, a white wine, should be served at room temperature. Shocked? We would have been, until an experience in 1981 challenged our beliefs about wine and temperatures and changed our wine lives.

We were at an excellent but claustrophobic wine store in Manhattan called Crossroads and a young salesman there told us we just *had* to buy a California Chardonnay called Bacigalupi, from the 1979 vintage. "Drink it at room temperature!" he gushed. "It's incredible!" We were doubtful, but we took it home, let it sit for a couple of weeks, and then, skeptically, opened it at room temperature. Our notes: "Delicious! Looks like Champagne, not golden like a Chardonnay. Buttery, woody nose. Big, citrusy taste up front, very peppery, but a big, smooth-as-butter finish. Thick and incredibly long-lasting. Amazing combination of tastes and qualities. ROOM TEMPERATURE. Absolutely luscious, big and fruity and plump. Huge finish."

Since then, we have found that big, rich California Chardonnays are almost always better at room temperature. These wines are meant to be bold. They're *American*, and their big flavors and verve are part of their charm. Chilling constricts those tastes, shuts them down tightly. Heat pumps them up, makes them effusive. Think aromatherapy. Think what happens when a woman applies perfume to pulse points—the throat, the wrists, behind the knees. Those places warm the perfume, releasing the fragrance that then envelops her in a cloud of sensuous scent.

On the other hand, some lighter reds are better when they are lightly chilled because the tastes are so wild and diffuse that some cool air focuses the flavors. Think here of a lovely tree whose symmetry is marred by errant limbs. Pruning those suckers enhances the tree's structure, allowing the tree to flourish. Wine that is too cold is like a denuded tree, the nightmarish handiwork of a tree surgeon on speed. Its lovely branches, and the flights of fancy they might inspire, are gone. Beaujolais, and especially Beaujolais Nouveau, is the classic must-chill red wine. But we've recently tasted several lighter Zinfandels and Pinot Noirs in which the tastes are so fresh, fruity, and diffuse that you can almost feel the wine bouncing around in your mouth. These wines would be more focused, and just plain more drinkable, if they were a bit colder.

How can you tell? Trust yourself. If you taste a wine and you're just not getting a lot of flavor out of it, it might be too cold; let it warm up and see what happens. But if you taste a wine, either red or white, and its flavors seem to be all over the map, try chilling it a bit. In fact, sometimes you'll taste a red wine and you'll think to yourself, "This tastes hot," even though you know it's not. Don't think of "hot" as just a temperature, think of it also as a taste. If you're tasting "hot," chill the bottle.

More generally, think of "cold" as pulling tastes together and "warmth" as letting tastes burst out. There's a big difference between "chilled" and "cold." If you can't even hold the bowl of a wineglass for more than a few seconds because the cold hurts your hand, that's too cold. If a wine tastes like ice going down your throat, it's too cold. A chilled wine should be refreshing, not numbing.

Even so, don't worry about overchilling wine in the refrigerator. There's no reason you can't put a bottle of, say, Sauvignon Blanc in the refrigerator today to drink sometime this week. If you take it out and it's too cold, you can always just leave it on the table and let it warm up. That's not a bad idea anyway, since it will show you how the wine tastes at various temperatures. That Sauvignon Blanc, for instance, might not be *better* warmer, but it definitely will be *different*.

Don't worry about underchilling wine, either, because that's easy enough to fix, too. Don't put the wine in the freezer. It's too easy to forget it's there. There's nothing quite so awful as suddenly leaping up and saying, "Oh my God! The wine!" and then find-ing it frozen, the cork pushed out by the icy juice (as you can tell, we've done this more than once. "I won't forget it," John always promises—before he does). And don't just drop the wine into a bucket of ice—that'll take forever to chill. Instead, fill a bucket with ice, add cold water, then the bottle. This will chill your bot-tle in ten minutes. With the ice bucket around, you can pop the bottle into and out of the cold water, experimenting with the dif-ferent tastes and temperatures.

One other thing: Restaurants almost always serve white wines too cold. They pour you a glass of wine you can barely taste because it's almost frozen, and then they drop the bottle into an ice bucket to make it *even colder.* This is usually a major tragedy, especially considering how much extra you pay for wine in a restaurant. We suspect restaurants do this because some diners insist on all of the trappings associated with wine drinking—you know, the whole show.

But just try this: After the waiter has poured you the first glass and you've told him you like it, just say, "But you know what? It's cold enough. Can you just leave it on the table, please?" This has two advantages. The first is that the wine will warm up and taste better. The other is that, when you're ready for another glass, if you're not in a place that's too precious, you can just pour it your-self, making your wine the simple drink-with-a-meal beverage it was always meant to be.

Here's a simple, and very rough, guide to serving tempera-tures:

~ Big white wines, such as California Chardonnays: Room tem-perature. ("Room temperature" really means "cellar tempera-ture," which is something around 55 degrees—cooler than most people keep their homes. Don't get hung up on this, but if it feels warm in your house, you might want to chill even a fine Bordeaux in the refrigerator for a few minutes just to get it down to "room temperature.")

~ Crisp whites, such as Pinot Grigio, Muscadet, Sauvignon Blanc, and Chenin Blanc, as well as Champagne: Well chilled. ("Well chilled" means cold. Leave it in the refrigerator for several hours, or in an ice bucket with water for at least a half hour.)

~ Good white Burgundies: Lightly chilled. ("Lightly chilled" means about a half hour in the refrigerator. Try to keep lightly chilled wines out of ice water, because they can quickly get too cold, but leaving them sitting on a little ice to keep them cool is fine.) Why are California Chardonnays better at room temperature but good Burgundies, which are also made from the Chardonnay grape, better cooler? To us, that's one of those marvelous mysteries of wine.

~ Big red wines, such as Rhône, Cabernet Sauvignon, and heavy Zinfandel: Room temperature.

~ Lighter red wines, such as Beaujolais, lighter Zinfandels, lighter Pinot Noirs, and some lighter Riojas: Lightly chilled. While this isn't always true, many light red wines *look* light, even in the bottle. It's not foolproof, but that's one way to try to tell if it's a lighter red wine before you open it. If that doesn't work, give it a quick taste and, if necessary, drop it into ice water.

SAUVIGNON BLANC
In Search of Fresh-Mown Grass

IN THE EARLY 1980s, after Dottie converted to Judaism, we joined a synagogue in Greenwich Village called the Village Temple. It was a warm, cozy, and lovely little temple, and we looked forward to attending services on Friday nights, even going once during a blizzard. We had a routine: We'd leave work—John was at the *Wall Street Journal* then, Dottie at the *New York Times*—meet each other, go to temple, then stroll over to West Fourth Street, where we'd walk down some steps to a charming, tiny restaurant called the Kitchen Witch. There we'd sit, talk late into the night about many things—sometimes religion—and drink a bottle of Dry Creek Vineyards Fumé Blanc, from California. And then, usually, we'd have a second bottle. (We were young.)

To us, that Fumé Blanc—more commonly known as Sauvignon Blanc—is what this wine should be. The "nose," or smell, was unmistakable: fresh-mown grass—not "hints" of fresh-mown grass, not "redolent" of fresh-mown grass, but like you're standing in the middle of a field. After it's rained. The wine had a little tinge of green, and in the mouth was crisp, aggressive, and almost haylike, herbal. The freshness and acidity, combined with that unique grassy quality, made this gulpable yet serious. We just loved it.

The Sauvignon Blanc grape makes some well-known wines in France, like Pouilly-Fumé and Sancerre. It also makes some great dessert wines, like the famous Château d'Yquem, in which it's blended with Sémillon (see page 269). One of the greatest dessert wines we've ever had was a 1978 Sauvignon Blanc from California's Robert Mondavi Winery, made from grapes that had been attacked by botrytis, the "noble rot" that makes some late-harvested grapes raisiny, concentrated, and sweet (see page 257).

As a dry wine, though, it's something different, the kind of wine, with lively acids, that was perfect with the Kitchen Witch's chicken and tarragon John always ordered. Sauvignon Blanc is so versatile that it's made in any number of styles. Sometimes winemakers give it a lot of barrel aging, the oak making it rich and creamy; sometimes they put it only in stainless steel, preserving the pure fruit and letting the grapes speak for themselves; and sometimes they put it in steel and oak.

Sauvignon Blanc has become popular as a simple, easy-to-drink, refreshing—and inexpensive—wine. It can be found everywhere. We decided in early 1998 to conduct a blind tasting—and we were disappointed with what we found. Most California producers, apparently in an effort to make Sauvignon Blanc more appealing to a greater number of people, had toned down or eliminated that vibrant grassy character. What was left tasted like lemon water. Why bother? Our notes about one of these wines read: "Nice and friendly, but stripped of character. Soft, could be anything. No varietal taste." When we ripped off the bag, the wine turned out to be a 1996 Field Stone—a delightful little winery whose wines we usually enjoy. There was this note on the front label: "A hand-crafted varietal blend with a crisp, non-grassy herbal and spice character." Jeez. When was the last time you saw a label that told you what something *didn't* taste like?

Our plan was to taste American Sauvignon Blancs. But we ran across Sauvignon Blancs from New Zealand and South Africa, so we threw in a handful as ringers. And the ringers were, in some cases, better than what we set out to taste. The wines from outside the U.S. had the real Sauvignon Blanc varietal taste that ones from California used to have. We could always tell which wines were from South Africa or New Zealand by their guts and gumption—and you could, too. One South African wine, a Thelema 1997 (expensive at $17.99), almost bit us on the nose with its aggressive bell pepper smell and taste. It was remarkable, but not necessarily—because of the price—a wine we'd recommend except to experience what this varietal tastes like straight up.

In the long run, our tasting yielded three American Sauvignon Blancs we could recommend. A Martinelli 1996 was very different from everything else—flat instead of crisp, filled with deep fruit, complex instead of simple. It was clearly a winemaker's wine—an interesting and memorable experience, more challenging than many of the others. The winery said the wine's special character was partly the result of oak barrel fermentation. We also liked the Kunde Estate Magnolia Lane 1996 California (Sonoma), a distinctive wine that tasted of wood, cream, and grass.

But the best of the tasting was a shocker. After navigating oceans of Sauvignon Blanc, we were beginning to think we'd never find one that was truly thrilling. Then, bingo, we hit it. Our notes: "Almost colorless. Soft nose, but nicely varietal. Delicate, flowery with a nice lemony finish. Good grapes. Terrific class, with wood, cream, and a tiny bit of fruity sweetness. Tastes incredibly expensive. This is a Sauvignon Blanc." We had tasted this wine blind in the same flight with Grgich, Silverado, and Chimney Rock, some of California's best vineyards. But to our shock, this was Chateau Ste. Michelle, from Washington State. The price? Get this: $8.99.

On the whole, though, that tasting was a disappointment, so we vowed to try again in 1999. In January, we trudged out on snowy days to find this summery wine. Our search, casual as always—we basically buy everything we can find—yielded an outstanding collection of the 1997 vintage. And we knew right off the bat, from the first sip, that this time things would be different. "Quite good," we wrote about that first wine. "Rich and creamy, a little wood. Some grassiness folded into cream, earth, and some smoke! Very attractive richness. Luscious, with hints of sweetness, like a 'dry Sauternes' if there were such a thing. Nutmeg, toast, and roasted almonds. Tastes expensive. So rich, so luscious, it's like a soufflé." This was the first time we had tasted the connection to those marvelous and famous dessert wines; it had fascinating hints of a family relationship. This turned out to be a Beringer that is widely available and costs only $12.99. It was an awesome achievement and we talked about buying cases of it.

Fortunately, it was not a fluke. Many of these wines had real character. Another one of them, a Freestone produced by Von Strasser Winery, was an excellent bottle of wine. It had real spirit—lots of grassiness, but in a beautiful, slightly creamy package. Several others also had that classic Sauvignon Blanc character. Wine after wine earned some praise:

"The real thing!" (Freestone)

"Real character." (Morgan)

"Good with food." (Gary Farrell)

"Simple in the best sense of the word." (Matanzas Creek)

"Real body, smoke, and oak." (Bernardus)

"Sweet, grassy fruit." (Kenwood)

And one was just knock-your-socks-off charming. It was clean, crisp, and refreshing, with excellent fruit and no pretense. This was simply lovely—and it knew it. It walked to the table unadorned, proud to be a simple, drinkable, fun wine. What was it? Well, it was once again the Chateau Ste. Michelle, from Washington State. It was not the best of tasting this time, but, at $9.99, it continues to be a great bargain.

So, what's the lesson here? Maybe 1997 was just a better year than 1996 or 1995. But maybe something more fundamental has happened. Back in our Kitchen Witch days, when American Sauvignon Blanc was newer, it was crafted with care by the few winemakers who produced it. When it became famous, everyone rushed it to market—sometimes working hard to make it into a wine it wasn't meant to be. Maybe the pendulum has swung back to where Sauvignon Blanc started out, to where it was proud to be what it was. Granted, it is a distinctive wine that needs some reins on its character, but not so much that it is rendered soulless. Whatever is going on, Sauvignon Blanc is back. Try a young, fresh one tonight.

Wine Notes

Sauvignon Blanc is a versatile white wine that tastes of fresh-mown grass. It can be made into many different styles, but should always display a unique character. Buy the youngest you can find. This is a great wine for a picnic, but also would add some spice to light fish and herbed chicken. Sauvignon Blanc gets crisper as it gets colder—at its best, it's like a bell ringing in your mouth—but at some point let your bottle warm up. Then you'll find all sorts of different, "flatter" tastes in there. All of the following are from the 1997 vintage.

Beringer Vineyards (Napa Valley) $12.99

DELICIOUS • *Best of tasting. Rich, grassy, creamy, and a little woody— even some smoke! There's some very attractive richness, with nutmeg, toast, and roasted almonds. It tastes something like a soufflé—airy and rich, but still with a haunting Sauvignon Blanc character. Tastes very expensive.*

Chateau Ste. Michelle
(Barrel Fermented; Columbia Valley, Washington State) $9.99

GOOD/VERY GOOD • *Best value. How can they do this for the price? Refreshing and clean, with lovely fruit. No pretense, just a very nice wine.*

Freestone (Von Strasser Winery, Napa Valley) $10.99

VERY GOOD • *The real thing, with grass on the nose and in the mouth. Classy, charming, and real. Aggressively varietal, with real spirit. Beautifully made.*

Matanzas Creek Winery (Sonoma County) $18.99

GOOD/VERY GOOD • *So clean, so fresh—good, ripe fruit and nothing but fruit. Varietal but controlled. This is a straightforward American wine.*

Bernardus Winery (Monterey County) $19.99

GOOD/VERY GOOD • *Real body, smoke, and oak, with both cream and grass. Heavier than most.*

Gary Farrell Wines (Sonoma County, Russian River Valley) $21.99

GOOD/VERY GOOD • *Lemony, with an attractive chalk-soil backbone. With good acids and some pepper, this would be good with food.*

Kenwood Vineyards (Sonoma County) $11.99

GOOD/VERY GOOD • *Real grass on the nose and in the mouth. Crisp, grassy, and round. Sweet, grassy fruit.*

Morgan Winery
(Barrel Fermented; Sonoma County–Monterey County) $12.99

GOOD • *Melon, grapefruit, and all sorts of fun tastes. Not "fine," but some real character.*

Silverado Vineyards $13.99

GOOD • *Tickles your nose. Delightful and light, with a little spritz. Hints of the varietal and flowers. A delightful house wine.*

PINOT GRIS

"Like Drinking the Cold"

ON ONE OF OUR cross-country train trips in the early 1980s, we stopped for a night in Portland, which is the end of one long train ride and the beginning of another. Walking around, we soon found ourselves in a tiny little wine shop, where the shopkeeper went on and on, extolling the virtues of Oregon wines and how they were The Next Big Thing. It was charming—and we didn't believe him for a minute. Oregon?

The rest, of course, is history. Oregon now is well known as one of America's up-and-coming wine regions. Many experts will tell you Oregon may be producing America's best Pinot Noirs, and they can indeed be lovely and filled with fruit. But when we think of Oregon, we think of a remarkable dry white wine called Pinot Gris that's one of the most drinkable and interesting wines made in America today. Winemakers all over the world do different things with the Pinot Gris grape. In Alsace, France, Tokay d'Alsace, a pleasant white wine, is made from Pinot Gris. In Italy, they make the ubiquitous Pinot Grigio. While we find most Pinot Grigio simple and unmemorable, Pinot Gris from Oregon is an incredible experience. It has a taste that's hard to describe: richer, fuller, and fruitier than Sauvignon Blanc, but lighter on its feet and more distinctive than Chardonnay.

That's why when a colleague of ours, Amanda Bennett, moved to Portland, we gave her two words of advice: Pinot Gris. As soon as she arrived, she bought a bottle and sent us this note:

> It reminded me of an experience I used to like a lot, when I was in Toronto. There was this German restaurant that used to keep some sort of not-too-sweet German wine in the refrigera-

tor and serve it really, really cold. I remember drinking it on the patio in the summer and thinking it was just like drinking the cold. The Pinot Gris felt a lot like that—like drinking the cold.

Truth is, there's nothing like having a Pinot Gris in Oregon, close to its source. There's something about its delicacy that sometimes doesn't travel well. Ditto for some Italian whites. Pinot Gris also can be a little hard to find, but, trust us, it's worth the effort. Even in and around New York City, which is a terrific market for fine wine, we found it hard to find many different Pinot Gris. But we found enough for a full tasting and to come to this conclusion: It's hard to go wrong. Even the wines that just rated "good" still showed more character and verve than most wines we drink. For instance, we liked the Yamhill Valley Vineyards '96 even before we tasted it because it smelled so rich and creamy. In the mouth, it reminded us of lemon-meringue pie, an interesting combination of acid and cream—a surprising taste we found in all of the wines. Amazing.

One truly memorable bottle was from a winery called WillaKenzie Estate. Check out these notes: "Cold, crisp, with soil and some chalk. BRACING in your mouth. Tastes a bit like Champagne without the bubbles. Fruit is so crisp it shocks your system. Almost a little menthol. Sort of crackles on your tongue. Round when you swallow, but jagged in your mouth. Really coats your tongue. More serious than Muscadet or Pinot Grigio. Nuttiness, too, like Champagne. Age worthy."

One of our other favorites was the 1996 from Eyrie, for years one of the consistently fine wineries in Oregon; in fact, Eyrie says on the label that it was the first producer of Pinot Gris in America. Experience shows: The nose was massive. The taste was complex, with layer after layer of flavors. Although not all of the layers were entirely pleasant, that kind of complexity in a white wine is remarkable.

We're happy to report that our favorite was a wine that is at least relatively available. King Estate Winery seems to have come out of nowhere, and fast. We see it everywhere, and sometimes more often than wines from more-established, better-known Oregon wineries. In fact, we happened to find both its regular Pinot Gris 1996 and its 1995 reserve, which made for an interesting tasting. Good news: The regular, which is cheaper, was better—which made it both the best of tasting and, at $11.95, the best value. It's a wine worth seeking out. "Fresh, vibrant nose," we wrote. "Explosive lemon-zest taste! Real character. Filled with fruit. Super-ripe grapes. Complex, with crispness yet depth. Is that wood?"

As we've said, many lighter white wines never see the inside of a barrel. They're fermented in stainless steel and then bottled to keep their freshness intact. But we were sure we tasted "wood" here. We called the winery and learned it was founded in 1992 and is now the largest winery in the state, producing about 100,000 cases each year that are sold in most places in the U.S. It made 30,000 cases of the 1996 Pinot Gris. And we did taste wood: 15 percent of the crush was aged in French oak for six months, then blended with the 85 percent of the wine put in stainless steel.

Remember: There are many styles of Pinot Gris. Some are fairly heavy and others are light as a feather. What they all have in common, though, is that they taste like you've just walked outside into a perfect fall day.

Wine Notes

Pinot Gris, from Oregon, is a bracing, crisp dry white wine that is sometimes hard to find, but worth looking for. Buy the youngest you see and chill it well. Pinot Gris comes in various "weights"—some seem to have lots of ripe fruit and some wood, while others are fresh and fruity. It depends on your own taste. While these are generally crisp white wines, they also tend to have layers of complexity that demand attention. This is a great wine to give as a gift or take to a friend's house for dinner, since most people haven't yet tried a Pinot Gris, and, as far as we can tell, just about everybody loves it when they do.

King Estate Winery 1996 $11.95

VERY GOOD • *Best of tasting and best value. Fresh, vibrant nose, with an explosive lemon-zest taste. Real character and "sweet" with super-ripe fruit. Crispness and depth combine into a wine of real complexity.*

WillaKenzie Estate 1997 $18.99

VERY GOOD • *Whoa! This is a bracing wine, so crisp it'll shock your system. It even tastes a little like nonsparkling Champagne. Rich and mouth-coating, lots of character.*

The Eyrie Vineyards 1996 $14.99

GOOD/VERY GOOD • *Layer upon layer of taste with a finish that's almost sherrylike. A big mouthful of lemon and cream.*

Yamhill Valley Vineyards 1996 $12.99

GOOD • *Nose is yummy, like creamy wood. It smells thick and tastes like lemon-meringue pie. Remarkably "big."*

Cristom Vineyards 1997 $15.99

GOOD • *Mid-range between the lighter and heavier Pinot Gris.*

Oak Knoll Winery 1995 $10.99

GOOD • *Crisp and fun and almost heavy with ripe fruit, but simpler than others.*

Elk Cove Vineyards 1996 $13.99

OK/GOOD • *If you want to taste the grape, this is it. It's fruity and simple and fun—so it will make you smile.*

King Estate Winery Reserve 1995 $15.99

GOOD • *It's lemony and pretty simple, but still very pleasant.*

You're an Expert on Wine;
We Can Prove It

You're an expert on wine. Maybe you don't think you are. But you are, and we can prove it. Just follow these ten easy steps.

1. Go to your local wineshop or supermarket. It doesn't have to be fancy.

2. Buy two bottles of the same kind of wine from different wineries. For instance, buy a Kendall-Jackson Chardonnay and a Glen Ellen Chardonnay, which shouldn't cost you more than $15 together. Or, if you want to make this more interesting, buy a Kendall-Jackson Chardonnay and, say, an Estancia Chardonnay. Together, those should cost maybe $20.

3. Take them home. Cut off the metal caps completely and take out the corks. Put the corks in your pocket. Do not look at them.

4. Put both bottles into identical bags. We find that our daughters' brown-paper lunch bags work perfectly. Twist the top of each bag tightly around the neck of the bottle, then tape it, leaving just an inch of the top of the bottle showing.

5. Put the corks back in (you should have no idea, at this point, which cork is going into which bottle). If you're trying white wine, put the bottles in the refrigerator. In any case, don't look at the bottles again for a while.

6. Number the bottles, No. 1 and No. 2. If someone else is there, and you've done the previous steps by yourself, let them do this.

7. Get out two glasses for each taster.

8. Pour No. 1 into the glass on the left. Pour No. 2 into the glass on the right.

9. Taste No. 1. Decide what you think about it. Taste No. 2. Decide what you think about it.

Know what? They're going to taste different to you. Maybe one will taste better than the other. Maybe they will taste equally good. But they will taste *different*. Don't open the bags yet. Keep drinking. You might find, as time goes by, that your opinion changes. First you liked No. 1 better. Now you like No. 2. Does this mean you're a wimp who can't make up your mind? No. It just means wine changes depending on its temperature, how long it's open, what you're drinking it with—and your mood.

Don't feel you need to be thinking about or talking about wine constantly. In fact, it's best if you completely forget you're doing a tasting. Too much talking and thinking can sometimes warp the experience, make it less genuine.

At some point, tear off the bags and see which wine is which. Maybe you liked the less expensive wine more; maybe you liked the "bad" vintage instead of the "good" vintage. And that leads you to step No. 10, which is the most important point of all:

10. Trust yourself. If you paid $8 for the Kendall-Jackson and only $5 for the Glen Ellen, but you liked the Glen Ellen better, don't say to yourself, "Gee, I guess I don't know anything about wine." You don't have a *problem*; you have a *bargain*.

There are a lot of wine experts out there. But there is no one—no one—who is more of an expert on *your* taste than *you*. Trust yourself. A good wine is a wine that tastes good to you. And don't let anybody tell you different.

VIOGNIER

Could This Be the Next Chardonnay?

WE ALWAYS SAY you should try a new kind of wine when you go out to dinner. Restaurants often offer wines that aren't widely available in stores, and there's sometimes a sommelier or a wine-loving waiter who can point you in whole new directions. That happened to our friend Laura Landro a while back, and she stumbled onto what some people think might be the next "hot" white wine in America. Laura is a senior editor at the *Wall Street Journal*, the author of the book *Survivor*, and someone who always sees trends early, so we pay a great deal of attention to what she says.

"I had it last week at the behest of the sommelier at Patroon restaurant," she said. "My husband and I were going over the list of the Chardonnays that we often go for and just couldn't get excited, felt it was the same old same old, wanted something different. So the sommelier suggested a Viognier, which we had never even heard of, and told us we would like it. He promised. So we did, and he was right! It was a little more complex than the usual Chardonnay but still had that rich, full-bodied taste we look for in a Chardonnay. I noticed it again just last night on the wines-by-the-glass menu at the SeaGrill in Rockefeller Plaza and decided to try it. Again it was quite 'yummy,' as you would say."

Chardonnay will always be popular, but for those who are looking for an alternative, some American winemakers, including very smart marketers like Kendall-Jackson, are putting money on Viognier. This is an unusual grape from the Rhône Valley of France that's so big and heavy it's sometimes blended into the region's massive *red* wines to take a bit of the edge off them.

In fact, the heft of Viognier (pronounced vee-oh-NYAY) is one thing that makes it perfect to drink even in winter. If you prefer white, this is what you should drink by the fire with hearty food. But be prepared for something really different. Viognier is a serious wine, often relatively high in alcohol. It tastes very much of minerals and earth—we think of it as tasting "dirty," although, obviously, it's not—and it will remind you of melons. The combination of crispness, dirt, and melons makes us feel like we're in the middle of a cantaloupe field on a sunny day.

Viognier is right on the cusp at the moment. Some wine stores carry a whole bunch of them, figuring it really will be The Next Big Thing. Other stores have given up on it. Some restaurants list it on the menu, often under a heading like "Alternative Whites" (they mean "alternative" to Chardonnay). We wondered what we'd find if we bought all of them we saw.

On the whole, we were both pleased and fascinated with our blind tasting. No one is making much Viognier yet, and it's clear that all of the wineries experimenting with this grape are giving it a lot of attention and care. Most of them were well made. While there were obvious differences—some were bigger than others, some were more "forward" in their fruit—almost all had "flat," earthy tastes and large personalities.

Consider the Viognier from Fess Parker Winery. (Yes, the actor who played Daniel Boone.) While it was not one of our top choices, it was a fascinating wine—"sweet" with fruit, with a nose of gardenias and spice. There was something about it that reminded us of chicken fat because it was a big, heavy wine, yet comforting and white. The wine was so unusual that we called the winery for some winemaker's notes: "This interesting wine was barrel fermented (77 percent) in neutral French oak barrels and aged approximately seven months sur lee [on the lees] and stirred every two weeks. One hundred percent malolactic fermentation lends a smoothness, adding to the complexity of the wine." Even the winemaker called this wine "interesting"!

By the way, if you're surprised that Daniel Boone is now making wine—and selling coonskin caps at the winery—don't be. While many winemakers are still, in effect, family farmers, the investment needed to go into the wine industry these days means more and more rich businessmen and celebrities are starting their own labels. There's Francis Ford Coppola at Niebaum-Coppola, for instance, and even the Smothers Brothers.

And all of them have a vision they pursue with grapes. Some wines taste as though they made themselves. What you taste seems like pure fruit, and indeed, no amount of fancy-schmancy winemaking techniques can overcome grapes that aren't good. All great wines start with great grapes. But sometimes a winemaker's vision leads to experimentation, and, like an alchemist, the winemaker tries a little bit of this, a little bit of that, to get the taste he or she (increasingly she) is looking for. We can't say enough about how highly individualistic and subjective all of this is. At the Fess Parker Winery and Vineyard, winemaker Eli Parker, Fess's son, was shooting for, as the notes say, "hints of pear, melon, light butter, vanilla, and toast" combined "with floral and mineral elements."

All three of our favorites had varying amounts of the tastes Eli Parker was after, and all three were from wineries with outstanding reputations. Joseph Phelps makes a Viognier called Vin du Mistral that's widely available, compared to many others. It's crisp, creamy, and fruity, with that underlying earthy taste that gives it real complexity. The Viognier from Calera—a winery that's justly famous for its Pinot Noirs—was the biggest of the bunch, rich and creamy with lots of earth and a little bit of sourness that gave it an added dimension.

Our favorite was from Qupé. Qupé has been a pioneer in making Rhône-style wines, such as Syrah, in the U.S. Its 1997, our best of tasting, was a beautiful balance of crispness, rocky soil, and meaty melon. Close your eyes, and you can imagine this is a red wine. How does all that fit together? You have to taste it to find out. That's part of the wonder and charm of Viognier.

The biggest surprise of our tasting was the R. H. Phillips EXP 1997, a lovely, serious, and very well made wine. Most of the Viogniers we tried cost more than $20, and we'd guessed this was one of the more expensive. Instead, it was the least expensive, at just $11.99. This would be a good place to start your knowledge of Viognier.

One last note: We always say you can't separate the taste of wine from the experience you're having while drinking it. A few months before our tasting, and before Laura's reading of the "hot scene," we sneaked out of work on a beautiful day to meet our friend Jim Stewart for lunch at a fancy Upper West Side restaurant. On the wine list, we were surprised to see a 1997 Viognier from Horton, a fine winery in Virginia. We ordered it, and it couldn't have been better—crisp and fun, with layers of complexity that made it a memorable experience. We found exactly the same bottle for this tasting, and, tasted blind against the others, it wasn't in the top rank. Maybe it was bottle variation. Maybe the wine was just better a few months earlier. But it doesn't really matter. If you asked us what was the best Viognier we've ever had, we'd still say that Horton on that day—and if the beautiful day, a few stolen hours together, and Jim's company made it so, well, that really doesn't change a thing.

Wine Notes

Viognier may be The Next Big Thing in white wines as more and more American winemakers try their hand at this grape from the Rhône Valley. This is not a frivolous white wine. In fact, it has so much heft and soul that you can drink it in winter with hearty foods. The taste of fruits and soil makes it an interesting alternative to Chardonnay. And its large personality makes it not for the faint of heart. This is white wine with a difference.

Qupé 1997 (Santa Barbara County, Ibarra-Young Vineyard) $25.99
VERY GOOD • *Best of tasting. This is the real thing from a classy producer of Rhône-style wines. It's not afraid to be a little bit harsh, and is
filled with earth and rocks. It's so meaty it seems like a red, but nothing
in the complex tastes is too pronounced, leaving the balanced taste of a
very good wine.*

R. H. Phillips Vineyard EXP 1997 (Dunnigan Hills) $11.99
GOOD/VERY GOOD • *Best value. Fruity, flat, and serious. A wine to
think about and talk about—at a great price.*

Joseph Phelps Vineyards Vin du Mistral 1996 $22.99
VERY GOOD • *A fine wine from a consistently excellent winery. Crisp yet
creamy, with lots of earth. That wonderful combination of richness and
flatness that seems special to a well-made Viognier.*

Calera Wine Company 1996 (Mt. Harlan) $25.99
GOOD/VERY GOOD • *Creamy, rich, and lovely, with those classic "flat"
tastes underneath the vibrancy. Sound contradictory? That's what makes it
such a fine wine. Another winner from a name always worth looking for.*

Alban Vineyards 1997 (Central Coast) $20.99
GOOD/VERY GOOD • *Lots of soil and sweet melon tastes, although the
melon might be a little bit on the overripe side. This tastes a lot like very
good, very dry honey wine, with a nice, warm finish that leaves you happy.*

Andrew Murray Vineyards 1997 (Santa Barbara County) $22.99
GOOD/VERY GOOD • *Holy cow! Massive, sherrylike, with huge
amounts of melon taste. It looks and tastes dark and rich. A very serious
mouthful of wine.*

Rosenblum Cellars 1997 (Santa Barbara County) $14.99

GOOD • *Fruity, pleasant, and simple.*

Fess Parker Winery and Vineyard 1997
(Santa Barbara County) $14.99

GOOD • *Sweet and chewy, with a very pronounced nose of gardenias and spice and a lot going on in the glass. It's a substantial wine that somehow reminds us of chicken fat—maybe because it has such weight even though it's white. And maybe that's why it seems so comforting.*

La Jota Vineyard Co. 1996
(Barrel Fermented; Napa Valley, Howell Mountain) $23.99

GOOD • *No real finesse, but plenty of "sweet" fruit makes it pleasant to drink.*

Preston Vineyards 1997 (Dry Creek Valley) $16.00

GOOD • *Crisp, lemony, and forward. Lots of vibrant taste. Clean and refreshing—this would be great with shellfish. But it lacks that varietal, special taste of many of the others.*

Horton Vineyards 1997 (Orange County, Virginia) $15.00

OK/GOOD • *Simple but quite pleasant. It's remarkable what's coming out of Virginia these days; try this unusual wine to find out.*

GEWÜRZTRAMINER
A Little Pepper with Your Wine, Sir?

THE ALSACE REGION OF FRANCE produces some of the classiest, most distinctive white wines in the world—and they're generally great bargains, too, because they're a little odd. Alsace is on the French-German border, and the wines themselves seem to have a split personality thing going on. They're mostly white, like German wines, and come in elongated German-style bottles; they're identified by grape type, like American wines, instead of by their place, like French wines; and the wines themselves have the restraint and elegance of German whites with some of the richness of character of French whites.

Sound interesting? Well, for just a few bucks, you can see for yourself. Alsace makes very dry, interesting wines like Riesling and Pinot Blanc. But you should start your journey into Alsace with something *completely* different: Gewürztraminer. This wine is so unusual that we'd been interested in wine for a few years before we heard of it. We remember that first encounter. It was during our first visit to the tasting room of Sebastiani Vineyards in Sonoma County, and we were slowly working our way through an awesome array of wines when, suddenly, one stopped us cold. Gewürztraminer. Huh? It was so distinctive we asked the woman behind the counter what grape the wine was made from. She looked at us blankly for a moment, then replied: "Well, Gewürztraminer." We didn't even know if that was one word or two.

It took us some time to figure out how to pronounce this—it's ge-VURTZ-tra-*mee*-ner, but everybody just calls it ge-VURTZ. And it took us even longer to begin to really appreciate it. It's not expensive, it's readily available, and it's the kind of white wine that inspires passion.

Gewürz can be very dry, a little sweet, or very sweet, but it is always spicy and fruity (*gewürz* means "spicy" in German). There's a rare, expensive Alsatian Gewürz called Vendange Tardive that combines high alcohol, lots of sweetness, and traditional Gewürz pepper-spice into an astonishing mouthful of taste. Imagine this, a 1976 Hugel Vendange Tardive we drank in 1991 with pork chops in caper sauce: "Light, spicy nose. Wonderful and wondrous taste. Clean Gewürz character with lots of spice. Yet creamy and *elegant*. Gorgeous, sensuous finish. Ripe and big, yet lots of finesse. Perfectly made, perfect age, with no hint of old age."

We've found over the years that even regular Gewürzes age beautifully. There were years, in fact, when we spent a lot of time searching for old Gewürzes. In 1987, when we visited a winery called Rutherford Hill in Napa, it had a 1977 Gewürz for sale on its list of "library wines"—the old stuff. We asked the people behind the counter how it was and they said they'd never tasted it. So we bought it, opened it right there at the tasting counter—it had turned a little dark—and drank it with them. Even at cellar temperature, it was delicious. The age—and, probably, the warmth—brought out its spicy, prickly, and austere tastes.

Alsatian wines in general age beautifully, which is surprising considering they're so delicious, charming, and drinkable in their youth. For Christmas 1998 we opened a 1976 dry Muscat from Alsace, made by Trimbach, and it was delicious. It was still full of that delightful orange-blossom taste that comes from the Muscat grape, but it had reached an elegant middle age, with plenty of maturity and many more years ahead of it.

Some California wineries make Gewürz and we've had some good ones over the years (we once had a Field Stone, from the 1980 vintage, that knocked our socks off: "Delicious, fantastic! Roses in the nose, incredible floweriness in the nose and in the taste. Happy, fresh, young, and incredibly fun"). But we've generally found American Gewürzes to be a bit sweet and clumsy. And since they tend to cost as much as the real thing from Alsace, why bother? The real thing is a natural wonder: extremely dry yet with an unmistakable pepperiness and a little taste of earth. Our notes from a 1976 Laugel Gewürz read: "Very HUGE. A Gewürz and an Alsatian all over. Much spice, yet crisp, clean. BOFFO and very, very dry." Or consider this, about a Beyer Gewürz 1983: "Delicious! Fruity and crisp, very varietal and fresh, yet actually with some cream. Beautiful!"

Clean, dry, crisp, fruity, and alive—and still filled with definite tastes of pepper and spices. This is what Alsatian Gewürz is all about.

For a blind tasting, we threw in a few American Gewürzes just to see what would happen. All of them dropped out of the competition early. They were pleasant enough, but lacked the taste of soil and the austere punch of the Alsatians. Among the Alsatians, the Trimbach 1993 was good, as always. This is our house Gewürz because, year after year, it's consistently reliable, available, and inexpensive. If you look for Trimbach Gewürztraminer, you can't go wrong. In this tasting, though, several were better.

The best of tasting, we're delighted to report, was one of the most inexpensive, and also one that's generally available, the Alsace Willm 1996. Our notes: "Classic nose, with lots of peachy fruit, aggressive flavors of pepper and spice. Smells like simmering spice, pretty, with a bit of sweet fruit. Light, with plenty of earth and restraint. A complete wine."

Under the umbrella of "classic" Alsatian Gewürz, we found many different tastes—wines others might like better than our favorite. The Lucien Albrecht 1996 was extremely dry, with lots of nice acids that would make it excellent with food. (A lot of folks think Gewürz is perfect with spicy food, such as Thai or Indian.)

We also tried a wine called Kientzler 1995 that was so aggressive Dorothy said, "It's like it wakes you up and slaps you around." It smelled and tasted like toast, with a little bit of spritz and a powerful, bracing taste.

These are beautifully made, unique wines that take your taste buds into whole new areas. Give them a try. More broadly, keep in mind that the white wines of Alsace are lovely and great buys—because only you know how good they are.

Wine Notes

Gewürztraminer is a remarkable grape that is at its best as a dry, austere yet spicy wine produced in the Alsace region of France. American wineries also make Gewürz, but we've generally found them to be simpler and often a bit sweet. Gewürz ages beautifully, so don't worry that much about the vintage. Many people find the spiciness of Gewürz goes well with Indian or Thai dishes.

Alsace Willm 1996 $10.99

VERY GOOD • *Best of tasting and best value. Smells "pretty," like simmering spice. Tastes of earth and pepper, yet light on its feet. That combination of lots of taste yet lightness is classic Alsace. This is a complete wine.*

André Kientzler 1995 $12.99

GOOD/VERY GOOD • *Smells of toast and flowers, and tastes like toast, too; remarkable. It's so bracing it wakes you up and slaps you around. This is a wine that's proud to be aggressive.*

Lucien Albrecht 1996 $13.29

GOOD/VERY GOOD • *So dry it's almost prickly. You can almost taste the vines. Nice acids make it perfect with food.*

Mittnacht-Klack 1995 $14.49

GOOD/VERY GOOD • *Wonderfully complex: sweet on the front of the mouth, austere on the back, tongue-coating in between. Tastes of peaches, pears, oak, and grapefruit.*

F. E. Trimbach 1993 $14.99

GOOD • *Crisp and dry, with a long, spicy finish. This is a name to look for. Trimbach is usually available and always reliable. This would be a fine introduction to what Alsatian wine is all about.*

Pierre Sparr & Fils 1996 $9.99

GOOD • *Fresh, flowery, lovely nose, but it's just a bit harsh in the mouth, with some mineral tastes. That gives it an interesting complexity, but makes it a little harder to drink than some.*

Léon Beyer 1996 $14.99

GOOD • *Nose is peaches and maple syrup, taste is prickly, herbal, and spicy. There are a lot of interesting tastes that haven't quite melded. Maybe with more age?...*

Kuentz-Bas 1994 $27.99

GOOD • *Lovely flower-garden nose. Really sweet and lovely, but probably too fruity-sweet for food.*

How to Judge a Wine Store
Without Saying a Word

Wine stores come in all shapes and sizes. Nancy's wineshop in New York City is a small jewel, with each bottle carefully selected, while Sam's in Chicago is the size of a football field and has everything you could ever dream of. We once dropped into a Harris Teeter supermarket in Atlanta with a wine collection that left us stunned. All three are excellent; just different. At some point, you simply must find a wine store you like and trust. How do you do that? It's easier than you think. Here's how to scope out a wine store in five minutes without having to say a word.

1. **The Chandon Test.** Chandon is the sparkling wine made by the ton in California by Moët & Chandon. Sometimes you can find the regular Brut or Blanc de Noirs for as low as $10.99. But if a shop charges more than $15.99, be careful. If prices are that much out of kilter on Chandon, who knows what the markup is for other wines? (Because of bizarre laws or distribution patterns, it's possible that Chandon is outrageously expensive throughout certain states. Check a couple of shops or newspaper advertisements and make your own decision about the drop-dead point.)

2. **Climate.** If a wineshop is really hot or really cold, walk out. It's not just that the wine is suffering—it's that the wine merchant doesn't care. Same thing for bright sunlight or harsh lighting. They're killers. (There are some very high-end shops where the wine on display is just for display; the wines you'll take home are in a cool basement somewhere. But that's rare.)

3. **"Do you like red or white?"** This is our all-time least favorite and yet most asked stupid question in wineshops. When you walk into a bookstore, no one attaches himself to your back and asks, "Fiction or nonfiction?" We sometimes murmur, "We

like everything," and try to ditch the guy. If he doesn't back off, we leave and wait a few months before trying again.

4. Déjà vu. Many shops have the same, tired selection. You'll never find something new and interesting there. If everything looks familiar, you've outgrown the shop.

5. Handmade signs. If merchants are into their wines, they want to share them. Signs on shelves often indicate an enthusiastic, down-to-earth staff.

6. Tastings. In states where this is permitted, tastings in stores are a great way to further your knowledge without buying a bottle of something. And they're a nice way for merchants to show you they appreciate your patronage and are invested in your expanding taste. Some stores offer free tastings all the time; others have tastings on Saturdays. Look for notices about them. (Again, because of various state laws, tastings might not be allowed where you live. Ask around.)

7. Case discounts. A 15 percent discount on a mixed case is a courtesy you should look for. Shops that offer discounts only on a case of the same wine are a bore. There is usually a sign about this.

If the store passes all of these tests and you decide to buy some wine, there are three additional points to look for as your relationship develops.

8. Trust. You need to find a merchant you can trust—but you also need to learn to trust your own taste. If a merchant has sold you something more expensive than you'd planned, and you don't like it, be skeptical about returning. Trust your own taste.

9. Look everywhere. Some supermarkets, in states where this is allowed, have wonderful selections. It sounds weird, but even convenience stores that carry wine sometimes will have something rare. No, it doesn't make any sense, but wine distribution doesn't make any sense.

10. Play the field. Try to cultivate several wine merchants. Stores have different strengths and weaknesses. One might be big on Australian Shiraz, another on old California Cabernets. Shop around.

There are many caveats here: With thousands of wineshops in America, no rules apply to all of them. Different states have different laws, prices vary widely, and what matters to people when they go about buying anything varies a great deal, too. But finding a wine store you trust—and where you feel comfortable—is an essential part of enjoying wine.

CHABLIS
The Case of the Stolen Identity

THERE WAS A television commercial several years ago in which one of those snooty voices endemic to wine ads talked about an inexpensive California white wine. The tag line at the end, in that ridiculous accent, was: "A better chablis." Poor Chablis! For years, it seemed like every cheap white jug wine in America was called "chablis," even though it had nothing whatsoever to do with real Chablis. Americans were in a frenzy over things wet, white, and cold—even if they were nondescript wines.

Remember wine coolers and spritzers? Then, by the time fake "chablis" was dying out, Chablis became best known as the drink of liberals who talked a good game about the downtrodden while enjoying a privileged life: the "Brie and Chablis crowd."

What a terrible thing to happen to one of the world's most remarkable—and, for the quality, one of its most affordable—white wines.

Chablis is one of the wonders of the wine world. Made from Chardonnay grapes in the Chablis region of Burgundy, it doesn't taste anything like California Chardonnay. Quite the opposite, in fact: It's famous for its crisp, steely taste and the way it goes with seafood. Chablis is one of those wines that wine lovers can often distinguish just from the smell. It has a flinty, chalky nose with an overlay of sourness. Yeah, we know that "sour" doesn't sound mouthwateringly good, but think of a tart green apple. It's that very lemon-sour quality, together with ripe fruit, perfect acids, and just the right soil, that makes Chablis such a crisp, delicious drink and a classic accompaniment with food (we conducted the following tasting over stone-crab claws and melted butter, which we recommend as one of the most sensuous meals you can imagine).

While some California Chardonnays seem styled like Chablis, especially those from Chalone and Grgich, many are plump and chewy, the antithesis of the classic, earthy austerity of Chablis. A good, well-chilled Chablis has a tartness, a flintiness, and a freshness that's like breaking open a very fresh head of lettuce. It's as edgy as a piece of ice in your mouth, with a tartness that explodes and a finish that's clean and bracing.

There are seven "Grand Cru" Chablis that attach their names to "Chablis" on the label. For instance, a label might say "Chablis Les Clos." More helpfully, it will say "Grand Cru," too. Then there are "Premier Cru" Chablis; you'll probably see a name right under "Chablis," such as "Fourchaume"—and it'll likely say "Premier Cru." There's no reason to memorize which is which, because it'll be there on the label. In any event, this is the kind of wine-expert stuff you really don't need to know to start enjoying Chablis. Our working assumption was that it is hard to go wrong just picking up any bottle of the real deal.

To test that theory, we bought a couple dozen Chablis at random from New York City wineshops, where we found it harder to find a good selection of Chablis than we had imagined. Americans don't drink a lot of Chablis, which means many wineshops only carry one or two, at best. But there's an upside to this: The lack of demand means almost all of the Chablis we bought were around $17—not much more than you'd pay for a good California Chardonnay, right?

In our tasting, the wines were generally good. All tasted better with food than without. A few were disappointing—thin, watery, and overly acidic, just an "OK" on our scale. On the whole, the 1996 wines were better than the 1995. Some of the simple Chablis wines showed as well as the more expensive Premier Cru wines.

The 1996 Montée de Tonnerre from William Fèvre's Domaine de la Maladière was good when we first opened it, and kept getting better as it got warmer. This surprised us. We had always found Chablis to be better colder because the tastes seem to crystallize better. But this one went down in our notes as "creamy, yummy, and toasty. A real 'holy cow' wine."

But that was merely preparation for a complex wine with a very basic label. The label, pale green on white, simply said Chablis 1996. In small letters, it said it was from a producer called Verget. It cost $19.99. "This is Chablis!" we wrote before we even tasted it, just from the smell. "Creamy, rich, toasty, even looks rich. Remarkable." One thing to watch for in any wine commentary is contradiction. If a writer describes a wine in contradictory ways, it doesn't mean he or she has had a few too many. It means the wine has the kind of complexity that makes a wine great. Consider our notes on this wine: "Butter, cream, lemon, sour, sweet fruit. Ripe grapes, good wood." On our rating scale, this rated a Delicious.

Now the bad news: While there are many different makers of Chablis, no one makes very much. When we called New York's importer of Verget, we found that only a few hundred cases had made it to the U.S. Don't let that dissuade you. Several of our randomly selected Chablis were quite good. So just grab any Chablis at around $18 to $20, chill it for an hour or two, and have it with seafood— maybe even just a simple pasta with shrimp. You'll wonder why it's been so long since you had the real thing.

Wine Notes

You're probably used to picking up a Chardonnay for dinner on your way home. Well, tonight, pick up a different kind of Chardonnay: a Chablis, the real thing, from France. It won't cost much more than your Chardonnay and it's a whole different ballgame. Especially if you're having seafood, you'll find that the crisp austerity of the Chablis complements the seafood much better than the plumpness of a Chardonnay. You could get fancy and look for a Grand Cru or a Premier Cru, but don't worry about it: Just buy a Chablis in your price range. We've had good luck with the 1996 vintage, but don't worry about that, either. Chablis is good when it's young and fresh, and it's good with some age on it, too.

Verget Chablis 1996 $19.99

DELICIOUS • *Best of tasting. Creamy, rich, and toasty, with butter, lemon, sweet fruit, and wood—and yet, at the same time, that classic Chablis tartness and mouth-cleaning freshness. Tart and rich like lemon-meringue pie. This is Chablis.*

Hamelin Chablis 1996 $14.99

GOOD/VERY GOOD • *Best value. Crisp and forward, like good grapes treated simply and well. Friendlier, less aggressive than some others; ready to drink now.*

Chablis Montée de Tonnerre Premier Cru 1996
(William Fèvre's Domaine de la Maladière) $17.99

VERY GOOD/DELICIOUS • *Colorless like water, but with a rich, sweet-fruit nose—an interesting contradiction. Wait a minute, wait a minute—as it gets warmer, it's toasty, aggressive, and big. Holy cow! What an experience!*

Chablis Premier Cru Vaillons, Louis Michel & Fils 1995 $29.99

VERY GOOD/DELICIOUS • *Lemony, fresh, aggressive nose. Pleasant, with plenty of character and cream. But quite young. The longer you save this the greater your reward.*

Château de Maligny Chablis Premier Cru Fourchaume 1995 $16.99

VERY GOOD • *This is one of our all-time favorites. It was our house Chablis for years. It's well priced, widely available, and worth looking for.*

It's chewy and rich, with a long, memorable "finish." It's probably more for-ward and ultimately less "serious" than some, but that's part of its charm.

Domaine Jean Defaix Chablis 1996 $16.99

GOOD • *Fruity, clean, and simple; just a lovely little Chablis.*

WHITE BURGUNDY
Yes, It's Worth the Trouble

IF YOU LIKE CHARDONNAY, get to know white Burgundy. If you don't like Chardonnay, you owe it to yourself to get to know white Burgundy. We know it's not easy. There are so many different kinds of Burgundy, from the famous Montrachet to the simple Mâcon. There are few simple château names, but instead a head-spinning array of Grand Crus, Premier Crus, village names, shipper names . . . eeek! It's enough to make you go straight to the California Chardonnay section of the wine store, where you'll find something easy like "Raymond, Private Reserve."

But white Burgundy is a special experience. It has inspired lots of exclamation points in our notes over the years. "Effortlessly wonderful! Nutmeg, fruit, and cream in perfect balance" (a 1992 Puligny-Montrachet). "One of the greats! Fruity, yet with lemon, earth, soil, and a tremendous lemon-cream finish. Despite all that, also crisp and clean and restrained, with a bit of sharpness. Tremendous complexity" (a 1983 Pouilly-Fuissé). "Great! Nose: Butter, straw, earth, herbs, rich. Taste: Huge, with a long finish. Clean, yet with a real bite to it. Vanilla. So big it's like a dessert wine. Take small sips" (a 1980 Meursault).

Thirsty yet?

Fine white Burgundy is made from the Chardonnay grape, but the wines are different from California Chardonnay. American Chardonnays tend to be powerful and plump; Burgundies tend to have more restraint, more layers of complexity, and better acids that make them better food wines. That's not to say white Burgundy is "better" than American Chardonnay; just different. Burgundy has a little taste of the soil, some chalk, and some "tar" that give an interesting structure to the wine. And, as we noted about that Puligny-Montrachet, one thing that sets white Burgundy apart is its effortlessness. These wines have an easy charm and elegance. While that doesn't mean you'll drink it and say, "Gee, this has an easy charm and elegance," what it does mean is that you're likely to find the wines easy to drink. They don't have the edges and self-consciousness of some California Chardonnays.

It's all of that together—easy to drink yet serious, big yet clean, creamy yet lemony, buttery yet crisp—that gives Burgundy its marvelous complexity. When white Burgundy is good, there isn't a classier white wine in the world, or one with a more beautiful, more sensuous finish that seems to last forever.

And you *can* afford it.

In early 1999 we decided to launch an experiment: If we bought several cases of white Burgundies at random, and spent no more than $30 a bottle, what would we find? We, and you, have a real advantage these days because there have been some excellent vintages recently. We ended up with wines from all over Burgundy, from $9.99 to $29.99. Some said "Premier Cru" on the label, which is usually a good sign, but others didn't. Some appeared to have been made by small producers, while others were made by big shippers, such as the ubiquitous Louis Latour.

We found this much across the board: The wines were quite good. They had a fairly consistent taste of lemon, cream, smoke, and vanilla. The wines we didn't like that much had more lemon and less of everything else. The ones we liked best tasted like crème brûlée—luscious, plump, and creamy on the inside, with an overlay of burnt sugar, a hint of lemon, and a taste of the soil. These were sensuous wines with some real texture and crisp acidity.

One after another was quite good. We had a fine Mâcon ("rich and creamy"), an excellent Saint-Véran ("velvety and soft"), and a terrific Saint-Aubin ("monster wine"), not to mention, of course, an outstanding Chassagne-Montrachet ("classy and harmonious"). All of those, by the way, are the names of the towns where the wines came from. Sometimes you might see a generic Bourgogne, which could be from anywhere, and sometimes you'll see a very specific single name, such as Montrachet, which means it's a "Grand Cru" (which you'll know by the breathtaking price). Usually, though, you'll see a place name, like Montagny or Rully, sometimes followed by a vineyard name or by "1er Cru." The more specific the name, usually the better the wine. But there are no guarantees.

For instance, we had two wines in the same "flight" that were equally good, in different ways. One was big, buttery, and almost American in its aggressive, fat tastes. The other was deeply elegant, with all sorts of shy hints of smoke, lemon, and spices in perfect proportion. The first turned out to be Pouilly-Fuissé—*this* is why it became famous, before it was ruined by fame. The other, the elegant wine, was a Meursault. Two very different wines, both excellent. This is why you should experiment with Burgundy. If you do, you're likely to have good luck.

But, that said, most of the wines in our tasting had something going against them: youth. Young white Burgundy, especially in good years, can be untamed—too much acid, too many disparate tastes competing for the attention of your taste buds. Sometimes it's only in the finish that you can taste the real potential of the wine. In our case, bottle after bottle—mostly from the excellent 1995 and 1996 years— simply hadn't had time to mature. What do we mean by that? It's very much like a person. In youth, sometimes people show wonderful attributes, but they haven't yet, as the saying goes, "amounted to any- thing." As people get older, they're able to tone down their edgier attributes while their best parts, if they're lucky, seem to come together into a real, rounder personality.

We thought of this while tasting one wine that was particularly excellent. "Oaky, flinty, creamy, with sweet fruit," we wrote in our notes. "Yet totally clean and fresh. Wow. It's clear just from the nose that this is something special, and it is. This is the real deal, fresh, creamy, delicious, and good with food." This turned out to be Pernand-Vergelesses Premier Cru 1995 from Rapet.

This wine is terrific. But it's not even close to its peak. We thought that if we bought a case of this, we'd probably drink a bottle a year for the next dozen years to see how it develops. Our guess is that it will be at its best in five to seven years. After that, it will move into a comfortable middle age in which charm and grace will replace its power.

None of this is to say you shouldn't rush out, pick up a white Burgundy, and drink it tonight. In fact, we think you're likely to find quite a few white Burgundies you'll enjoy more than your usual Chardonnay, and at the same price, too.

Wine Notes

There have been several good vintages of white Burgundy in a row, so now is a good time to try some. There are so many different Burgundies out there that it's daunting to choose one. So keep this in mind: The more geographically specific the name, the better chance you have that the wine will be excellent. So a label referring to a broad region, such as Bourgogne, is ranked lower than one referring to a specific village name. Ranked even higher are the Premier Cru vineyards; these will have the name of a vineyard and the village where it comes from (and also, helpfully, will probably say "1ᵉʳ cru" or "Premier Cru" right on the label). Higher yet are the Grand Crus, which are individual vineyards, too. Grand Cru labels are shorter than the Premier Cru labels. The Grand Crus only have the vineyard name and the appellation "Grand Cru" on them (another way to know it's a Grand Cru will be the astonishing price). But there are no guarantees, and, as you can see below, good wines come from all over Burgundy, so be bold. Be sure to chill these well; their tastes seem to get sharper and better focused with some chilling. As with American Chardonnay, the wine will change as it warms. And remember that good white Burgundy improves with some age. These would be good wines to "lay down."

Pernand-Vergelesses Premier Cru 1995
(Domaine Rapet Père & Fils) $27.99

DELICIOUS • *Best of tasting. It's clear just from the nose that this is special—it's oaky, flinty, creamy, and filled with sweet fruit, yet totally clean. This is the real thing. And it's great with food.*

Mâcon Villages 1997 (Trénel Fils) $9.99

VERY GOOD • *Best value. Rich, creamy, woody taste, with a lovely finish like Key lime pie.*

Saint-Aubin Les Charmois Premier Cru 1996
(Bernard Morey et Fils) $29.96

DELICIOUS • *Wow! Rich, heavily oaked, with huge, sweet fruit. A huge, fruity monster wine that's SO young. So rich now, it's just too aggressive. Great in five years.*

Bourgogne Hautes Côtes de Nuits 1996
(Domaine Gros Frère et Saur) $19.99

VERY GOOD/DELICIOUS • *Refreshing, bright tastes, with nutmeg and cream underneath a sharp exterior. Wakes up your mouth.*

Chassagne-Montrachet "Les Charrières" 1996
(Michel Colin-Deléger et Fils) $29.99

VERY GOOD • *Fresh and fruity, with a real crème brûlée taste—yet some tar and soil that give it a special structure. Classy and harmonious.*

Château-Fuissé Pouilly-Fuissé 1996 $26.99

VERY GOOD • *Big, fat, and scrumptious like a California Chardonnay. Like melted butter.*

Meursault 1996 (François Mikulski)   **$29.99**

VERY GOOD • *Classy and restrained, with smoke, spice, and lemon, but in balance. Very, very elegant.*

Rully Premier Cru Le Meix Cadot 1996
(Vincent Dureuil-Janthial)   **$29.99**

GOOD/VERY GOOD • *Lots of lemon and earth, with a lovely sour-cream finish. Hints of grapefruit. Still quite young, but it's already a perfect match with seafood.*

Mâcon-Pierreclos 1996 (Guffens-Heynen)   **$18.49**

GOOD/VERY GOOD • *Aggressive cream-lemon tastes with a surprising amount of pepper. There's a lot going on in the glass. Good buy.*

Saint-Véran "Les Bruyères" 1997 (Jean Goyon)   **$14.99**

GOOD/VERY GOOD • *Velvety and soft, with cream, lemon, and an easy elegance. Finish is a bit weak and watery, but this is still a steal.*

Chassagne-Montrachet "en l'Ormeau" 1996 (Brenot)   **$29.99**

GOOD/VERY GOOD • *Smoky lemon nose and luscious taste. Sensuous and plump. A lot there. Yum.*

Savigny-Les-Beaune Premier Cru "Les Hauts Jarrons" 1996
(Maurice Écard et Fils)   **$27.99**

GOOD • *Nutmeg and cinnamon on the nose and a very different taste, with real depth, backbone, and spice. Fascinating.*

Montagny Premier Cru "La Grande Roche" 1996
(Louis Latour)   **$12.99**

GOOD • *Simpler than others, but with similar hints of lemon, earth, and chalk. Very pleasant—and a great deal.*

Etienne Sauzet Bourgogne Blanc "Chardonnay" 1996   **$29.99**

GOOD • *Lemony and pleasant. Lovely, well made, and unpretentious.*

Saint-Romain (Verget)   **$18.99**

GOOD • *Toasty nose. Pleasant. A good, simple white wine.*

MUSCADET AND VOUVRAY

Cheap White Wines, with Class

YOU SPEND $7 OR $8 on an everyday white wine without much thinking about it, right? Well, what if we told you that you could buy a better wine, with more character, for the same money—and that it was from France, no less? Well, you can. And it's easy.

It's Muscadet, the crisp white wine made in great quantities in the Loire Valley of France. Just as the Rhône Valley is associated with big, heavy reds, the Loire is known for lovely, often inexpensive whites: Muscadet, Vouvray, Sancerre. We often take Muscadet for granted because it's everywhere and so affordable. It's dry and a little musty, with enough fruit-acid taste to go really well with food. Drunk young and well chilled, it's perfect with light, white fish. It's also exactly the kind of wine you'd take to a summer picnic: fun, gulpable, and refreshing.

Muscadet's taste is a little difficult to describe because it's so "flat." The best description we've seen is from the famous British wine writer Jancis Robinson, who writes that Muscadet is "almost bubbling with neutral-flavored fruit." Muscadet is made from the Muscadet grape, which is formally called Melon de Bourgogne. A few American wineries are beginning to make a "Melon" wine, and they're interesting but not cheap. (They're not easy to sell, either. A California winery executive told us he once made a "Melon" wine no one would buy—because they didn't want a wine made out of melons!)

Muscadet isn't a wine to linger over or debate. It's just fun. It's the kind of wine you'd want to have in the cozy little bistro down the street. That said, it's also not a simple bar wine, because it has some sharp edges and acidity that make it perfect with food.

We decided to pick up a whole bunch of inexpensive Muscadets for a blind tasting on the assumption that pretty much all young Muscadets—the younger the better—would be good. We were right. There were a few disappointments—one, from 1994, we drank only to assure ourselves that youth was a virtue; a couple of others had so much of that musty quality they went over the line to "wet dog." (We use the term "wet dog" a lot to describe a smell, and sometimes a taste, that's like—well, like a wet dog. This is not a good thing.)

All of the rest were at least very nice; not the kind of wines you'll always remember, but fun, pleasant, altogether winning picnic wines. They tasted slightly different from one another, but also were clearly related.

While millions of gallons of Muscadet are produced, many of them are produced in limited quantities. One we often see, though, is Château de la Chesnaie, and it's consistently good, with classic, understated Muscadet tastes. In this tasting, several were slightly better. The Château de la Chesnaie is likely to remain our house Muscadet because of its year-after-year reliability. But the better Muscadets had some extra tastes and a little bit of special crispness that made them stand out.

The very best of the tasting was an absolutely clear choice. The La Nobleraie 1997 had it all: It was fresh, crisp, and satisfying, with a thirst-quenching, sprightly taste that showed real character. There was nice lemon on the nose and in the mouth, but it still had that classic Muscadet "flatness" that makes it good with food, especially seafood. For only $5.99, it was a surprisingly memorable wine, with so much personality it was impossible to ignore.

If you're looking for something with a little more character than Muscadet, it's worth checking out another white wine from the Loire called Vouvray. It's a more distinctive wine than Muscadet, made from the Chenin Blanc grape. Chenin Blanc, you say?

Poor Chenin Blanc. Just as with poor Chablis, every cheap white jug wine in the world, for a time, was called "Chenin Blanc," although much of it wasn't—not even close. That made Chenin Blanc as declassé as a grape could be. When was the last time you showed up at someone's house with a bottle of wine and exclaimed, "I brought a Chenin Blanc"? In fact, some courageous California winemakers have made serious Chenin Blancs (the best we ever had was from a winery called White Oak in Sonoma). But Chenin Blanc grapes most naturally hit their highest notes in France, in wines like Vouvray.

Vouvray can be sweet, dry, or sparkling. But it's generally delightful and it is truly—we know this word is overused, but it truly is—unique. It smells fruity and creamy, but packs a powerful green-apple tartness. Imagine what the skin of a very fresh green apple smells and tastes like. Vouvray has a great deal of body—almost like it's thick—and yet, at best, it's clean, crisp, and lemony. Well chilled on a hot day, it's particularly refreshing.

We visited several New York–area wine stores and bought a whole bunch of different Vouvrays, and one thing became clear: If you're looking for some kind of consistency, this is not your wine. Vintages matter; styles vary; producers have different visions. But it's worth the effort to try a couple of Vouvrays, because a good one is something you will remember.

While the tastes weren't consistent, the quality was. Most rated "good" on our scale. It was clear real winemakers were at work here. The wines had character and charm, time after time, which is a lot to ask for bottles that cost about $7 to $19.

The first wine we tasted was Domaine Bourillon-Dorléans La Coulée d'Argent 1996. "Sweet/tart!" we wrote. "Pungent, pearlike nose. Great nose. Fresh-smelling like a flower garden. Rich at front, sour at end. Refreshing, clean, fruity, classy, elegant." As we drank it, though, it got less flowery and even more elegant, with even classier, more restrained tastes.

Then there was the Champalou Cuvée des Fondraux 1996 ($12.99). We wrote it was "crisp, aggressive, with a fruity, sour nose. Long, luscious/tart finish. Creamier than No. 1, but just as good in its way. Surprisingly light, but with lots of tastes of peaches and pears. Well chilled, it all comes together."

Both Muscadet and Vouvray are inexpensive and widely available. Buy the youngest you can find, chill it well, and try it. There's not a lot of risk—and there are possibly great rewards.

Wine Notes

Muscadet is the always available, generally inexpensive dry white wine from the Loire Valley in France. If you're having any kind of white fish tonight, this will make your dinner better. Buy the youngest you can find and chill it well. If you think of it, look for the words "Sèvre-et-Maine" on the label; that's the area that often makes the best ones. You shouldn't have to spend more than about $9.

La Nobleraie Muscadet Sèvre-et-Maine Sur Lie 1997
(Sauvion et Fils) $5.99
VERY GOOD • *Best of tasting; best value. Lovely, crisp, clean nose with a lot of fruit. A crisp, aggressive wine, almost biting in its crispness. Lively, young, fresh, and everything you want in a Muscadet.*

Clos de la Senaigerie Muscadet Côtes de Grandlieu
Sur Lie 1996 Sèvre-et-Maine Sur Lie 1996 $7.99
GOOD/VERY GOOD • *Lovely. Very much like the wine above, but with less fruit.*

Château du Cléray Muscadet 1996 $8.49
GOOD/VERY GOOD • *Real Muscadet taste, with some acids that make it especially good with food.*

Morilleau: Prieuré Royal Saint-Laurent Muscadet
Côtes de Grand-Lieu Sur Lie 1996 $7.99
GOOD/VERY GOOD • *Fresh and fruity, with surprising and subtle hints of lemon, melon, and peach.*

Château de la Chesnaie Muscadet Sèvre-et-Maine
Sur Lie 1996 $5.99
GOOD • *Often available and always reliable. Want to know what an everyday Muscadet tastes like? This is it: young, fresh, lemony, a little musty, and totally drinkable.*

Domaine de la Pepière Muscadet Sèvre-et-Maine $5.99
GOOD • *A little like the wine directly above. Fresh and young.*

Wine Notes

Vouvray is a unique white wine made from Chenin Blanc grapes in the Loire Valley of France. It can be sweet, dry, or sparkling. In youth, it tastes like a big bite into a very fresh and crisp green apple, which makes it perfect, well chilled, on a hot August day. But Vouvray also ages well, so if you happen to see an old Vouvray, it's worth a try.

Domaine Bourillon-Dorléans La Coulée d'Argent 1996 $13.99
VERY GOOD • *Best of tasting (tie). Smells like a bouquet of flowers, with a riot of tastes: rich at the front of the mouth, sour at the back. It's refreshing, clean, and classy, with that sweet-tart taste so special in a Vouvray.*

Champalou Cuvée des Fondraux 1996 $12.99
VERY GOOD • *Best of tasting (tie). A crisp, aggressive, fruity, sour nose. Taste is luscious and yet surprisingly light, with all sorts of hints of*

peaches and pears that come together in a long, memorable finish. Yum.

Domaine de Vaufuget 1996 $6.99

GOOD/VERY GOOD • *Best value. So dry it's almost austere, with a great deal of lemony class.*

Domaine du Clos Naudin, Sec, Foreau 1996 $18.99

GOOD/VERY GOOD • *This is a very serious wine, with acid, chalk, and even wood tastes in lovely balance. This one requires a bit more thought than most.*

Valentin Fleur 1996 $7.99

GOOD/VERY GOOD • *Soft, spritzy, creamy, with "sweet" green-apple and nectar tastes.*

Jean Sauvion 1996 $6.95

GOOD • *Simple and lemony, but refreshing on a hot day.*

Cherry Picking
Wine Tastes Better When It's a Steal

Wine lovers, no matter how successful or rich, love to "cherry pick." This means finding a rare or expensive wine at a bargain price. When wine lovers get together, they spend half their time talking about the great bottles they had—and the other half talking about the great bargains they found. Somehow, a wine just tastes better when you got it on the cheap. We once spent an evening crying with laughter as Bill Plante, the elegant longtime CBS News White House correspondent and wine lover, told us about rushing down the aisles of a giant Costco store early in the morning because it was selling Tignanello, one of Italy's most famous red wines, for just $30.

When we think of cherry picking, we think of some great Burgundies we found for $1.99 each and a 1970 Château d'Yquem we found for just $30. And we think about this:

One of the famous wines of the '70s was something called Ice Wine from Chateau Ste. Michelle in Washington State, now one of the state's biggest wineries and still one of the best. Ice wine—real ice wine, because there are fakes out there—is rare. Winemakers, usually in Germany (ice wine is derived from the German word *Eiswein*), leave a few grapes on a few vines after all the others have been harvested. Then they wait for frost. When the grapes freeze, only a tiny amount of concentrated, sweet juice remains. From this, they make precious amounts of very expensive, and exquisite, wine. The fact that Ste. Michelle had made an ice wine from its Riesling was remarkable. It was so rare it was sold in half bottles, and ordinary mortals, like us, couldn't hope to ever taste it.

We were living in Miami at the time, and we went to a Cuban restaurant called 27 & 27 every weekend, sitting at the counter, nursing our café con leche and reading the newspaper. In the middle of the counter, where the waitresses worked, was an island where they cut that delicious Cuban bread and kept desserts in a refrigerated case. On top of that there were always a couple dozen bottles of wine, mostly Spanish and mostly just for show. One morning, John saw something new. He couldn't believe it. It was the Chateau Ste. Michelle Ice Wine 1978. For $3.50.

Cherry picking is a very delicate art. When you make a great discovery, it's very important not to appear excited. You might raise the curiosity of the shopkeeper, who might then jack up the price. John whispered to Dottie what he'd seen, his lips barely moving. She, too, was agog—quietly. After a couple of minutes, we called over the waitress. "Um," said John, "that looks like an interesting wine. Is this price [his voice was so tight he could barely talk] corr-ect?" The waitress, of course, didn't have a clue. So she held up the bottle and, in Spanish, yelled something across to the man at the other end of the restaurant. Soon, everyone who worked there crowded around our bottle, and us. They didn't much care about the price. They wondered who was interested in wine at nine in the morning. Three dollars and fifty cents was indeed the correct price. We bought two.

The first we drank for Christmas in 1986: "Delicious! Sweet apricot nose, golden rich color. Burnt orange. Intense nectar taste. Huge, long finish. Sweet, rich, and luscious." We still have the second bottle. And even if we never drink it, it has been worth far more than $3.50.

But then, of course, there's Lu's. If you ever want to see a silly grin come across our faces, just say, "So, tell me about Lu's."

We were at a Shell's City liquor shop in Miami in 1985 when we spied a Champagne we'd never seen. It was a horrible little label, bright red and white, that just said "Lu's." No vintage. But it said it was from Épernay, one of France's great Champagne towns, and it looked real, and was just $9.99, so we bought it. Oh, man. It was delicious: nutty, creamy, with a real sense of fullness and richness that could only come from age. We went back and bought a case.

Lu's quickly became our house wine. We kept a bottle in the refrigerator all the time. On any whim, we'd give one to friends, who would then rush out and buy a case of Lu's. When one Shell's City store would run out of Lu's, we'd find another that still had some and buy a couple more cases.

Finally, sadly, it became harder and harder to find Lu's, and then it disappeared. We even sent a letter to Lu's—just "Épernay, France"—but it was returned, undeliverable. And that was the end of that, until several years later.

One day we were spending a few hours looking through a wine store, trying to find something new and interesting. There on the shelf was a very expensive Maxim's Champagne, with a lovely, artistic label. "We've never seen this before," we said. "Is it new?" The shopkeeper explained that Maxim's had tried once before to break into the South Florida market. "They brought their 1964 in here a few years ago," he explained. "But it was so expensive nobody would buy it. So they slapped some sort of awful label on it and basically gave it away. It was some stupid name. I can't remember it." He yelled across to one of his associates: "Hey, remember that '64 Maxim's? What did they call it?"

And the associate yelled back, from across the shop, "I think it was Lu's. Yeah, that's it. They called it Lu's."

GERMAN WINES
Imagine the Taste of a Rose

QUICK: You're at a wine store staring at these three labels. Which would you pick?

No. 1. Georg Albrecht Schneider 1997er Niersteiner Paterberg Riesling Kabinett. Qualitätswein mit Prädikat. Rheinhessen. Gutsabfüllung.

No. 2. Weinkellerei Carl Graff Ürzig a.d. Mosel 1996 Mosel-Saar-Ruwer Ürziger Würzgarten Riesling Auslese. Qualitätswein mit Prädikat.

No. 3. Weingut Dr. Bürklin-Wolf. 1996. Wachenheimer Gerümpel Riesling Spätlese. Pfalz. Qualitätswein mit Prädikat.

If you answered *any* of the above, you're right. All three are delightful, beautifully made German wines. But if, like a lot of people, you answered *none* of the above, well, then, this chapter is for you.

We certainly can't blame you. German wines seem just about impossible to figure out. *Wachenheimer Gerümpel?* That sounds like the punch line of one of John's father's jokes. But figuring out German wines is easier than you think. Just knowing which wines come in green bottles and which in brown bottles takes you halfway there. By discovering the great wines of Germany, you'll also discover the wonderful, versatile Riesling grape, truly one of the wonders of the wine world.

We spent the first few years of our wine lives together without ever drinking a fine German wine. We thought they were simple, sweet, inexpensive, and forgettable. They were Blue Nun, which in our youth was so widely known it engendered a knockoff called Blue Monk. But then something opened our eyes.

We're always preaching that you must find a good wine merchant, someone whom you trust—and someone who cares enough about you (and about wine) to try to introduce you to new tastes. Many years ago, on our third visit to a store called the Wine Cask in North Palm Beach, Florida, a friendly merchant named Art Gadarian quietly asked us, "Do you like German wines?" We told him that, in our limited experience, we had found German wines sweet, simple, and not really suited to food. "Try this," he said, and he handed us a bottle of 1975 Steinberger Kabinett from Rheingau. We can still taste its remarkable combination of backbone, aggressive fruit, pear-apple charm, and soil.

We began to dabble in better German wines and were amazed. Consider these notes from a Rüdesheimer Berg Rottland Spätlese 1971, a Rheingau we bought from Art (for $8.99) in 1980: "Delicious! Pure gold. Big nose, burnt almost, with peaches and cream. *Big*, spicy, creamy (got creamier with air in mouth). Incredibly *long*, spicy, smooth finish. Strong peaches. Fluffy! Incredible complexity of nose and taste. Coldness made it crisper!"

Riesling is grown all over the world—some American wineries make fine Rieslings—but it reigns in Germany. It has a crisp acidity, a whole cornucopia of fruit tastes (apples, peaches, pears, grapefruit), and a bouquet of flowers on the nose and the tongue. Imagine if you could taste the essence of peach nectar without any of the heaviness— or if you could actually taste what a bouquet of flowers smells like. Even dry Riesling has a "sweetness" about it that's not from sugar but from the very vibrancy of the grape. And sweet German Riesling is unlike anything else.

One of the pleasures of drinking German wines is that they seem so effortless. You taste the grape, not the winemaker. You can't sense any gears turning. There are no fingerprints on it. As Chardonnay falls out of fashion among some aficionados, who find it too heavy, too obvious, and too much an extension of the winemaker, more are turn-ing to Riesling because of its purity. It's clean, it's crisp, and it tastes like grapes, not like wood. It tastes like nature. And German wines have a self-confidence that makes them easy to be with. Their crisp-ness and acidity make your taste buds water, so some people find them perfect with food.

We sometimes drink German wines with dishes like chicken with creamy mushroom sauce or pork with sautéed apples and plums. But on the whole, we find their delicate, flowery tastes best enjoyed on their own, as an apéritif, an after-dinner wine when the girls are finally asleep, or on a sunny day with a picnic in Central Park. Still, whether it's with food or standing alone, German wines are a wonder, and you don't need a German-language dictionary to enjoy them.

The labels needn't be as daunting as they appear. Just remember, for starters, two broad categories: the wines of the Rhine River (such as Rheingau, Rheinhessen, and Rheinpfalz, or Pfalz, traditionally in brown bottles) and the Mosel River (Mosel-Saar-Ruwer, traditionally in green bottles). Rhine wines have a little more pepper and backbone; Mosel wines seem more flowery (and, by the way, it's MO-zuhl). The words "Qualitätswein mit Prädikat" mean the wine has met the high-est government requirements. The first name on the label, like "Nier-steiner," just means it's from Nierstein.

In very simple terms, you can think of the words Kabinett, Spätlese, and Auslese as guides to sweetness, from the driest (Kabinett) to the sweetest (Auslese). In fact, these terms are guides to ripeness and "weight"—that's how you can have a "Trocken," or dry, Auslese—but if at first you just think of them as guides to sweetness, you'll be fine. It's important to remember that even a Spätlese or Auslese isn't "sweet" in the kind of cloying way you might be thinking. All good German wines are so clean, so crisp, and so beautifully made that the sweetness is fundamental to their charming taste, not a film of sugar blanketing the taste.

There are higher grades of sweetness—Beerenauslese, Trocken-beerenauslese, and Eiswein—but they're rare and expensive. They also, by the way, last forever. For Christmas 1998, we drank a bottle of Trittenheimer Apotheke Beerenauslese from the 1975 vintage. It had turned golden, with a nose of burnt almonds and peaches. Even at that level of sweetness, the wine was vibrant, not cloying or clumsy. It was light and frothy instead of thick, with a clean, light, orange-nectar finish. Yum! So don't rule out buying a Spätlese or an Auslese just because it's sweeter than a Kabinett. Also, keep in mind that German wines are often lower in alcohol than other wines.

There are so many different vineyards, so many regions, and so many different producers you'd go crazy trying to get it all straight. After you've had one good German wine, remember just one word from its label and look for that again. After our first Steinberger, from Rheingau, we just looked for Rheingau for a while. At some point, we discovered wines from Nierstein, so we bought everything we could that said "Niersteiner." In other words, you don't have to be an expert on German wines to enjoy them. To test that thesis, we bought dozens of German wines, at random. Our only criteria were that they cost less than $20 and be made from Riesling. (Most German labels now say "Riesling" on them, but most German wines sold in the U.S. seem to be made from Riesling anyway.) We were very pleased with the results. Wine after wine was delightful and beautifully made. In our very first "flight" of six wines, we had trouble deciding among three—an unusually high success rate for any kind of wine. Our three favorites of this flight were the three indecipherable wines at the beginning of this chapter.

Of those three, it was a tough call, but we ultimately decided we liked the Carl Graff Ürziger Würzgarten Auslese, from Mosel, best from that first flight. At first, it seemed a bit simple and sweet, but as it opened up, it was very satisfying—rich in the mouth, almost like fluffy egg whites, with a nose like a bouquet of fresh flowers. It had some taste of soil that gave it real backbone. And while we'd generally recommend that German wines be served well chilled, the wine showed more class and character as it got warmer, which was remarkable.

Here are some descriptions that kept coming up in the tasting:

"Delightful."

"Totally lovely."

"Like nectar."

"Light on its feet."

"Charming."

"Like a bouquet of flowers."

"So clean."

"Refreshing."

"Peachy."

"Crisp."

"Pure pleasure."

Actually, that last term—"pure pleasure"—is how Dottie described our best of tasting when all the flights were done. It was a Zeltinger Schlossberg Riesling Spätlese 1997 from Selbach-Oster. It had a little bit of spritz, but the spritz turned out to be integral to its charming tastes. It had hints of all sorts of fruits—pineapple, lemon, peaches, and oranges—and yet, in our mouths, there seemed to be little body there but the slightest hint of bubbles. And inside each bubble was a universe of fruit nectars. Marvelous!

This wine was at the upper reaches of our budget—$19.99—but was worth far more than that. In general, German wines tend to be great bargains because they're not popular. They should be.

Wine Notes

Many wineshops carry only a few German wines, and they're off in a corner gathering dust. Don't buy them there! These are charming, ephemeral wines, and if they've been kept poorly, they might have been harmed. Find a store with a nice selection of young, fresh German wines. Look for "Riesling" on the label. If you're buying a wine to have with dinner, you might be better off with one that says "Kabinett," because that is generally the driest, but don't shy away from the sweeter designations (Spätlese and Auslese), because they're delightful, flowery, peachy wines. Chill well, which will make the wine crisper—although, as an experiment, you might try letting a bottle warm up. You'll be surprised to suddenly taste some earth and a bit of tough backbone that's carefully hidden most of the time but actually gives these wines their surprising depth. Don't ever judge a German wine by the first glass; these wines are so different from what you're already comfortable with that it takes a while to get used to them. By the second glass, you'll be seduced.

Selbach-Oster Zeltinger Schlossberg Riesling Spätlese 1997 (Mosel-Saar-Ruwer)   **$19.99**

DELICIOUS • *Best of tasting. Like the most charming person you've ever met. Pineapple, lemon, peaches, and orange, wrapped in a slightly spritzy package with a bow on top. Pure pleasure.*

Georg Albrecht Schneider Niersteiner Paterberg Riesling Kabinett 1997 (Rheinhessen)   **$9.99**

VERY GOOD/DELICIOUS • *Best value. It tastes like peach-pear nectar, with hints of grapefruit, yet it's so light in your mouth that it's more of a thought than a taste.*

Carl Graff Ürziger Würzgarten Riesling Auslese 1996 (Mosel-Saar-Ruwer) $13.99

VERY GOOD/DELICIOUS • *It fills your mouth, like fluffy egg whites, with the taste of a bouquet of flowers. Yet, warmer, it shows some surprising heft. Serious wine.*

Schloss Vollrads Riesling Qualitätswein 1996 (Rheingau) $14.99

VERY GOOD • *Very, very classy, with everything going for it: acid, fruit, earth, and a lovely lightness. So easy and self-confident.*

Schumann-Nägler Riesling Spätlese Geisenheimer Kläuserweg 1997 (Rheingau) $17.99

VERY GOOD • *Clean, refreshing, and peachy. It's sweet, but so very light on its feet. Who wouldn't like this?*

Joh. Jos. Christoffel Erben Ürziger Würzgarten Riesling Kabinett 1997 (Mosel-Saar-Ruwer) $16.99

VERY GOOD • *Colorless, crisp, and spritzy. Absolutely delightful. Yes, it's sweet, but it's so crisp that it's like biting into a perfect apple.*

Dr. Bürklin-Wolf Wachenheimer Gerümpel Riesling Spätlese (Pfalz) 1996 $17.99

VERY GOOD • *Delightful. Crisp, like apples, with a spritz that wakes up your mouth. Marvelous apéritif, but with enough soil to give it some attractive backbone. Could stand up to food.*

Dr. Bürklin-Wolf Wachenheimer Rechbächel Riesling Kabinett (Pfalz) 1995 $14.99

VERY GOOD • *Pretty and golden. It's like apples, grapefruit, and sunshine. It's toasty—it tastes amber. It's still young, but intellectually engaging. A sophisticated wine, great in a few years.*

**Schumann-Nägler Johannisberger Erntebringer Riesling
Kabinett 1997 (Rheingau)** **$11.99**

GOOD/VERY GOOD • *Tastes like a fresh green apple, with more body
and acid than most. This is probably the best food wine of the bunch.*

ITALIAN WHITES

... and Blue Suede Shoes

IF WE HAD WRITTEN THIS BOOK just a few years ago, we probably would have skipped a chapter on the white wines of Italy. Until recently, Italian whites, at least the ones imported into the U.S., were hidden off in a corner somewhere—an Always Elvis kind of wine.

Always Elvis?

When people visit our house, they're sometimes intimidated by our large wine collection. They figure our cellar is filled with rare treasures from France and irreplaceable liquid gold from California. That's when we pull out our bottle of "Always Elvis." The label, black and bright gold, shows The King, in his later years, singing into the microphone. On the back is a poetic tribute to Elvis, "Written for all the Fans Worldwide, BY THE COLONEL." What's inside is an Italian white wine called Frontenac Blanc d'Oro. We bought two bottles of this, for $3.29 each, at a Grand Union in Miami in 1980. We opened one right away. Here are our notes, in their entirety:

"Slight sparkle. Little character."

That pretty much summed up Italian whites back then, when you saw them at all in U.S. stores. Italy, after all, is known for its red wines: Chianti, Barolo, Dolcetto, and so many others. When you thought of dinner at that little Italian place on the corner, years ago, you thought of red wine, regardless of what you were eating. But in just the past few years, white wines from Italy have exploded onto the scene in the U.S. Everywhere you turn, you hear: "I'll have a glass of Pinot Grigio." Even bad wineshops offer a huge array of Italian white wines, most of them inexpensive, in an effort to satisfy Americans' insatiable thirst for cold white wines.

What are these gazillion Italian whites? It's often impossible to say. Unlike the French, whose wines come from specific, formal viticultural regions that are known for their specific styles, Italian winemakers can pretty much produce whatever wine they want, from wherever they want. It's basically a free-for-all—despite various government and industry efforts over the years—which only confuses consumers. "Pinot Grigio," for instance, doesn't tell you much, since it's simply the name of the grape and could come from just about anywhere.

Bianco, for instance, just means "white." Well, you can tell that just by looking at it. Even when geographical regions or zones are on the labels, they're not much help. And the quality designations—from Denominazione di Origine Controllata e Garantita (DOCG) to Denominazione di Origine Controllata (DOC), then down to Indicazione Geografica Tipica (IGT) and vini da tavola (table wine)— aren't hugely helpful because they include some of the country's best and worst producers.

We love all wine, of course, but we've found Italian whites over the years to be so simple, so much like lemon water, that we just haven't made them a regular part of our lives. Our favorite description of Italian whites is from Tom Stevenson in *The New Sotheby's Wine Encyclopedia,* which is an excellent reference book: "Freshness, crisp acidity, and purity of varietal character personify the wines of the northeastern regions of Trentino–Alto Adige, Friuli–Venezia Giulia, and the Veneto, but beware the mass-produced wines, which are so clean and pure that they lack any fruit."

Our serious education began at a charming restaurant in Manhattan called Le Madri, which was so eager for company in the dog days of August that it offered an outrageous deal: Come in, have lunch, and—for free—drink all you want of a huge array of Italian wines served by the importers themselves. So there we were, on three successive Fridays, indulging in four-hour lunches. We may have overdone it, but we learned something important: Some Italian whites— whether Pinot Grigio or Soave—are better than others. A lot better.

These had a depth and a sophistication we hadn't seen outside Italy, and we suspect, from the price, that not many of these are available in wine stores in the United States. But which is which and what is what and how in the world can you tell? We went on a journey to find out. We bought Italian whites by the dozen, over a period of several weeks, to try to reach some conclusions.

We bought dozens under $10, a few between $10 and $15, and just a couple above that as ringers. We figured most people these days are buying the cheap stuff—and, in any case, the cheap stuff is surely what they're getting when they order that "glass of Pinot Grigio" at the bar. We tasted them blind in "flight" after flight, night after night. We tasted Orvietos and Soaves and Pinot Grigios, Vernaccias and Pinot Biancos, and more.

We found, as Tom Stevenson suggested, that most of these wines simply lacked fruit—and, therefore, much character. The Soaves were, on the whole, simple, with spritz and a taste of lemons. None that we had rose very far above that, although the Bolla Soave 1997, which you see everywhere, had some cream on the nose. The Orvietos went from one that was basically dead in the glass, and couldn't be revived, to a Ruffino Orvieto 1997, also ubiquitous, that we found "delightful," with some real body. Not nearly as nice, but OK, was the Orvieto Antinori 1997, which we nailed as the wine closest to what we've been served in restaurants. It was "pleasant and unmemorable," basically neutral, a heck of a thing for a wine to be. (And our guess is most restaurants charge more for a single glass of this than they pay for an entire bottle.)

The Vernaccias and Pinot Grigios spanned the gamut, from lemon water to well-made wines like the Isonzo Pinot Grigio 1996 (Nando) that tasted of earth and fruit and had real backbone. We searched desperately for some notation on these bottles that would have hinted at which we might expect to be good and which would be nondescript, for something the impressive ones had in common. Were the better ones of the same grape type from the same part of Italy? Were they all estate bottled? We even laid all of the empty bottles on our bed, hoping some marker, until then unnoticed, would leap out at us, standing back at a distance. We found zip. Nada.

In general, we'd urge you to skip your Pinot Grigio next time and try a Pinot Bianco. Many of the Pinot Biancos had some real character, with hints of melons and a kind of "dirty" taste that added some texture. Still, these wines, again, ranged from simple to the more complex, like the Alois Lageder Pinot Bianco, Alto Adige 1996, about which we wrote: "Sweet with flat-fruit tastes; tastes like a white Bordeaux."

One of the more expensive wines we threw in as a control was a Cornarea Roero Arneis 1997. Arneis from Roero, we've learned over time, are of good quality. While not expensive in the scheme of things, this one, at $16.99, was at the high end of a range that started as low as $6.99. We had it, as it happened, during the last blind flight and we said in our notes that it was a "real wine with some bite."

After tasting dozens of Italian whites and finding most simple and charmless, we tried a radical experiment. We went out to dinner at one of our favorite Indian restaurants and ordered a bottle of inexpensive Pinot Grigio. We thought maybe the flat, lemony, simple taste of the wine might somehow come alive when paired with fiery Indian food. We were wrong. The wine added nothing to the food, and vice versa. It was very much like ordering a bottle of sparkling water with dinner.

In fact, that may be the point. After tasting several cases of Italian whites in blind flights, we arrived at this disturbing conclusion: Since the marketplace is flooded with so many Italian whites that taste like sparkling water with a slice of lemon, a lot of people must be treating this like a hip, alcoholic version of Perrier with lime. Gee. If that's what you really like about these wines, here's our advice: If you feel you must have a glass of something as you circulate at a party or at a bar, or if you'd like something cold to drink with your lunch, order the fizzy water and lemon and forget about it. It even has fewer calories. Perhaps if enough people have the courage to drop the charade and part with these faux wines, Italian winemakers will get the hint and either turn out better wines or ship their spritzy stuff elsewhere.

On the other hand, maybe people are drinking bad Italian whites because they think that's what Italian whites are supposed to taste like. In fact, they're supposed to be better. While the average quality of our wines was not good, we did find several exceptions, wines with some style, some fruit, some body, and some class. In other words: *You don't have to settle!* We wish we could offer more guidance about how to tell the good from the bad, but what we can tell you is that if your Italian white wine is simply a cold drink and not something you're truly enjoying, try another. The prices are low, so you can afford to take a couple of chances.

For those of you who really like Italian whites, and who have had your eyes opened, as ours were at Le Madri, all we can say is good luck on your search. There are gems out there, but the Italian wine industry hasn't done much to help you find them. For the same amount of money and a lot less angst, try a French Muscadet.

Wine Notes

Italian whites can range from simple, lemony bubble water to complex, full-bodied wines. There's not a lot on the labels to help you figure out which is which. But there are a couple things you'll want to remember: Buy younger vintages and drink them well chilled. The high acidity of most of these wines makes them good with food, especially seafood. At least theoretically, Denominazione di Origine Controllata e Garantita (DOCG) is the highest-quality category, followed by Denominazione di Origine Controllata (DOC) and then Indicazione Geografica Tipica (IGT)—but, as you can see from this list, those really don't guarantee much. If you're used to drinking Pinot Grigio, try a Pinot Bianco, which generally seems to have more character, although its flat, melonlike tastes might not be for everybody.

Alois Lageder Pinot Bianco, Alto Adige 1996 DOC   **$9.99**

VERY GOOD • *Best of tasting. Crisp and fresh, "sweet" with flat fruit.*

Isonzo Pinot Grigio (Nando) 1996 DOC   **$8.99**

VERY GOOD • *Best value. Real taste, warms your mouth. Earth, nutmeg, and backbone. Sage and herbs and body.*

Terrazzo Esino Bianco 1997 DOC   **$7.95**

VERY GOOD • *Clean, lemony, with some cream. Very nice and highly drinkable.*

Vigneti del Sole Pinot Grigio Delle Venezie 1997 IGT   **$11.99**

VERY GOOD • *A little cornucopia of fruits like grapefruit and melon, but just hints of everything. Light, pleasant, and shy. Charming, a bit like caramel apples, with a little cream on the nose.*

S. Quirico Vernaccia di San Gimignano 1996 DOCG   **$8.95**

GOOD/VERY GOOD • *Chalk and wood. This is real wine, crisp but with some fruit and flavor. This would be sublime with grilled fish.*

Kris Pinot Grigio Delle Venezie 1997 IGT   **$8.99**

GOOD/VERY GOOD • *Pleasant and lemony, but with some body and some depth. Drinkable, with real mouthfeel.*

Cornarea Roero Arneis 1997 DOC   **$16.99**

GOOD/VERY GOOD • *A real wine with some bite, some spritz, and some fruit. Pleasant.*

Ruffino Orvieto Classico 1997 DOCG   **$6.99**

GOOD/VERY GOOD • *Crisp, biting nose. Clean, crisp, lemony, simple, and pleasant, with some "sweet" fruit. Delightful.*

Decoding the Wine List

It's Easier Than It Looks

Ordering wine in a restaurant should be one of the pleasures of eating out. Instead, for too many people it's a chore, something to be dreaded. The wine director of one of America's most famous restaurants once told us that often when he hands the wine list to people, he feels he's tossing them a hot potato. He mimicked the recipient of the wine list virtually throwing it to someone else at the table. "No, YOU do it." "No. YOU!"

This is a tragedy. After all, you're spending a lot of money to eat out. The experience should be special. And wine helps make dinner special. Not only that, but right there on that wine list— hidden, like a piece of gold in a mine shaft—are treasures you probably won't see anywhere else. Wineries, importers, and shippers like to see their wines on fine restaurants' wine lists. It's good exposure for them, and it's likely the wines will be treated well, too. Restaurants want to have impressive wine lists so they can offer wines that equal their spectacular food.

So there you are at the restaurant, and you've been handed this seemingly incomprehensible list, filled with languages from all over the world. What do you do? Truth is, it's easier than you imagine. Don't think of the list as one big Tower of Babel. Think about how you decode things every day in your life. That's what you need to do with any wine list, no matter how thick. Just go through these seven simple steps. Think of them as a kind of Gaiter/Brecher Secret Wine List Decoder Ring.

1. Take your time. A few seconds after handing you the biggest wine list in the world, the waiter will come over and ask, "Have you made your selection?" or "Do you need help?" Just look up, smile, and say, "You have such an interesting list. It'll take me a few minutes to decide." At this point, the waiter will think you know what you're doing and will leave you alone.

2. Decide if you want red or white. If you're with a date or business colleagues, just ask: "Hey, do you like red or white?" If it's lunch, the answer will almost always be white. The rest of the time, the answer will usually be "Whatever you think." So if it's lunch, go with white. Otherwise, think about what kind of restaurant you're in. Look at the menu. Fish restaurant? White. Steak joint? Red. This single decision cuts the wine list in half. (If we're at an unfamiliar restaurant, we ask to see menus right away so we can make a quick determination if we're more likely to order "white" food or "red" food.)

3. Does the restaurant specialize in a certain type of wine? If there are twenty Italian wines listed and five American wines, the owner cares more about Italian wine. Go with it.

4. Eliminate the showcase wines. Many restaurants that have huge lists specialize in expensive French "first growth" wines, like Château Lafite-Rothschild. Are you going to order those wines? Of course not.

5. Now, among what's left, look for wines you already know— and cross them off, too. Hey, if you can buy the same wine from the corner wine store for half the price, it's not going to be much fun drinking it at a restaurant, is it? There are exceptions to this cross-out-the-familiar advice: If this is a make-or-break business meal or if you're proposing marriage, you might want to go with what you know is a sure thing. Otherwise, look for something new. Remember that restaurants often have wines on the list you won't see anywhere else. Sometimes they're cult wines, small-production wines rationed by the winery to certain chichi restaurants. They're not available in wine stores at any price. In fact, that's part of their allure. Most wine lovers will never even see them. In any case, ordering something you've never seen before and may never see again makes the whole issue of "markups" irrelevant.

6. Decide what you're willing to spend. Maybe you had planned to spend $25, but there's just about nothing on the list at $25. Think about $35. Whatever the price—and be flexible; c'mon, you're eating out—decide what you're willing to spend and mentally strike out everything else.

7. You've decided red or white, focused on what the restaurant specializes in, eliminated the showcase wines, crossed off wines you already know, and decided what you can spend. How many wines could possibly be left? Just a handful, we'd guess. So pick two or three. At this point, say to the waiter, "I can't decide among these wines"—and, wait, the next sentence is the key. Do not say, "What would you recommend?" Sad to say, in many restaurants, the waiter really won't have a clue and will simply choose one. Instead, ask, "What can you tell me about them?" This may flummox the waiter—who will then send over someone who actually knows something about wine. Ignore what he says. Instead, watch his eyes and his body language. You'll know which wine he is most excited about.

Order it. And don't worry about it. If it's not terrific, it's still something new and different. And if it's special, well, maybe something like this will happen to you:

A little French restaurant called Entre Nous opened on Lexington Avenue in New York City in 1980 and, instead of posting its menu in the window, posted its wine list. This is our kind of place, we figured. So, for our first anniversary, John dropped into the restaurant and secretly planned a special dinner with Bernard, the chef-owner. John looked through the wine list and decided on a fine Burgundy for dinner—a Domaine Duchet Beaune Cent-Vignes 1969—and told Bernard the food was up to him.

When we showed up, the wine was already on the table, open, and Bernard had prepared a spectacular meal, with duck as the main course. The rare duck paired with the rich, round, perfect Burgundy was everything an anniversary celebration could possibly be. In fact, it was a once-in-a-lifetime experience, quite literally: When John called a few weeks later for new reservations, the man on the other end of the line did not sound at all like Bernard. Entre Nous had been replaced by a Chinese restaurant.

We looked, but we never found Bernard.

RED
WINE

CABERNET SAUVIGNON

The Meaning of "Glassiness"

WHEN PEOPLE ASK US about the best bottle of wine we've ever had, we tell them this story.

Our wedding in 1979 was a family affair, just seventeen people, in the backyard of Dorothy's family's home in Tallahassee, Florida. As soon as the ceremony and sit-down dinner were over, we rushed to Jacksonville to catch a train. We spent our wedding night in one of Amtrak's deluxe sleepers with what was left of two cases of Taittinger Champagne, headed for Napa Valley.

It's a mistake to make too many plans when you visit wineries. You never know when you'll run into a winemaker who can talk and pour for hours. But we knew there was one winery we had to visit. Every day, we were told, Beaulieu Vineyards sold a limited number of its 1968 and 1974 Georges de Latour Private Reserve Cabernet Sauvignon at the winery. Wine people considered these among the greatest wines ever made in California, the ultimate triumph of the vision of the great winemaker André Tchelistcheff, one of California's true giants. But, outside of the winery, these wines could no longer be found.

We got to Napa, checked into the then-new Harvest Inn—all wood, brass, and fireplaces, perfect for a honeymoon—and immediately headed for Beaulieu. It wouldn't be long before the winery closed, and we figured we might have already missed our chance for that day. We burst into the tasting room and asked if they had any more of the '68 and '74 for sale. The daily allotment of the '74 was gone, but there was one bottle left of the '68. So we ran downstairs to the cellar, bought the bottle, and went back to the Harvest Inn, which had a vineyard out back. We borrowed a corkscrew and two glasses from Richard, the proprietor, told him it was our honeymoon, and asked if he'd mind if we walked among the vines.

We paid $35 for that bottle and it sure didn't look like much. Those were the days when wineries thought labels were less important than the wine in the bottle, and this was a label for its time: plain white with red lettering. Cheap, simple, utilitarian. But we'd heard there were wonders inside. It was mid-April and "bud break" had begun. The dark, gnarled vines sported new green stalks with tiny, embryonic, closed-tight-as-fists buds.

Spring is a special time in a vineyard. In winter, everything seems so dead, so brown and dreary. Nothing happens until bud break. By fall, the vines are filled with big, green leaves and plump, dangling fruit. On that April day, we were surrounded by Cabernet vines, and, in our minds, we could see them almost vibrating with life. The earth beneath us was fertile, dark, fragrant, and newly turned. We sat down between rows of vines, enveloped in the stillness of the vineyard, feeling very much in love and lucky to be alive. Dottie held the glasses as John opened the bottle and poured a tiny sip. The smell was glorious: incredibly fruity, ripe, and red, still, at eleven years old, very much a wine of youth and power.

It's hard to describe that first sip. It was fruit. Pure fruit. Perfect fruit. But this was the amazing part: With each sip, the wine changed. There is a quality to Cabernet we call "glassiness." It's hard to describe, but by glassiness we mean it has a sharpness, like a pin-focused, clear, distilled taste that fills your mouth with distinct layers of flavor at the front and leaves a lingering depth of flavor at the back. You know what a pane of glass looks like when it's clean and glistens in the sunlight? We think of Cabernets like that. Other people refer to it as "brightness." This wine was bright: alive, vibrant, sometimes sharp, sometimes huge, sometimes coy. Sip after sip, as the sun disappeared behind the mountains surrounding Napa Valley, the wine just kept getting better.

We will never have a better wine. Was it because we were on our honeymoon? Because we were sitting among vines on a perfect day? Of *course* it was. It's impossible to separate a great wine from a great experience. Years later, we met André Tchelistcheff at a wine dinner at the Plaza in New York City. Even then, nearing ninety years old, he was vibrant, with sparkling eyes and unabashed passion. Bright, like his wines. We told him the story of our honeymoon and got him to sign that label. When we asked how he knew 1968 would be such a great vintage, he looked at us and a big smile crossed his small face. He lifted his hand, rubbed his thumb and forefinger together, and said, "How did I know? I crushed a grape in my hand and I tasted it. And I knew."

Cabernet Sauvignon is the most consistently wonderful red grape in the world, the grape of the great "first growths" of Bordeaux and of those famously expensive, impossible-to-find California Cabernets. This is the classic wine to have with dinner, because its complex structure makes almost all foods more interesting. Even inexpensive Cabernets have way too much class to drink at the bar as a throwaway glass of wine.

Every couple of years, some new winery bursts on the scene with the latest must-have Cabernet. They're good, but much of their cachet is based on the fact that *you can't actually buy them*, which is nuts. Some of these wineries have messages on their answering machines that say, "No, we don't have any wine to sell; no, you can't get on our mailing list; and no, you can't leave a message." Holy cow! Truth is, if you're willing to spend $40 or $50 on a Cabernet, there are outstanding "Cabs" out there you can really find. We have had, over the years, dozens of outstanding Cabernets, but the Heitz Cellars Martha's Vineyard 1968, one of America's most famous wines, was one of the greatest. We drank it on New Year's Eve 1993. Consider these notes:

"Huge nose, like tar. Look is so *rich it looks like Cognac.* Intense fruit on the nose with raspberries and cherries. Thick, no hint of age. Taste is *perfect,* incredible. HUGE, RICH, with an incredible explosion in mouth that goes from chest to ears. Really! Wow! Like a *young* Latour! Bold. Smells, looks, and tastes thick, but it's not. Tingle in the nose. Nose is *overwhelming*. Completely forward taste."

Now *that* is wine. But as we discovered in a tasting in late 1998—a tasting with remarkable and unintended consequences—Cabernet does not have to be expensive to be excellent.

We decided we'd try dozens of American Cabernet Sauvignons under $20 to see, generally, how they were. As always, our mission wasn't to find the "best" Cabernet for under $20. There are hundreds of Cabs, from many different vintages, and it would be impossible to declare a best. Instead, our goal was to discover, in general, whether you can expect to get your money's worth by spending $20 or less on a Cab right off the shelf.

We were in for a huge surprise. The wines were, overall, quite good, and we were pleased American wineries still obviously take their Cabernets very seriously. But one stood out. It stood out so much, in fact, that we were sure there had been some sort of mistake.

We keep our wines in our wine closet very carefully. We separate the wines we drink for our *Wall Street Journal* column—we call them "Joanne's wines," because our boss, Joanne Lipman, pays for them—from our own private purchases. The night before, we had had one of our own wines—a 1982 Château Grand-Puy-Lacoste from Bordeaux. It was just great, everything a fine old "claret" should be. Well, we were convinced that somehow, instead of putting one of Joanne's Cabs into a bag for the blind tasting, John had picked up another bottle of that '82. "Lovely, complex nose, very much like an aged claret," we wrote. "Tastes like a real claret, rich yet filled with crisp layers of taste. Alive in your mouth. Dust, soil, and oak."

At the end of the tasting, we ripped off the bag fully expecting to see an old Bordeaux from our own stash. Instead, it turned out to be a Gallo Sonoma, from the 1992 vintage. Cost: $9.99.

Gallo?

All of us started somewhere with wine. We drank Mateus in college.

Our first bottle together was Cold Duck. But, to some extent—metaphorically—everyone started with Gallo, and nobody's proud of it. It's like looking at pictures of yourself when you were in your twenties. "Oh my God, look at that hair!" Not only that, but for those of us who came of age in the '60s, Gallo's epic battles with the late labor organizer César Chavez—not to mention its reputation as a ruthless competitor in the marketplace—made the company as unsavory as its wine.

We had recently read about how Gallo really is making good wines, but we didn't believe it. Gallo is a big advertiser and a major player in the industry; we weren't sure how much that had influenced the coverage. Well, we admit it: We were wrong. The '92 had the advantage of being one of the oldest wines we tasted, but it came right off the shelf of an everyday wine store, and we saw it at other wine stores around New York. Gallo made 43,000 cases of it, which is a lot, and wine stores say they were still getting it by the case in early 1998.

We first wrote about this wine in late 1998, and it created a sensation. We were deluged for weeks with calls, letters, and E-mails asking how to find it. Wine stores that usually sell out of whatever we write about by the evening the column appears sold out hours earlier. Gallo itself went on a mission to find every possible bottle and set up a special contact for anxious wine drinkers. One sad reader told us he'd gone to his wine store to get a bottle and found a line of people asking for it.

All of this is flattering, but it misses our ever-present Essential Point: There are plenty of good Cabernets out there. If you pick one up today—almost any one—and pop it open for dinner, you're almost sure to have a better dinner.

On the other hand, Cabernets (and the wines made from it, like Bordeaux) are the classic made-to-be-cellared wines. Good Cabernets will live for decades, and even inexpensive, well-made Cabernets get better and better with some age. In 1994, we opened a 1971 Cabernet from Chateau Ste. Michelle in Washington State. If you asked any expert if this was one of the great Cabernet makers in America, the answer would be no. But age does wonderful things to good wine. Our notes: "Delicious! Despite a low fill, nose is huge and room-filling. Big, massive, with an amazing nose of tobacco. Oddly, it's like a terrific old Burgundy. Rich and sweet and mouthfilling, with round textures. Lots of layers, from fruit to vibrancy. Raspberries. Not at all old, maybe even young."

Still, that wasn't perfection. This was:

On a Saturday morning in 1986, a wine-drinking friend of ours in Miami named Bob Radziewicz called us, breathless. "There's a little wine shop out on the Tamiami Trail that's selling seventy-eight Diamond Creek for fourteen dollars a bottle!" he yelled into the phone. In minutes, we were headed way out to western Dade County where, in a little strip shopping mall, we found a liquor store that, incredibly, was selling one of America's most famous Cabernets for $14.19. (It had been marked up twice. Under the $14.19 label were labels for $12.19 and $13.19.) We bought several bottles and kept them for years, until August 1998. Then we opened one. Here, uncensored, are our notes:

Cork smells great. It's so sweet with fruit that bugs have gathered around the glass! Awesome, sweet nose with lots of chocolate. Black color. Taste is simply awesome, soft yet enormous. Fruit without a single hard edge. Absolutely perfect on first sip. Only age will accomplish this perfect combination of fruit and softness and depth. Plums, cherries, wood, tobacco, chocolate, with an awesome finish more in the mind than in the mouth. Perfect NOW!

After ten minutes, gets backbone and verve under the fruit. Awesome grapes. Even the empty glass is awesome!

After one hour, it's rich and creamy and chewy without a hint of decay. It's mouthfilling in a fluffy kind of way. Deep, dark, rich, very California. Aged, powerful, big, bold, elegant—a Sean Connery kind of wine.

Rich, round, sensuous, and plump with layers and layers of fruit, plums, and taste.

It's simply perfect. Perfect.

There is no wine that can attain perfection as consistently as Cabernet Sauvignon. But you don't need perfect tonight, just a good, classy bottle of wine. For less than $20, Cabernet Sauvignon can be that wine.

Wine Notes

All regions of California are making surprisingly good Cabernet Sauvignon for less than $20. Almost all Cabs will benefit from some air, so pour a glass or two and let the wine sit for a while before you drink it. Age does wonderful things for Cabernet, so feel free to buy older vintages. Better yet, find an affordable young Cabernet you really like and lay it down for a couple years to see what happens. To us, the classic Thanksgiving wine is an old Cabernet, which has the richness to stand up to the gamier parts of the meal and the elegance to stand up to the lighter ones. All of the following except the Columbia Crest are from California.

Gallo Sonoma 1992 (Sonoma County) $9.99

DELICIOUS • *Best of tasting and best value. Lovely, complex nose, very much like an aged claret. Rich, yet filled with crisp layers of taste. Alive in your mouth, with tastes of dust, soil, and oak.*

William Hill Winery 1995 (Napa Valley) $12.99

VERY GOOD • *Lovely color, just like a Cab, rich and elegant. Young, viney nose. Rich, plump, lots of fruit. Tastes expensive. Long, elegant finish. Very Cab, with real aging potential.*

Liberty School 1996 (Coastal Oaks) $13.99

VERY GOOD • *Big, rich, creamy nose. Coats your tongue with creamy Cabernet taste. Sensual. The real thing.*

Villa Mt. Eden 1995 $11.99

GOOD/VERY GOOD • *Grapey, pleasant, and "sweet," with huge, forward fruit. Simple, without much complexity, but utterly drinkable.*

Cartlidge & Browne 1995 $9.99

GOOD/VERY GOOD • *Crisp and Beaujolais-like. Light and drinkable, not at all "serious," but with a depth of flavor on the finish that's quite nice.*

Columbia Crest 1994 (Columbia Valley, Washington State) $18.99

GOOD/VERY GOOD • *This is a wine with real edge—nothing simple about it. A great deal of character, but you have to go to it because it won't come to you. Don't even taste it for an hour. And if you can cellar it for a few years, it will be terrific.*

Gallo Sonoma 1994 (Barrelli Creek Vineyard) $19.99

GOOD • *Fine nose, with berries, tobacco, and chocolate. Deep purple. Rough-hewn. This is a classy California Cabernet, but it needs some time. Lay it down and it will reward you in a few years.*

Glen Ellen Winery 1996 (Proprietor's Reserve) $5.99

GOOD • *Light, fruity, simple, and nice. Nothing special, but, at the price, a very pleasant bottle of wine.*

Hess Select 1995 (The Hess Collection Winery) $13.99

GOOD • *Like a Syrah. Pleasant. Real character.*

Hawk Crest 1995 $10.99

GOOD • *Very pretty. Berrylike nose. Grapey, simple, and perfectly nice.*

Glass Mountain 1995 $9.99

GOOD • *Grapey, pleasant, and simple. A fine picnic wine.*

Tessera 1995 $12.99

GOOD • *Classy and fruity, but not deep.*

Decanting
When to Do It, and How, and Why Not

You've heard you should sometimes let a wine "breathe." But the truth is that simply removing the cork and letting the wine sit open doesn't do much at all, since very little air is getting to the wine to help it breathe or unfold. If you really want the wine to breathe, you need to pour a glass or two and let the bottle and the glasses sit for a while. Or decant it.

Truth is, we rarely decant wines. We enjoy experiencing everything a wine can show us, from that first sip of sometimes tight fruit to that gracious last taste, when the wine, almost spent, bestows its final kiss. We don't like to hurry that process. To speed it along by pouring the wine into a decanter so it can get a blast of air would be, for us, like entering a theater during the second act of a play. How much we would have missed!

Our only exception is when the wine is "throwing" a lot of sediment. That's when we pour off the clear wine, separating it from its sometimes sludgy stuff. But this kind of decanting has to be done carefully, because once air starts getting to a wine, the wine can change very quickly, and with tragic consequences. Yes, tragic. Listen to this:

As we've said, one of the most famous Cabernet Sauvignons in California is Heitz Cellars Martha's Vineyard. The 1974 is among the most prized old Cabs ever made. It is a wine no mere mortal would ever see—except for one Christmas, when we visited John's parents in Jacksonville, Florida.

We learned long ago that out-of-the-way wineshops are often great places to find wines that have been forgotten and are ripe for cherry picking. OK, you're right: Basically, we're hoping to take advantage of some sleepy merchant who's unaware. So we rarely pass a wineshop in a place like Jacksonville without running in. One day, in a neighborhood called San Marco, we saw a little wineshop and braked to take a look. There, sitting on a counter right next to the Soave, was a 1974 Heitz Cellars Martha's Vineyard. We had never seen one. It was one of those moments when organ music seems to swell up in the background. Then we saw the price: $125. One hundred and twenty-five dollars—far more than we could afford on journalists' salaries. We each touched the wine, and then we left.

John's father loved books. Through decades of marriage and raising three sons, John's father would spend whatever he could on rare books. He was surely the best-read car salesman in Jacksonville, and the only one with a first edition of *Tristram Shandy*, but the story John grew up with was about the book his dad *didn't* buy. It was a book of Picasso prints. At some point back in the '40s, he found it in a bookstore for $100. John's mother put her foot down. They could barely afford food, John's mother said. No way was he spending $100 on a book.

Picasso's book became very famous. Copies were sold at auction. It was mentioned in Picasso retrospectives. With each passing year, its price would rise. Throughout fifty years of marriage, John's father never stopped telling John's mother about the current price. So it was, in Jacksonville, that Dottie looked at John, pale behind the wheel of his Chevrolet, and said: "If we don't buy that bottle, it will always be your Picasso book." We walked back into the store and she bought it for him for $125. As we drove away, the entire staff of the store stood outside and waved.

Many years later, on Thanksgiving Day 1995, we decided to open it. We carefully decanted the bottle, which had developed some real sediment, giddy at the pleasure that awaited us. The first sip was spectacular—"awesome, concentrated fruit," we wrote. Then, the phone rang. It was an old friend from Miami, calling to say he was in town. We hated to be rude, but we couldn't wait to get back to the wine. Finally, after ten minutes, John got off the phone—Dottie had waited for him, like a nut—*and the wine had gone downhill!* It was still quite good, but the sweet intensity had evaporated. Poof! In its place was a more ordinary Cabernet richness. We were distraught. Totally inconsolable. We made a solemn vow to never, ever answer the phone again when something even barely approaching the specialness of that Martha's Vineyard was in our glasses. Civility has its limits.

We tell you this as a warning, before we tell you the best way to decant a wine, so you'll remember that, especially when decanting an older wine, you need to be vigilant so you won't miss it at its peak.

There are three reasons some people decant a wine. One is to make sure it gets plenty of air. You might want to do this because the wine is young, and air will blow off the rough edges; then you can taste the good stuff underneath that ordinarily only age would show you. Or you might do it because the wine is old and needs some air so it can open up a little after years of being tightly wound in the bottle. The second reason to decant a wine is if the wine is throwing sediment. If the wine has been properly handled, so that the sediment is all on the side or on the bottom, decanting allows you to pour the good, clear wine off the sediment. The third reason to decant a wine is that it's just a pretty cool thing to do; that's usually why restaurants do it.

That said, if you are going to decant, forget the candle and the rigmarole, unless you're trying to impress a date. If you are, great. If you're not, follow these steps:

~ First, be sure to stand the wine up for a day or two so all of the sediment moves to the bottom.

~ Get a flashlight with a flat bottom so it will stand up with the light flashing toward the ceiling. Get a decanter with a fairly wide mouth.

~ Open the wine carefully so you don't disturb the sediment.

~ Hold the bottle in one hand and the decanter in the other.

~ Lift the decanter and the bottle, so the flashlight is shining through the bottle just under the neck. Start pouring. You should be able to see the wine glistening through the bottle.

~ When you see sediment begin to flow into the neck of the bottle, stop! That's it. You've done it.

One last thing: Some people throw out the wine at the bottom of the bottle that has the sediment. This is a shame, because much of the soul of the wine is there. If you're squeamish, when you've finished the rest of the bottle, just pour the sediment through a coffee filter into the decanter. Then drink it. If you're not squeamish, just drink the sediment. To us, it's always an appropriate way to honor a fine wine's very last gasp.

ZINFANDEL

America in a Bottle

WE WERE HEADED down to the Florida Everglades in the winter of 1986 to get a good look at Halley's Comet. The air would be crisp and cold as we lay on the ground trying to see this once-in-a-lifetime ghost image. What wines would we take along? Zinfandels, of course. They would be big, bracing, warming, we were sure. And we were right. We wrote of our favorite on that trip, a Sherrill Cellars "Oct. 29th Zinfandel" from the 1974 vintage: "Portlike, shy nose with lots of ripe fruit and some sweetness. Real body. Hot in the middle. Huge, sweet at the end. Hot. Tastes like it's on fire."

This was California Zinfandel in the 1970s: wild, unrepentant, large—a John Wayne kind of wine. It's not for nothing that Zinfandel is known as the only uniquely American fine-wine grape.

There's not too much about American winemaking that's uniquely American, after all. Chardonnay, Pinot Noir, and Cabernet Sauvignon grapes make great wines in the United States, but they're more commonly associated with white Burgundy, red Burgundy, and Bordeaux. American wines are often aged in French oak. And the most famous event in American Chardonnay history happened only in comparison to France. When a Chateau Montelena Chardonnay, from California's 1973 vintage, beat all of the great white Burgundies of the same vintage in a tasting in 1976, it was a sensation. Virtually everyone who touched that Montelena later became famous. To this day, people will point at someone who stomped some of those grapes, lower their voice to a whisper, and say, "You know, he did that '73 Montelena."

American grapes—true American grapes—generally don't make very good wine. If you've ever tasted Concord grapes, you've tasted native American grapes, which are usually of the variety *Vitis labrusca.* In his classic book *The Wines of America,* the late Leon Adams says the very first American wines were made from native American grapes in John's hometown of Jacksonville between 1562 and 1564. We always thought that rather cool.

Vitis vinifera grape types like Pinot Noir, Cabernet Sauvignon—the classics—are the best. They were bred in Europe over centuries to make wonderful wines, and were brought to California more than two hundred years ago. What makes Zinfandel so special is it's a genuine *vinifera,* a fine wine grape, but it's American and only grows well in the United States. That's why many wine writers think it should be served with Thanksgiving dinner for an all-American bash, its dark pepper-fruit taste complementing the turkey. (We think old American Cabernets are the way to go on turkey day, but that's another story.) Nevertheless, it seems pretty clear Zinfandel is some sort of offshoot of an Italian grape. The tastes are too similar to be just happenstance. That's no coincidence, either, since so many of America's pioneering winemakers were Italian.

We've always loved Zinfandel, although it was never clear exactly what was in the bottle. Would this be a simple, elegant Zin that would taste a little like a Cabernet? A kick-ass, primitive Zin? A late-harvest Zin, with high alcohol and even some residual sugar? Or maybe even a Beaujolais-like Zin that needed to be chilled? (Not to mention White Zinfandel, of course, which is discussed in its own chapter, see page 211.) We loved Zinfandel so much, in all its variations, that when we began our book of wine notes way back in the mid-'70s, our second section of notes, after the first section on Cabernet, was on Zinfandel—not Merlot, not Pinot Noir. Truth is, years ago we had one marvelous Zin experience after another, from the Ridge Jimsomare 1970 ("awesome") to the Amador Foothills 1982 ("classic") to the Sutter Home Late Harvest 1980 ("sweet, big, long, clean finish") to this, a 1984 from A. Rafanelli:

"Delicious! One of the greats. Huge and classy, like a late-harvest Zin but with the class of a Cabernet. Almost black in its taste, with awesome intensity, yet lots of layers and character. Ready to drink now. A huge, memorable, blackberry wine."

Yum! But how are they now? In mid-1998 we began a large tasting of Zinfandels under $20 to find out. And frankly, we were disappointed. Most just weren't well made. They were simple, grapey, and lacking character. We never would've guessed that most were Zinfandel; instead, they tasted like some sort of cheap grape, harvested too young and rushed out of the winery with little care or thought. Almost all of the wines we tasted, even those that cost close to $20, would be better chilled, which is fine for Beaujolais, but not a compliment to a red wine that should have some weight, and certainly not a compliment to the noble heritage of Zinfandel. There were some exceptions, of course, as you'll see in the Wine Notes that follow.

Zinfandel shouldn't have to be expensive to be good. Over the years we've had oceans of inexpensive Zinfandels from Louis M. Martini Winery that were excellent when purchased and became even better with some age. But we figured maybe these days you just have to spend over $20 to find a really good Zin. So we conducted a new tasting where price was no object. We bought dozens of Zins that cost between $20 and $50. We were pretty disappointed again. So many seemed clumsy and poorly made.

Fortunately, there are still some Zin producers who make the real thing. Ridge Vineyards, for instance, has been making outstanding Zins for years. If anyone sets the standard for Zin, it's Ridge, and our blind tasting confirmed why. "Deep, dark nose with intense highlights and a massive, raspberry/chocolate nose," we wrote. "Chewy, like red meat. Spicy." This is classic California Zinfandel.

At the same time, some newcomers are making a mark. Friends kept telling us we had to find a Rosenblum Cellars Zin—and they were right. "Grapey, Zinlike, with some real heft to it," we wrote. "Very Italian. Young, serious wine, but with lots of life and zest."

Zest! That's what Zinfandel should be all about. When you taste a Zin, you should taste America—young, vibrant, with unlimited potential to get even better. It's worth trying until you find a Zin like that—but, we're sorry to say, the hunt might take longer than it should.

One last note: Zinfandel—good Zinfandel—is meant to age. In 1986, we bought a Mirassou Zinfandel from the 1966 vintage, and kept it for another seven years, when we opened it as a treat for John's mother. "Look is old, tired, very orange, and clear," we wrote, alarmed that this twenty-seven-year-old-wine had gone over the hill. "But nose is marvelous. At first, it's a lot like an old Burgundy, but with time there's *lots* of sweet fruit. Luscious and gorgeous."

It was also an old Zin that led to one of our most memorable, and bizarre, wine experiences. On February 15, 1980, John was visiting St. Petersburg, Florida, for a newspaper-writing seminar and, naturally, he dropped into local wineshops, where he found something he'd never seen before: Woodland "California Zinfandel." It was nonvintage, but the simple label said: "To combine the best qualities of separate vineyard areas and vintages, Woodland Zinfandel was blended in August 1974. The wine is ready for immediate consumption but will repay the cellarer handsomely for allowing it to age in the bottle for a few years."

The wine had no price tag and the shopkeeper had no idea how much it was because, incredibly, he had never noticed the two bottles of Woodland, had no other bottles of Woodland, and knew nothing about the winery. John bought the two bottles—they settled on a price of $3.35 each—and we opened one right away. It was so good we tried to find out who the mysterious Woodland was. John sent Woodland a letter, but it was returned. So he sent a letter to the Wine Institute, a California trade group. "Please," he wrote, "can you tell us *anything* about Woodland? This is driving us crazy."

On March 12, 1980, a J. V. Ingalls wrote back from the Wine Institute: "This was a label used by Montcalm Vineyards of Acampo (later merged into The Felice Winery). Both firms no longer are in business, which probably accounts for the mystery. Your dealer must not sell much wine if a bottle stayed on his shelf that long...."

Obviously, we couldn't bear to open that second bottle. But by May 27, 1996, we couldn't stand it anymore. Remember: This was "blended" in 1974, lost in a wineshop until 1980, and then moved, with us, from Miami to New York, back to Miami and back to New York. It was at least twenty-two years old.

"Delicious!" we wrote. "Remarkable after all these years. Intense and raisiny, *very* much like an Amarone, with lots of intense fruit and a real black hardness. Not at all over the hill."

Is it worth the trouble to find, and maybe cellar, a great Zin? What do you think?

Wine Notes
Under $20

St. Francis Vineyards and Winery 1995 (Sonoma County Old Vines) $19.99
VERY GOOD/DELICIOUS • *Best of tasting. Big, rich nose. Meaty, chewy, with guts. A serious wine, rich and plump. Even some cream. Very fine.*

Zabaco Vintners 1994 (Sonoma County) $8.99
GOOD/VERY GOOD • *Best value. Lovely, Beaujolais-like fruit. Light, grapey, and pleasant. A bit harsh on the finish, but on the whole quite nice. Chill it slightly.*

Alderbrook Vineyards and Winery 1996 (Gamba Vineyard) $15.99
GOOD/VERY GOOD • *Tar, pepper, and real bite in the nose. Tastes expensive, with a long, pepper-fruit finish.*

Steele Caves 1995 (Catfish Vineyard)   **$17.99**
GOOD/VERY GOOD • *Grapey and sweet with fruit, with real hints of wood. Still green—needs some age—but it has more fruit than most.*

Joseph Swan Vineyards 1995 (Zeigler Vineyard)   **$18.99**
GOOD/VERY GOOD • *Finally, a real Zinfandel: rich, fruity, powerful, and edgy, with hints of mint and hot peppers. There's some real fire there. Untamed, as a Zin should be.*

Newlan Vineyards and Winery 1994 (Napa Valley)   **$14.99**
GOOD/VERY GOOD • *Very pleasant and drinkable, but a bit light and watery. Chill it slightly.*

Over $20

Ridge Vineyards 1996 (Paso Robles)   **$24.99**
VERY GOOD/DELICIOUS • *Best of tasting (tie). Deep, dark nose with intense highlights of raspberries and chocolate. Chewy, meaty, like a rare steak, but restrained on the finish.*

Gary Farrell Wines 1996
(Sonoma County, Old Vines)   **$39.99**
VERY GOOD/DELICIOUS • *Best of tasting (tie). Plummy and good, very pleasant. Real guts yet delicate—wow! Fine, yet fruity and plump.*

Selby Winery 1995 (Sonoma County, Old Vines)   **$23.00**
VERY GOOD/DELICIOUS • *Best value. Creamy and soft, very drinkable but still with real character. Berrylike, not deep. Cranberry hints remind us of Pinot Noir. So charming it could hurt you.*

H. Coturri & Sons 1996
(Sonoma Valley, P. Coturri Family Vineyards)   **$27.00**
VERY GOOD/DELICIOUS • *Color is dark and forbidding. Big, heavy Zin taste, but beautifully made. Blackberries and bricks. This is the real thing.*

Bannister Winery 1995
(Russian River Valley, Rochioli Vineyard)   **$23.99**
VERY GOOD • *Hold on to your seats! Intense fruit, almost prunelike. Dry as a bone, yet intensely tight and fruity.*

Rosenblum Cellars 1993
(Napa Valley, George Hendry Vineyard)   **$24.99**
GOOD/VERY GOOD • *Some real heft to it. Quite Italian. Young, serious wine, with life and zest. Berrylike, sweet fruit, but with some backbone, too.*

THE MERLOT PHENOMENON
For Just a Few Dollars More

BOOM!

That was the sound of Merlot exploding onto the American scene a few years ago. We've seen fads before—White Zinfandel, wine coolers, Vanilla Ice—but we've never seen anything quite like this.

Consider: In John Melville's *Guide to California Wines*, written in 1960, he covered all the bases and all the grapes. The index lists "Riesling, Emerald" and "Riesling, Gray." There's "Sparkling Malvasia" and "Mondeuse." But there's not a single mention of Merlot. Put into perspective, that omission isn't really surprising because, back then, Merlot was known mostly as a blending grape. Winemakers used its deep, flat, red flavor to round out the sharper, harder, more tannic edges of grapes like Cabernet Sauvignon. The French use it that way in many of the great Bordeaux wines, such as Château Lafite-Rothschild. But while Merlot has stood quite well on its own for decades in the Pomerol region of Bordeaux—it makes the great Château Petrus—it was virtually unknown in the U.S. as a stand-alone wine until fairly recently.

Certainly, some tried. According to the Wine Institute, a San Francisco–based trade organization, Louis M. Martini Winery released the first California Merlot. The winery says it was a blend of the 1968 and 1970 vintages and was released in 1972. In 1982, we opened a bottle of Sterling Vineyards Merlot from the great California vintage of 1974. "Delicious," we wrote. "Elegant yet very big. Flat and silky. Years left. Lots of wood, lots of power. Huge, long finish. Small sips."

But things quickly went crazy. In 1987, California wineries crushed 6,782 tons of Merlot; just one decade later, the figure was 201,707 tons. We imagine one reason for this is Merlot's essential "flatness." It is smooth and easy, without the complexity or the edges of a Cabernet Sauvignon. Merlot is a dark wine, with even-toned flavors, that tends to be approachable and friendly at an early age. You know Ben Stein, the nerd who's made a career of being a boring guy with the flat, monotonal voice? He's Merlot. All across America, Merlot has become the red equivalent of "a glass of Chardonnay"—simple wine with no rough patches and not enough taste to trouble anybody. But when a wine suddenly enjoys that kind of popularity—especially because of its essential blandness—what happens to its quality? In our experience, bad things. Remember Pouilly-Fuissé? It's a lovely white wine from France that became wildly popular in the 1970s. Suddenly, boatloads of it arrived in American stores, much of it underripe and overpriced. Soon the boom busted. Is the same in store for Merlot? We decided to conduct a tasting to find out. In the long run, though, it turned out one tasting was not enough.

There's an old episode of *Columbo* in which the detective is trying to solve a murder in the wine world. At some point, he goes to a wine store and asks the shopkeeper: "How can you tell a good wine from a bad wine?" The wine merchant looks at Columbo dismissively and responds: "The price." We generally had not found that to be the case.

Merlot was the exception.

For two blind tastings, one in early 1998 and one in early 1999, we zipped through New York–area wine stores and bought dozens of Merlots from California that cost under $20. Then we conducted "flight" after flight of blind tastings. We were disappointed. In fact, in some cases, we were pretty well grossed-out.

"Charming but raw."

"Green and bitter."

"Just heat and alcohol."

"Saltwater nose."

"Grain alcohol."

"Kool-Aid."

"Not very pleasant."

It was clear many wineries had jumped on the Merlot bandwagon to make a quick buck. They were picking mediocre grapes, giving them too little care, and shipping them out as quickly as possible. Wine after wine tasted like second-rate Beaujolais—fruity and acceptable as a slightly chilled gulping wine.

Many more of the wines were perfectly acceptable and inoffensive. In fact, that might be what bothered us about them: Many seemed to aspire to nothing more than inoffensiveness. Time after time, we'd pour a glass, start talking about something else, finish the glass, and then say, "Wait a minute. How was that wine?" We'd missed it entirely. No wine should be so lacking in character.

Fortunately, there were exceptions in both tastings. The 1995 Kunde from Sonoma County was the best in the first tasting. It had a rich, pleasant, woody-fruity nose and several deep layers of ripe, well-rounded tastes that made it both a fun wine to drink now and a good bet to lay down in the bottom of your closet for a few years. As our notes said: "Young, but some depth on the nose. Vibrant, spirited. Well made. Nice and fruity. Friendly, comfortable, mellow."

The best value in the first tasting was a Bogle Vineyards 1996. It tasted of vanilla and wood, which was one hint it was a well-made wine with some complexity. The price: just $9.99.

There were more winners in the second tasting than the first. The Franciscan 1996, for instance, was a remarkable glass of wine, so dark it looked like Manischewitz, and filled with rich, creamy, "sweet" fruit. As we wrote in our notes: "Classy, rich, and full of attitude. This is not your usual 'glass of Merlot.'" We were sure the Talus 1996 was expensive, but it cost just $8.99. And our best of tasting was an outstanding bottle of wine, a bottle that easily could have held its own against far more expensive Merlots. It was rich, classy, and young, filled with fruit and yet challenging in its tastes, with some pepper and spice and real personality. This was truly a wine that made you notice it, and it turned out to be the 1994 from Frick, which cost $18.99.

We wondered, though, what would happen if we went upscale. So, for months, we picked up every Merlot over $20 we could find. Again, we conducted "flight" after flight to try to reach a conclusion. And this was it:

What a difference a few bucks makes!

Wine after wine was deep, rich, plump with ripe fruit—serious wine made by serious winemakers. This is not the wine you think of when you order "a glass of Merlot." In fact, if what you really like about Merlot is that it's so simple, soft, and drinkable, stay away from these. This is the real thing, with intense, "flat" tastes that grow and change in the glass and inside your mouth—reminiscent of what their French cousin, Pomerol, can be in a good year. Many of these engage your intellect; attention must be paid. If you're not up for a challenge, stay with the simpler stuff.

These are the kinds of wines that explain for themselves why they cost more. Good wines cost more to make: There's the price of good land, the years-long attention to the vines, serious oak barrels, small yields (which means trimming back vines so you get fewer, but better, grapes), a good deal of personal care. That doesn't mean all expensive wines are worth it. In fact, the ones we liked best in this tasting were at the lower end of our price range.

While we tasted wines that cost as much as $58, and included many well-known makers (Duckhorn, Matanzas Creek, and so on), the best of tasting was a surprise: Burgess 1995. Price? $28. Burgess has been a classy producer for years, but it's not one of California's best-known names. "Black wine!" we wrote. "Huge, deep-fruit blackberry nose. Yet the taste is soft, creamy, rich, and ephemeral. Wow! What a satisfying gulp of wine. A nice, round mouthful with no hard edges. Stains your mouth, but is pleasant and mellow. Delicious."

The best value, at only $20.99, was Steltzner 1994. You may have never heard of this winery, but it's worth looking for. On the rare times we see it, we grab it because Steltzner has never disappointed us. Its wines have real character, and because the winery isn't very well known, Steltzners tend to be good buys. This was no exception. It was a gorgeous color, classy and complex, with the kind of tastes that usually come only from age. As it stood open, it got even better, indicating this will be a wine worth holding on to.

That's an important point about all of these wines. Age is a wonderful thing for big, rich, classy wines. After some years, they gain a depth and personality that just aren't possible in youth. The problem is that you'll rarely find these wines well aged, and if you do, they'll cost a fortune. These are wines to save, if you can.

It's a funny thing about wine: Sometimes the "best" wine doesn't taste best because it's just too young. In fact, one wine we tasted might turn out to be the best of the lot, but not for some years (Dorothy thinks a couple, John thinks ten). It was a Beringer Howell Mountain 1993, which cost $49. It was an absolute Godzilla of a wine—for now, intense, green, and almost bricklike. But as minutes ticked by, it was clear that beneath the youthful power there was layer after layer of taste—wood, vanilla, tobacco, blackberries. This is a wine made with real confidence for real wine lovers.

This wine, we think, might well be a classic, though at the moment it only rates a "good/very good." In the long run, it may well become a wine that's not only delicious but truly exciting. And that's not just true of expensive wines. Some of our very best wine experiences have involved inexpensive red wines we've aged for many years. It's always fun to yell something like "Can you believe we only paid $4.99 for that in '76?" In this case, consider this: In our second tasting of under-$20 Merlots, we began one round of tasting before dinner and tasted a 1995 Hess Select. "Black wine," we wrote about the color. "Light taste, though. It's watery! Very disappointing."

Then we went to dinner. Two and a half hours later, we tried the Hess again, and "Oh my," we wrote. "It's rich and wow. Dark, fruity, and plump, like an expensive Merlot, with lots of vibrant fruit. Finishes to a very nice, fruity, dry taste." If you could cellar this wine for a few years, you'd have one spectacular bottle—and you'd say, "Can you believe we only paid $14.99 for this in '99?"

Wine Notes

If your "glass of Merlot" is simple and unmemorable, try something else! Too many Merlots under $20 are little more than glass-fillers, smooth and inoffensive, but some are quite good—and for just a few dollars more, you can have a great experience. All of the following are from California except the Chateau Ste. Michelle and Columbia Crest, which are from Washington State. Many lighter, inexpensive Merlots we tasted need to be drunk right away, and in some cases would be improved by chilling them slightly. But the good stuff—even some of the better inexpensive Merlots—should age beautifully. If the Merlot you open seems light and its taste diffuse, try chilling it; if it seems heavy and almost chewy, leave it alone and let it "breathe" for a while. (The "Under $20" index includes tastings in 1998 and 1999.)

Under $20

Frick Winery 1994 (Dry Creek Valley) $18.99
VERY GOOD • *Rich and classy, with the brightness of a young Cabernet Sauvignon. Still quite young, but with so much fruit that it's already excellent. This is a challenging, serious wine worth far more money.*

Hess Select 1995 (Napa Valley, The Hess Collection Winery) $14.99
VERY GOOD • *Looks great, but it's watery and thin in the glass. But wait: almost three hours later, it's simply awesome—rich, dark, fruity, and filled with "flat" fruit, like a very expensive Merlot. It's vibrant in your mouth but leaves a lingering, dry, and very wonderful "finish." A real stunner.*

Kunde Estate Winery 1995 $17.49
VERY GOOD • *Nice, friendly nose, with some tobacco and tar. Very young but with some guts. Fruity. Real wine.*

Franciscan Oakville Estate 1996 (Napa Valley) $19.99

VERY GOOD • *So dark and grapey it looks like Manischewitz. But, wow, this is the real thing: still young, with interesting notes of tar. Classy, rich, and filled with attitude. This is not your usual "glass of Merlot."*

Brutocao Cellars 1995 (Mendocino) $18.99

GOOD/VERY GOOD • *This is the perfect "glass of Merlot," something soft, pleasant, and so very drinkable.*

Talus Cellars 1996 $8.99

GOOD/VERY GOOD • *Tastes expensive, with the seriousness of a Cabernet Sauvignon and a little bit of an edge. This is a great buy.*

Quail Ridge Cellars 1995 $18.99

GOOD/VERY GOOD • *Simple at first, but after a full hour it develops some real body, with fruit, tar, and cream. It's both creamy and crisp—interesting. There's some real class here.*

Blackstone Winery 1997 $11.99

GOOD/VERY GOOD • *Hot and metallic at first, but lovely and fruity later. Some guts.*

Chateau Ste. Michelle 1994 (Washington State) $15.99

GOOD/VERY GOOD • *Rich and pretty, with spices on the nose. Vibrant and fruity.*

Forest Ville Vineyard 1996 $6.99

GOOD/VERY GOOD • *It's friendly, it's comfortable, it's mellow—and it's really cheap.*

Columbia Crest Winery 1995
(Columbia Valley, Washington State) $13.99
GOOD/VERY GOOD • *Looks and smells of age, a little dusty. Filled with mature, rich fruit, but with a finish that's a little hot.*

Markham Vineyards 1995 $19.49
GOOD • *Fruity, but alcoholic and harsh. Maybe with some age...*

Bogle Vineyards 1997 $9.99
GOOD • *Classy looking. Taste is simple, red, and a little creamy, then opens up to some richness, plumpness, and creamy wood.*

Bogle Vineyards 1996 $9.99
GOOD • *Charming. Vibrant and Beaujolais-like. Some vanilla and wood, but simple and nice. OK, maybe a little superficial, but still fun to be with.*

Taft Street Winery 1995 $12.99
GOOD • *Sweet, fruity nose. Like Beaujolais. A bit hard, but maybe that's good for the future.*

Grand Cru Vineyards 1996 $8.99
GOOD • *Grapey, sweet, and earthy. It's an interesting wine, with some seriousness of purpose.*

Forest Ville Vineyard 1997 $7.99
GOOD • *Some sweet, creamy fruit, with a bit of backbone and a hint of tobacco along with nice, sweet fruit. Good deal.*

Beringer Vineyards 1996 Founders' Estate $9.99
GOOD • *Dark, rich, and filled with "sweet" fruit. Very pleasant.*

Kunde Estate Winery 1997 (Sonoma Valley) $14.99

GOOD • *Intense, raisiny, and serious. No "sweet," giving fruit, but instead a tightly wound intensity. This is a wine to lay down for a few years.*

Over $20

Burgess Cellars 1995 (Napa Valley) $28.00

DELICIOUS • *Best of tasting. Huge, black wine, with a powerful, blackberry fruit nose. Yet the taste is soft, creamy, rich, and ephemeral. Balanced, round, warm, and complete. It stains your mouth yet is pleasant and mellow. This wine takes you someplace very nice.*

Steltzner Vineyards 1994
(Napa Valley, Stags Leap District) $20.99

VERY GOOD/DELICIOUS • *Best value. Gorgeous color with plenty of fire. Soft, pleasant, and bursting with ripe fruit. Classy and complex. Tastes more mature than it is.*

Swanson Winery 1995 (Napa Valley) $23.99

VERY GOOD/DELICIOUS • *Whoa! Rubber, vines, and tar on the nose. Tough, leathery, and young. Classy and crisp, yet big and fruity. An intense experience.*

St. Francis Vineyards Estate Reserve 1993 (Sonoma Valley) $30.00

VERY GOOD/DELICIOUS • *Classy and complex, with more layers of taste than most.*

Gundlach-Bundschu Winery 1995
(Rhinefarm Vineyards, Sonoma Valley) $21.99
VERY GOOD • *Intense, ripe berries, yet a very dry finish. Powerful, strong, almost Portlike. Good enough for a significant occasion.*

Fisher Vineyards 1994 (RCF Vineyard, Napa Valley) $30.00
VERY GOOD • *A bit too much alcohol taste but still plump and "sweet" with fruit, with a sensual, creamy finish.*

Newton Vineyard 1994 (Napa Valley) $28.99
VERY GOOD • *Soft, fruity, and approachable. Sweet with fruit; hints of peaches, interestingly. After an hour, gorgeous, classy and rich, indicating real aging potential.*

Beringer Vineyards 1993
(Napa Valley, Howell Mountain, Bancroft Ranch) $49.00
GOOD/VERY GOOD • *Not the best wine of the tasting, but maybe the most exciting. Black as night. Smells and tastes at first like blackberry wine. Hard, green, and basically undrinkable at first. Hard as a rock. Later, it begins to sweeten out. Real class emerges, a real confidence. It's like concentrated wine, with layer upon layer inside. Could be one for the ages.*

The Perfect Wine to Drink Tonight

Right now, how many bottles of wine do you have in the house?

If you're like most people, the answer is probably "none,"except for maybe that special bottle Uncle Harry gave you for your wedding that you're saving for some special occasion. And that's a shame. Maybe you intended to pick up a bottle to have with dinner tonight, but you were running late, or you were too busy or too tired. So instead of enjoying a wine, you had soda instead. How sad.

Truth is, you can have the perfect wine on hand for any meal if you just go out today and buy twelve bottles—one case. Not only will this eliminate the hassle of picking up a bottle on your way home every night, but it will be cheaper, both because you won't be in a rush and vulnerable, and because you will probably get a discount on the case. Storage? Don't worry about it. (See page 148.) Here's the perfect mixed case. We've focused on generally available wines that you have a good chance of finding in a good wineshop.

1. Champagne. Sometimes you have a bad day. Sometimes you have a good day. In every day, there's a reason to pop open a bottle of bubbly. So you must have a bottle of Champagne—or American sparkling wine—in the house. And don't rule out having it with dinner. Its crispness is great with some butter or cream sauces. An American sparkler is just perfect as a house bubbly. Try Scharffenberger/Pacific Echo or Piper-Sonoma. They'll cost about $12.

2. Cabernet Sauvignon. If you're having any kind of serious meat dish, like filet mignon or perhaps a veal chop, a California Cabernet will enhance the flavor. Overall, California Cabernets are quite good. They come in all prices, but we've found that Gallo of Sonoma is good and inexpensive, and Fetzer is always reliable. Either should cost about $10.

3. Chardonnay. Yes, it's great with any kind of "white meat" dish, like chicken. But if you choose carefully, it's also a wine that will make you feel better when you come home hot and tired and just want something to remind you of life's pleasures. You can stick one in the fridge for a few days so it will be ready to drink when you're ready to drink it. Then let it warm up a bit. We enjoy Estancia's regular bottling, which usually costs about $10.

4. Zinfandel. This is what we drink with Dorothy's meat loaf. But it's also perfect with that pizza you've ordered in. And with grilled hamburgers. You want something red, fun, zesty—and inexpensive. Again, there are great Zins that cost plenty, but for a keep-it-handy Zinfandel, we've always relied on Louis M. Martini Winery, which will cost about $8. Zabaco, which costs about the same, is also quite good.

5. Muscadet. This is an inexpensive French white that you can find everywhere. Buy the most recent vintage you can find. If you're having any kind of white fish or shellfish, Muscadet is a classic accompaniment. It's not a wine to linger over, but it's hard not to feel like you're in a French bistro when you're drinking it. We like Château de la Chesnaie Muscadet de Sèvre-et-Maine Sur Lie for about $10.

6. Alsatian Gewürztraminer. The wines of Alsace, in France, aren't very well known, which is good—that keeps prices down. And the Gewürztraminer grape isn't well known, either. It's peppery, has real backbone, and, in the hands of Alsatian winemakers, it's crisp and delicious. There are few wines better with pork and sautéed apples. Some people also think this dry wine, well chilled, is a perfect match with Indian and Thai food. Just look for a producer named Trimbach. It will cost about $13.

7. An inexpensive Italian red. These budget Italian red wines always make us feel as though we have a red-and-white checkered tablecloth on our dining room table, with a little candle in the middle. They're perfect if you're going to throw together a spaghetti dinner or make lasagne. Spend around $7 on anything you haven't had before. We've had luck with Santa Cristina, a Sangiovese from the Antinori people. It's $7—a great buy.

8. Bordeaux. There are times you just want something a little better than usual. When John makes his famous brisket in his sainted Grandma Helen's special pot, it would be sacrilege to serve anything less than a fine red. Over the years, we've never been disappointed with Château Gloria, which will cost about $25.

9. German Riesling. Riesling is the wonderful, fruity grape that makes those delightful German white wines. Truth is, we don't keep these around to drink with anything, but to enjoy when we come home from work. Look for the words "Riesling" and "Kabinett" on the label, buy the most recent vintage you see, and spend $10 to $13. We like Georg Albrecht Schneider Niersteiner Paterberg for just $9.99.

10. Rioja. What in the world would you have with Mexican or Cuban food? Or, for that matter, your turkey sandwiches the day after Thanksgiving? We like to buy an inexpensive red Rioja, from Spain, and chill it slightly. There are plenty of them, but you can't go wrong with Marqués de Cáceres. It should cost around $10.

11. Beaujolais. The light, fruity taste of Beaujolais, slightly chilled, is always perfect. Try it with salmon or even roast chicken. Buy the most recent you can find. Georges Duboeuf's wines are ubiquitous—and only about $6.

12. Dessert wine. You don't think you need a dessert wine, but you do. Dinner's over, the children are finally asleep, and that Bordeaux was even better than you expected. How about just a small glass of something sweet? Look for any half-bottle of Muscat from Robert Pecota Winery in California. The half-bottle will probably cost about $11—and you'll find it's a perfect way to top off a wonderful evening.

PINOT NOIR
The Queen of Wines

IN OUR EARLY YEARS of drinking and learning about wine, we heard that America couldn't produce a great Pinot Noir. All California Pinots, we were told, smelled like sulfur or rotten eggs and were harsh in the mouth. So went the conventional wisdom in the '70s, and our early tastings confirmed it. "Not good. Over the hill. Ironlike, thin, very little fruit," we wrote in our wine notes about a 1970 Mirassou, from California. Of the next year's vintage of the same wine, we wrote: "Even worse. Hardly drinkable."

It was hard to believe these wines were made from one of the world's greatest red-wine grapes, the one used to make all of those fabulous, and very expensive, red Burgundies from France. If Cabernet Sauvignon is the king of grapes—big, rich, deep, and "masculine"—then Pinot Noir is the queen. When you look at it, its color is somewhat light, but filled with a shimmering vibrancy. Put your nose in the glass and you might smell raspberries, cherries, and maybe some lilacs. When a Pinot is especially rich with fruit, we often call it "jammy" or "jamlike."

At the same time, Pinot has a special depth and richness that belie its lightness. In a good Pinot, you can smell, and taste, a hint of cream. And there should be a haunting, hard-to-put-your-finger-on taste of the earth, what the French call "goût de terroir." What do we mean by that? Think about standing in the middle of a field after rich, dark soil has been tilled, or in your garden after it has rained. The smell of that earth—clean and fertile and chock-full of minerals—is something you can almost taste, something that you almost feel deep in your soul.

Swirled around in your mouth, a good Pinot should have a velvety, rich texture. When you swallow, it should leave memories of warm, fruity flavors. There are few more classic pairings than a simply roasted chicken and a good Burgundy. The chicken is smoky and dark on the outside, but juicy and vibrant on the inside. A good Burgundy—or a good Pinot Noir—should be like that. But in the long run, all of those tastes should be in balance, none of them obvious. The flavors should be ephemeral, more in the mind than in the mouth. Even in Burgundy, that is hard to do. But in California, we were assured, it was just about impossible. The grape itself was too hard to grow, too finicky, and too delicate. The climate wasn't right. And U.S. winemakers, while skillful with big, muscular wines like Cabernet Sauvignon, just didn't have a touch that was light enough to make wines that should be elegant instead of powerful.

On November 24, 1981, we discovered we had been misinformed.

If you really love wine, one of the unfortunate facts of life—a real downer—is that you're going to kiss plenty of frogs before you find a prince or a princess. We drank some bad Pinots in the '70s, but in 1981 we found a 1978 Pinot from a winery called Raymond in California. Our notes: "Delicious! Fantastic! Chocolate liqueur nose. Big, luscious, rich. Very much American (bold, assertive, brash), but not at all a Cabernet or a Zin. Definitely a Pinot: Lots of 'sweet,' flat fruit, a full wine. Very young, many years ahead of it." We had found a prince.

There are some experiences as a wine drinker that change your life, and this was one of them for us. It was as though suddenly everything had gone into lovely, soft focus. Ah, yes. Clearly, some American winemakers could successfully decode the mystery of the Pinot Noir grape, at least sometimes.

Much later, we discovered that some pioneers had it right all along. In 1992, we discovered an amazing thirty-year-old bottle of Pinot Noir made by an old curmudgeon named Martin Ray. "It's gorgeous," we wrote in our notes. "Rich Pinot nose, sweet with fruit, with just a hint of oak. Much less chewy or oaky or dark and rich than you'd expect. Primarily classy, big fruit. Very Pinot, very much a fine Burgundy. Remarkably, not even a hint of old age. Ready to drink. Spectacular."

It's pretty well accepted now that some small, high-end producers are making outstanding Pinot Noir, both in California—where the Carneros region of Napa and Sonoma is a hotbed of good Pinot— and in Oregon, where Pinot Noir has quickly become the state's best red wine. If you're lucky enough to find Williams Selyem from California, for instance, or Cristom or Domaine Drouhin from Oregon, you're in for a treat.

The more important question, though, is whether you can just drop into your local wine store tonight and find a reasonably priced, good Pinot Noir to have with your roast chicken. To answer that question, we bought several cases of Pinots that cost less than $30 per bottle.

The answer was a shock.

We had earlier done tastings of relatively inexpensive Merlots and Zinfandels, and, as we reported in previous chapters, were often disappointed. We would have guessed that Pinots would be even more disappointing. But we were wrong. The average quality was very high—and there were some terrific bargains.

Our first "flight" of six wines was instructive. During this first flight, with bottles all carefully wrapped in brown paper bags and numbered, it was clear No. 6 was the best. "Hard and serious," we wrote. "Deeper than the others. An earthy finish, a real winner. Bigger, heavier, nothing awkward. Smoky, expensive-tasting, plump. Creamy, rich, and chewy."

When we took off the bags, it turned out we'd been tasting wines up to $26.99. But what was No. 6? Napa Ridge 1996. Cost: $10.99.

The competition for best of tasting was intense. The runner-up was no surprise: Saintsbury. We liked the regular bottling at $14.99, but we liked the Reserve, at $19.49, even more. Saintsbury is consistently one of our favorite Pinots. Remember that name. An even more venerable Pinot producer, however, turned out to be the winner. "Great nose. Has depth, richness, guts, and yet still that Pinot life," we wrote. "Smells expensive. Wow! Holy cow: Just as good as it smells. Like a fine Burgundy. Even some tobacco. The essence of class."

When we tore off the bag, this turned out to be an old friend: Chalone, one of California's first great Pinot makers. While this wine was not inexpensive—$26.99—there is, as we keep saying, a big difference between price and value. Some inexpensive wines are bad values, and some expensive wines are great values. This is the latter, because it's easily the equivalent of a $50 Burgundy.

How well does Pinot age? Some of the lighter ones in the Wine Notes will probably do fine for a couple of years, but then lose their charm and have little to replace it. Better, bigger, richer Pinots, though, get better and better as the years go by. We had a 1966 Inglenook in 1987 (with duck; one of our favorite pairings), and it couldn't have been more perfect: "More gold than red," we wrote, "without a hint of decay." And consider this: We bought a bottle of 1977 Chalone Pinot Noir way back in 1981 for the then outrageous sum of $30. We didn't open it until March 10, 1996, to drink with a roasted turkey. Our notes on this nineteen-year-old wine:

"Wow! First taste is massive, huge, powerful. Intense fruit, totally forward. Classy and very varietal. After one hour, thins out, loses fruit—a little over—but still very good. A real powerhouse Pinot."

Two Chalone Pinots, vintages 1977 and 1996, and both "Wow!" This is a wine to look for. Drink it today—or save it until the year 2018. It'll be great either way.

Wine Notes

All of the following wines are from California except for the Woodward Canyon, which is from Washington State. Oregon also makes some fine Pinot Noirs, although none rose to the top in this tasting. In general, California Pinots from the Carneros region have a lot going for them. Good Pinot Noirs age beautifully, so if you see a bottle that's a few years old, it's worth a try. Serve it at room temperature, and don't let it "breathe" before you drink it: Often, that very first taste after the bottle is opened is pure, sweet fruit. In time, the wine will get better, richer, and deeper, but that first sip is so very lovely.

Chalone Vineyard 1996 $26.99
DELICIOUS • *Best of tasting. Worth the price just for the nose—elegant and expensive. And it tastes just as good. The essence of class. It's hard to go wrong with Chalone.*

Napa Ridge 1996 $10.99
VERY GOOD • *Best value. A serious wine, big, deep, and heavy. Smoky, plump, and creamy. Tastes very expensive, as if it received great care. This is a seriously good deal.*

Saintsbury Carneros Reserve 1994 $19.49
VERY GOOD/DELICIOUS • *Big, rich, and "sweet" with fruit. Beautifully made—light on its feet yet with layers and layers of complexity. Creamy and approachable. This is always a name to look for in Pinot.*

Jekel Vineyards 1994 $13.99
VERY GOOD/DELICIOUS • *Like a big piece of raspberry cream pie, plump, fruity, and fine.*

Rabbit Ridge Vineyards Russian River Valley
(Partners Reserve) 1994 $22.99

VERY GOOD · *Sharply defined tastes, with some hard edges, like fine cheekbones. Serious wine. This winery is a real comer; keep an eye out for it.*

MacRostie Winery Carneros Reserve 1995 $24.99

VERY GOOD · *Dark and very serious. A big, chewy wine, velvety, rich, and sensuous, with a memorable berry-cream finish. We don't see MacRostie wines often, but we're always impressed.*

Saintsbury 1997 (Garnet) $14.99

VERY GOOD · *Light and jammy, but with character. Well made and still young.*

Tria Winery 1996 (Carneros) $22.99

VERY GOOD · *Beautiful, deep color with so much life and fire. Chewy. Rich nose with some heat. Rich and mouthfilling.*

Cambria Winery and Vineyard 1996 (Julia's Vineyard) $24.99

GOOD/VERY GOOD · *Very pleasant, very feminine, but not one you'll remember forever.*

Robert Mondavi Winery 1993 (Carneros) $25.00

GOOD/VERY GOOD · *Creamy, rich, and luscious at first, but it turns a bit alcoholic after a while.*

Raymond Vineyard 1995 $18.99

GOOD/VERY GOOD · *Very pleasant at the front, quite lovely. But the finish is a bit metallic. Still, that first taste...*

Gundlach-Bundschu Winery 1996 (Rhinefarm Vineyard)   **$18.00**

GOOD/VERY GOOD • *Looks like Beaujolais and smells like cherries. Fruity, fun, and nice, with a bit of vanilla cream that adds some character. Very pleasant.*

Woodward Canyon Winery 1995 (Walla Walla Valley)   **$30.00**

GOOD/VERY GOOD • *If you want to taste what sweet Pinot fruit tastes like, this is it. It's a fulfilling mouthful of wine, although the finish can be a little harsh.*

Kent Rasmussen Winery 1995 (Carneros)   **$27.99**

GOOD/VERY GOOD • *A yummy, rich nose, like roast chicken. A lovely Pinot, lighter than most, but extremely drinkable.*

Taking Wine to a Friend's House
Ten No-Lose Suggestions

"I'm going over to a friend's house tonight and he really knows wine. What do I take?"

Over the years, we've been asked this question more than any other. In our column, we said if a dinner guest brings a bottle of wine to your home, for heaven's sake, open it. To not open it would be rude. Have it as an apéritif, add a cheese course. Find a reason to open it. If you don't, we said, your guest will infer that you think one of two things: (1) This stuff is so bad I'd never be caught dead serving it, or (2) This stuff is so good I certainly wouldn't want to share it with *you*.

Well, you can't imagine the torrent of letters we received, and how many ways readers dissented from that advice. What if the host planned the meal around a specific wine and your wine didn't complement the food? Wouldn't your wine be an "arrogant intrusion"? We've heard wine called many things, but "an arrogant intrusion"? And then there was this sentiment: Sometimes I bring wine as a gift. It's not to be opened right then and there.

So let's try this again. You've been invited to dinner by someone who knows wine, and, this being your friend, you'd like to bring something he or she would enjoy. Simply ask, "Can I bring some wine?" If your host says yes, ask, "Red or white?" This exchange should establish an understanding that you're bringing a wine to be served at the dinner party.

If your friend says, "Gee, that's sweet, but we've got the wine all planned," you can still bring a bottle of wine. Just say to your host when you arrive: "I heard this was great. You might not want to open it tonight, but keep it and think of me when you do."

This urge to bring something, we suspect, is partly the end result of years of indoctrination by mothers like Dottie's who insisted that one should never arrive at a friend's home empty-handed. But it also springs, we'd insist, from a love of wine, the

~ *125* ~

fun of discovery, and the desire to share something wonderful. How could that ever be unwelcome?

So, what do we tell people who ask us what to take? You don't want to take something your host buys by the case. But you also don't want to take something your host would scoff at. Go to a good wine store, someplace with a large, ever-changing selection. You want something that will make your friend say, "Gee, I always wanted to try this," or "What an interesting bottle." Plan to spend somewhere around $30 (we're assuming this is a fairly serious affair). If you take a white, don't buy it chilled in the store if you can help it—the bottle could've been in that refrigerator for years—but do chill it before you take it to dinner so it can be served right away.

Find out something about the wine so when you hand it over you can offer some sort of reason why you chose it. It really is the thought that counts, and if you can say, "I haven't had this, but I heard it's the best Shiraz in Australia," or whatever, it will add to its enjoyment.

Here are ten wines you could bring along that are sure to impress your host:

~ Château Léoville-Barton or Château de Sales. These are outstanding red Bordeaux wines. While both are generally available, they're not as well known as many other "clarets," so that makes them a more special offering to your host.

~ An expensive Chianti from Italy. Even wine lovers don't often buy themselves an expensive Chianti, and it's a shame. They are very special wines. Look for anything around $25; if you see something from the 1996 vintage, grab it. Your friend will say, "That was a great year, but I haven't had any '96s yet. Thanks!"

~ A good Shiraz from Australia. Wine lovers know Australia is making some outstanding Shiraz, but most folks haven't tasted some of the better stuff. Older vintages are better, since Shiraz tends to be huge in its youth, but don't worry about it.

~ An expensive Zinfandel. Everybody likes Zinfandel, but there are so many inexpensive Zinfandels out there that even wine lovers don't often enough spend real money on one, such as Ravenswood or Ridge or Rosenblum (just remember "it started with an R. . ."). "Wow," your host will say. "I forgot how good Zinfandel can be."

~ Sonoma-Cutrer Russian River Ranches Chardonnay with a little age on it, Pezzi King Chardonnay, or Beringer Private Reserve Chardonnay. We guarantee your host will be thrilled to get any of these Chardonnays. The Pezzi King, which is a terrific wine, might be the most prized of the three because it's hard to find. So if you see it, pick it up.

~ Château Musar from Lebanon. This is hard to find. But if you really want to impress your friend, it's worth looking for. It's a remarkable red wine from the Bekaa Valley that has the character and class of a Bordeaux but a totally different taste. We have had many vintages of it going back to the early '70s and loved every one. Sometimes you can buy it for very little, because wineshops don't know what it is, and sometimes you can buy it for a great deal of money, because wineshops know exactly what it is. Find a bottle of this and you will be invited to dinner again.

~ Burgess or Steltzner Merlot. Merlot is the wine of the moment, so you can't go wrong with it, if you spend $20 or more. The advantage of these two Merlots, from California, is that they're not well known. Chances are your host has never had them. And he or she will be impressed with their depth, class, and richness.

~ Pinot Gris from Oregon. Buy the youngest you can find, chill it well, and as soon as you show up ask, "Can we open this right away?" It will be light, fresh, fruity, and different, which will immediately jump-start the evening and likely earn you the gratitude of your host. Remember that this is the same grape as Italian Pinot Grigio, which should give you something to talk about, too, because everybody drinks Pinot Grigio.

~ Chablis, the real thing from France, crisp and flinty. If your host is serving seafood, this wine will be a winner—and much appreciated.

~ Robert Pecota Moscato d'Andrea Muscat Canelli from California or a Tokaji (pronounced toh-KYE) from Hungary. If you asked your host if you should bring a dessert wine, he'd say no. Most people, maybe including you, don't think they like dessert wines. And that's why you should take along one of these. These are sweet, yet light on their feet and charming. This wine will leave your host, quite literally, with a good taste in his or her mouth.

ROMANTIC RED BURGUNDY

Easier Than You Think

WE LOVE WINE. We're willing to try anything, and we find something to like about almost everything. We think it's a mistake to decide you only like white wine, or dry wine, or French wine. There's a whole wide world of wine out there that's constantly in flux. All that's why, when someone asks us about our favorite wine, we always say, "We like everything." But if you really pinned us to the wall, if you absolutely insisted that we tell you what we think is the greatest wine in the world, we would tell you that it's red Burgundy, from the Burgundy region of France.

If you truly want to know wine better, you have to taste a fine Burgundy. We know it's daunting. We know people willing to spend $400 on an old Château Latour who have never spent $50 on a Burgundy, and we can understand why. When you buy a fine Bordeaux, you pretty much know what you're getting—one château, one winemaker, a consistent vision. Burgundy isn't like that. There are hundreds of growers, most of whom sell their wines to big *négociants*, who bottle and ship the wines. The wine itself isn't called something simple, like Château Giscours or Kendall-Jackson Chardonnay, but is instead called by its place name, like Santenay. Vintages make a big difference. Few wine merchants know much about Burgundy. So each bottle is a little bit of a gamble. And on top of all of that, everybody knows Burgundy prices are ridiculous. *Geez!* How could this wine possibly be worth the trouble?

Well, it is. Red Burgundy is the wine we always recommend for

Valentine's Day, because we consider it the most romantic wine in the world. It's "feminine" and sensual, with a creamy roundness wrapped around a hard core of ripe, "forward" fruit. A good Bordeaux or Cabernet Sauvignon can shout; Burgundy whispers. Good Burgundy always reminds Dorothy of a kiss, of red velvet and, as she puts it, "of all sorts of warm, gooey stuff, like chocolate fondue." It doesn't have to cost a fortune, either.

Let's start at the beginning, with an old French winemaker in a beret. We had never been to France, so in 1984 we planned a trip— to winegrowing regions, of course. At that time, we had little experience with Burgundy, for all the reasons above, so we decided to spend some time there. It's a funny thing about the red wines of Burgundy. As difficult as they are to get to know, many wine lovers get a kind of goofy expression on their face when they talk about them. One Wall Street financier, a rational man, once told us he had a Burgundy so perfect that, right there, after the first sip, he got down on his knees and prayed. Some people travel to Lourdes or Jerusalem for a religious experience. We traveled to Burgundy.

It was a great trip. We'd been warned that the French were hostile. John speaks no French and Dottie just a little, from college, but the people of Burgundy couldn't have been nicer. We have found, all over the world, that winemakers speak a common language. Whether it's Italy, Pennsylvania, or France, winemakers appreciate genuine interest in their art, and a sincere and lusty *"ummmmm"* transcends all traditional languages.

Every time we saw someplace that looked like a winery, we'd knock on the door, Dottie would say a few words about tasting wine and we'd be invited in. No visit changed our life more, though, than the one with the wiry old man with an unfiltered cigarette who was sitting alone inside a tiny room when we knocked. He didn't speak English, but he knew why we were there and he motioned for us to follow him. He opened a trap door in the room. A ladder led to a cellar. We followed.

For a wine lover, this was heaven. We were in Gevrey-Chambertin, the epicenter of great Burgundy, the village named for one of France's greatest wines, Chambertin, in a tiny cellar surrounded by wine. It was dark, it was cold, it was musty—and it couldn't have been more wonderful. He opened a bottle and poured us glasses and our lives would never quite be the same after that. Only God could adequately describe a great Burgundy, but here's a broad idea:

Fine Burgundy is made from the Pinot Noir grape, which gives it a cherrylike vibrancy and a "forward" fruit taste, as we discussed in the chapter on American Pinot Noirs. But combined with the soil, the winemaking know-how, and the traditions of Burgundy, Pinot grows into something grander: It develops a depth and a richness that give it infinite layers of taste. There's chocolate, raspberries, tobacco, and soil, but all in balance, giving the wine a kind of Queen Elizabeth regality. You know the rich, red velvet that surrounds kings and queens? That's what a great Burgundy tastes like. Underneath it all is a taste of the earth that binds it all together. And the taste lasts forever. After you swallow, all of those tastes somehow seem to get *more* pronounced in your mouth and in your throat. And the smell, even of an emptied glass, is pure bliss.

Consider these notes, made the next night during dinner at a restaurant called La Rôtisserie du Chambertin. We'd ordered a bottle of 1961 Gevrey-Chambertin for $40. This was a great year, and we couldn't imagine our good fortune in being able to taste a 1961—then twenty-three years old—that had been waiting for us in the same cellar all these years. Watch the time go by in these notes:

"Almost orange, persimmon looking, very orange at the edge. Big, fruity nose—massive. Taste at 9:10 P.M. a bit *too* 'sweet' and muscular, better at the back. Needs air. Almost jamlike sweetness. No real hint of age at 9:15. Years left, very fruity and young-tasting. No dusty taste or brown in look or taste. Really dries mouth. Lots of tannins left. Dry, fruity, very Pinot, no wood taste, just fruit, but best at back. 9:30: Richer, bigger, almost like cherry wine. Still a long finish, but fruitier. 9:35: Pepper comes in. 9:45: Nose is unbelievable. Not 'deep red' like a claret or California, but big. Austere yet fruity, very dignified, stately, not at all plump. Regal. 10:15: Dusty nose, finally. 11:00: Huge, lots of fruit, almost sweet yet austere at the same time. 11:30: Still lots of fruit, long, red finish. Terrifically elegant, great character. Rich and austere at the same time. *Great finish*, long and red and hot and Pinot."

Of all the wines in our wine notes, thousands of them, this is the only one that rated "Fantastique!" If you looked at our notes over the years, you'd find more exclamation marks and flat-out wonder on the Burgundy pages than any other. But still, if you asked us what was the greatest Burgundy we ever had, we would tell you this:

We bought a bottle of the 1982 from the old man in Gevrey-Chambertin—it was about $5—and packed it in our suitcase for the trip back to New York via London. On our one day in London, we wandered into Hyde Park to drink it and happened upon a small lake with rowboats. We're old hands at the rowboats in Central Park in New York, so this seemed like something we could handle. We rowed out with our glasses and our wine. Soon we were surrounded by ducks and swans. The sun was bright and the beautifully tended grounds were the greenest we'd ever seen. There in the boat, we opened the old man's wine, poured it, and it was, and will always be, the greatest Burgundy we ever had.

But, wait, let's come back to earth here. It's 1999 in America. Is Burgundy just the stuff of great memories, or can you walk into a wineshop in the U.S. and buy a Burgundy for a reasonable price that will knock your socks off? We were determined to answer that question. We set an upper limit of about $30 and chose a wide variety of red Burgundies.

There are many different kinds of Burgundies, from generic Bourgogne to the awesomely expensive Chambertin and Romanée-Conti. If you really try to understand all of Burgundy, it'll make your head hurt. There's a whole book, for instance, just on Romanée-Conti! Our question was a simple one: Without studying the difference between Santenay and Ladoix and Gevrey-Chambertin, could you simply go into your wineshop, plunk down $30, and find out what Burgundy *really* tastes like?

The answer, we're delighted to report, is yes.

The very first wine we opened in our blind tasting was prophetic. "Cherry/soil nose," we wrote. "Nice, sweet-cherry finish. Awfully pleasant." This wine—which turned out to be a Labouré-Roi Gevrey-Chambertin 1995—rated only a Good/Very Good, but it was an auspicious start. Only two wines later, with No. 3, we seemed to hit an early jackpot:

"Pretty, with a big, serious, Burgundy nose. Raspberries and cream on nose. Purple at the edge. Cherry-berry. Huge, creamy fruit, round, lovely. Vibrant, rich, round, and berrylike, with fruit that's alive and 'feminine.' Beautifully made, harmonious. Doesn't taste oaky, but you know the wood is there. It sparkles in the glass! It looks like red glass sliding around! There's fire in it! It's like velvet in your glass, like a fine ruby. Dottie says, 'I've never seen a prettier wine.' After half an hour it's sweeter with fruit!" This wine, which turned out to be a Guyon Gevrey-Chambertin 1995, rated Delicious, and we couldn't imagine a better one.

We were wrong.

One reason it's easier to choose a Burgundy these days is that recent vintages were good years, on the whole. In good years, Burgundy can be deceptively drinkable in its youth. What we mean is that good Bordeaux wines, when young, are virtually unapproachable; no one would misunderstand why it's a good idea to let a fine Bordeaux age. But because Burgundies tend to have more "forward," approachable tastes, they tend to taste good even young. That makes it hard to appreciate how very much better they are going to be with age. One thing we discovered in our tasting was what a tragedy it was to be "tasting" these wines, as opposed to drinking a whole bottle. We would conduct our blind tasting, take our notes—and then come back around to wines that were completely different from how they tasted on the first round. These are wines to drink, not taste.

One wine we tasted, for instance, was nothing short of high art. It was a Beaune-Bressandes 1994 from Albert Morot. "Whoa!" we wrote. "Light-looking and light at first in the mouth, with a remarkable, big, rich, creamy finish that belies everything about it. Wow! What an achievement. Totally unassuming, hiding what it has. Spice. Pepper. Older cherries. Velvety and highly textured." This is embarrassing, but Dottie said this wine reminded her of light bondage—ripe cream and fruit straining, with great spirit, to be released from a tightly wound structure. Ahem!

It was a tough call, but we decided the best of tasting was a Nuits-St.-Georges Les Pruliers 1996 from Chicotot Georges. "Hints of tar, big. This is *very* serious," we wrote. "Big, tar wine. Holy moly! Sweetness under the tar. Could be great in time. Sweet and earthy, with layers you taste in back. Now, the tar is gone, replaced by fruit. Lots of guts, but easy on the finish." This is a terrific wine we believe will be great in a few years.

Red Burgundy is the kind of wine that can change your life. Like love itself, it is risky and it might require a few false starts. But it's worth it. And getting there really is half the fun.

Wine Notes

There is nothing in the world quite like a red Burgundy—but "Burgundy" covers a lot of territory, from generic Bourgogne (which we'd avoid) to the astonishingly expensive great wines such as Romanée-Conti. There are some hints on the label. For instance, if a wine says "Premier Cru" or "1ᵉʳ Cru," that's a good sign. It's also a good sign if there is a vineyard name attached to the name of the locale, such as Pommard-Epenots or Nuits-St.-Georges Les Pruliers. Vintages matter, too, but recent vintages—the ones you are likely to find in stores—have been good. However, if you try to remember all of this, you'll never buy a Burgundy. So our advice is to plan to spend around $30, go to a store with a good collection of Burgundies (many stores carry only a few in a dusty cor-

ner; watch out!), and just pick one up from a recent vintage. Be sure to pour a couple of glasses and then let the rest air for at least an hour, if you have the time. Or, if you're willing to linger, taste it when you first open it and then take small sips for as many hours as you can. These are classy wines that will be different with every sip.

Nuits-St.-Georges Premier Cru Les Pruliers 1996 (Chicotot Georges) $29.95

DELICIOUS • *Best of tasting. The Les Pruliers at the end of the name indicates a specific vineyard, and while this is no guarantee of quality, this wine is terrific. It's filled with powerful, tarlike fruit that, over time, begins to soften into classic Burgundy "sweetness." This has the potential to be a great wine in a few years.*

Santenay 1996 (Domaine Bachelet) $15.95

GOOD/VERY GOOD • *Best value. At first, this seems fine, but not serious. Then, with some air, it begins to get rich and memorable. Bottom line: In a few years, this is going to be one excellent wine. And for the price, that's really something.*

Gevrey-Chambertin 1995 (Antonin Guyon) $29.95

DELICIOUS • *A beautiful wine, both in the glass and in your mouth. Creamy, sensuous, and round, alive in your mouth. Simply beautiful, and one of the most romantic wines we've ever had.*

Beaune-Bressandes Premier Cru 1994 (Albert Morot) $32.95

DELICIOUS • *Wow! It seems so unassuming: Light in the glass, and in the front of the mouth—and then, pow, a remarkable hit of rich, creamy wine, especially in the back of the mouth and on the finish. Spicy, with some pepper, yet still velvety and highly structured. The high art of Burgundy winemaking.*

Gevrey-Chambertin 1995 (Bouchard Père & Fils) $29.95

VERY GOOD/DELICIOUS • *Big, deep, and creamy nose. Deep-dark, rich Pinot fruit. Richer than it is elegant. Even earthier than most. Some real heft here, with hints of tobacco and a heaviness that's a little more like a Cabernet. Quite an experience.*

Santenay Clos de Tavannes Premier Cru 1996 (F. & D. Clair) $24.95

VERY GOOD/DELICIOUS • *Thick, rich, and creamy. Deeply sensuous, with all sorts of cherry-raspberry tastes and a long, long warming, red-berry finish. Young and mouthcoating.*

Pommard-Epenots Premier Cru 1995 (Domaine Caillot) $29.95

VERY GOOD/DELICIOUS • *The essence of character and class. Already tastes mature and mouthfilling. This is what Burgundy tastes like.*

Gevrey-Chambertin 1995 (Labouré-Roi) $20.95

GOOD/VERY GOOD • *A very nice wine from a reliable shipper. Most Burgundies have some cherry taste, and this had more than most. It's like a big piece of cherry cream pie.*

Chambolle-Musigny 1995 (Antonin Guyon) $29.95

GOOD/VERY GOOD • *A very pleasant bottle to drink right now. Ripe and ready.*

Chambolle-Musigny 1993 (Louis Jadot) $28.50

GOOD/VERY GOOD • *Dry, austere, and very serious. Hints of chocolate, but with a core of very tightly wound fruit. Much fruit and beautifully made, so the fruit remains intense. It even* looks *dense.*

Vosne-Romanée 1996 (Domaine François Lamarche)   **$29.95**

GOOD/VERY GOOD • *Cherrylike and rich, vibrant yet flat at the end.
It has a little lemon, a little bite, that's interesting and unusual, and
might make it even better than most with food.*

Chambolle-Musigny 1995 (Louis Jadot)   **$29.95**

GOOD • *"Sweet" with fruit but simple. Fun to drink, but expensive for
the experience.*

Invite Your Friends
to a Wine Tasting; Yes, You

You can throw a successful wine-tasting party. It's easy, it's fun, it's educational—and you and your friends will have a terrific time. It needn't be formal, snooty, or stuffy. Here's how:

~ Tell everyone who's coming to bring a bottle of the same kind of wine and set a price range—say, Chardonnay under $12. Couples can bring one bottle.

~ Tell them to put the wine in a bag with their names on it before they come over.

~ Have a bottle of your own, in a bag. When people walk in, give them a glass of your wine (no more than two ounces; remember, this is a tasting) and put theirs on the table (or, if white, in the refrigerator). Have plenty of heavy finger foods around and put out bottles of sparkling water and glasses, periodically encouraging your guests to eat and to drink water.

~ When everyone's finished with the first wine, pour the second—and, white or not, leave it on the table. And so on.

What you'll find is that at the beginning people will be embarrassed to say anything about the wine and seem a little shy about the whole thing. What a difference a couple of glasses make, though. By the third glass, the noise level will increase. Your guests will probably be talking about everything except the wine. And soon they'll be helping themselves (that's why you left the wines on the table).

By the fourth glass, your guests will start to interrupt themselves to comment on the wines—"Wow, Jim, I really like the one you brought!" It doesn't matter if they don't think they know anything about wine; they will know which one of these they like the best. Soon, people really will be talking about the wines. Keep opening until they've all been poured. Then it's time to . . .

~ Take the bottles out of the bags. You don't have to take any sort of poll of the best or the worst; it doesn't matter. Everyone will enjoy seeing who brought what, and finding out how much everything cost.

At the end of the night, you'll find that the wine tasting itself has been incidental to the evening. In fact, all that the tasting of wines has done is get your friends' minds off more pressing matters—like work—so they could relax. In the long run, that's what a wine-tasting party is all about: good conversation and good friends—not just wine. But don't tell anyone that. It'll be our secret. And please, if your friends are driving, be very careful. Have a designated driver or call a cab. You want everyone to be around for the next vintage.

BORDEAUX
More Affordable Than You Think

COMPARED TO MOST of the wine world, Bordeaux is easy to understand. In most cases, there's an actual estate in this region of France that makes an actual wine that has a fairly consistent style every year. If you buy Château Gloria one year and you like it, you can be pretty well assured you can buy Château Gloria every year and like it, though some years will obviously be better than others. The most prominent grapes are Cabernet Sauvignon, which everybody is familiar with, and Merlot, which everybody is *really* familiar with.

And yet Bordeaux is so famous, so microscopically examined, such a point of reference for wine experts (what other wine gets people into heated arguments about the relative merits of 1929 vs. 1945?) that it's easy to be intimidated about it. Whole books have been written about individual estates. Aficionados can explain at depth the differences among the various Bordeaux regions, such as Pauillac, St.-Estèphe, St.-Julien, and Graves—not to mention the differences among the great "First Growths" (see next chapter).

Relax! Bordeaux wines are classy, elegant, and approachable, and they don't have to be expensive. You don't have to know everything about wines from Bordeaux to enjoy them. But they are worth getting to know well, because they're really special. "Class" is a word often used to describe a "claret," which is what the British call red Bordeaux. The wines have an amazing complexity. They have a crispness, with layers of red tastes, and at the same time a depth you taste especially on the "finish." You're likely to smell and taste tobacco, leather, and dark wood, like you're in Churchill's personal humidor. These are wines, even the inexpensive ones, that can't be quaffed, because they seem to disappear from your mouth in stages and leave tastes behind that you would miss. You don't want to rush through these and miss any of their nuances.

You can experience Bordeaux's wonders without having to pay an arm and a leg. Here's how: Buy clarets from great producers in bad years; buy wines from producers you've never heard of in good years. No wine is hyped more than Bordeaux in good years. This sends the prices of the famous producers, such as Château Lafite-Rothschild, through the roof. Right? Of course. Bam! Out of sight! On the other hand, aficionados avoid great Bordeaux producers in so-so years, which brings their prices down. This phenomenon is good for the world.

When we were young, just starting out our careers as journalists, we couldn't afford fine Bordeaux. But both 1980 and 1984 were considered so-so years. So, when we saw the 1980 Château Mouton-Rothschild, one of the great "first growths," we pounced on it. It was just $19.95 and it knocked our socks off. We declared it "Great! Fantastic. Absolutely wonderful nose, full of cinnamon, fruit, wood, more classy than powerful. Taste: Very fruity, full of cinnamon. Round, rich, elegant, surprisingly ready to drink. Big yet not 'powerful.' Not really assertive or forward, but big with fruit and spice, with a long, red finish." We went out and got a second bottle for even less—$18.99—and it was just as good. This is also how we enjoyed the 1974 Château Latour and 1973 Mouton-Rothschild. On our budget, these were pure bliss.

But "first growths" like those are a rare and special pleasure because, even at lower-than-usual prices, they're still pricey. So, what works best is this: Start with far more reasonable clarets, the châteaux most of us have never heard of. Many Bordeaux wines are made by little-known, small châteaux that produce fine, reasonably priced table wine that's meant to be drunk fairly young. But in an exceptional year like 1995, these wines are often better than good; they're really, really good—and reasonably priced. After all, people have been making wines in Bordeaux for more than 1,500 years for a reason: The soil, climate, and vines are special. Even the "minor" wines often have an easy sophistication and depth. These probably will cost you somewhere between the $10 to $20 you'd pay for a pretty good California Cabernet, but they'll be better.

Of course, they aren't nearly as good as those from top makers, and none of this should obscure the fact that great wines from great years are life-changing experiences. But those wines are not only expensive, they also need a great deal of age to achieve their best possible taste. So, in a good year, lesser-known châteaux have three things going for them: (1) They're available sooner, since they don't get as much care or as much time in barrels; (2) They're ready to drink now, instead of a decade (or two) from now; and (3) They're affordable.

To check our theories, we asked a wine merchant to select and send us two cases of 1995 Bordeaux wines under $20. What we found made us very happy. A couple were just OK; most were delightful and drinkable now; and three tasted age-worthy—wines we could store for a couple of years. The best of the bunch was a Clos Magne Figeac from St.-Émilion, which cost $12.95. It showed lovely fruit and nice balance, especially after being open for a little while. The most remarkable buy was a Château Peyraud, from Premières Côtes de Blaye. At $6.95, it was ready to drink, slightly grapey, with some real depth of flavor— lovely and fun.

Because they are from small châteaux, you might not find these two wines. But the important thing is to look for small châteaux in good years and pick them up.

Of course, there is a mid-range, too. Early on, we found we liked the taste of Château Gruaud-Larose, from St.-Julien. To us, it had just the right combination of dark richness, complexity, and approachability. So, over the years, we've had more vintages of Gruaud-Larose than any other Bordeaux. We also routinely enjoy Château Gloria, from St.-Julien, and, for a bit more money, Château Pichon-Lalande, from

Pauillac. These are the kind of mid-range Bordeaux wines that make a dinner special. After all, sometimes you want to splurge a little. You're having company over for your world-famous beef tenderloin. Or you've been invited for dinner and volunteered to bring the wine. Or maybe you just—finally—have a night alone together. At special times like these, you want to spend more than usual, but you don't want to mortgage the house. This is the time for a good mid-range Bordeaux.

We love California wines. They're usually very good, generally not intimidating, and rarely in short supply. But if you're going to spend a little more on a wine than you ordinarily would—and especially if you're preparing for a special occasion—there's something about red Bordeaux wines that makes moments memorable. Partly it's the wine itself, which tends to have depth and complexity that demand attention. Partly it's the centuries-old cachet. And partly it's because most of us don't drink good Bordeaux very often, so when we do it's a big deal.

So let's say that tonight you've decided to spend $20 to $40 on a Bordeaux. What should you get? We conducted a tasting to find out.

To begin with, if you really like Merlot, here's a good steer: Château de Sales (we had the 1993 for this tasting). It was the only Pomerol of the tasting, which means it was the only wine made predominantly from the Merlot grape, and it was immediately recognizable. It was soft, flat, fruity, classy, very much a Merlot. But it lacked the complexity of our other favorites, and for that reason we've never been huge fans of Pomerol. Still, it's a wine most people would like a lot. In fact, since our tasting, we've served it extensively, and people are just crazy about it. (We found it for just $19.95, but it's usually higher than that, sometimes double that price.)

The Château Gloria we had for this tasting, the 1993 ($23.95), was as lovely as always—a bit fat and flabby, but ripe and approachable. If you can't remember the name of any other Bordeaux wine, remember Gloria.

Our third favorite was a shocker. In a tasting of well-known names, we wouldn't have expected the 1993 Château de Fieuzal, from Pessac-Léognan, in Graves, to show very well. In fact, it was remarkably classy—as elegant as it could be, with rich undertones of fruit and wood. At $24.95, it was a bargain.

The top two wines are a matter of taste. The 1993 Château Duhart-Milon, from Pauillac ($33.95), was a monster wine—huge, rich, and plump. It smelled and tasted of cream, which made it almost sinfully sensuous. Ripe fruit, perfect wood, just the right age—this is a big, rich Bordeaux you really should taste.

But it wasn't our favorite. That was Château Léoville-Barton 1993, from St.-Julien. It was lean and muscular, with classic, deep, fruitwood Bordeaux tastes. Simply gorgeous. This was everything a good Bordeaux can be, and you owe it to yourself to try to find a bottle. Yes, it was $37.95, and we know that sounds like a lot. But is it so much more than you would pay for wine at a restaurant? Eat home tonight—and pretend you're eating out. Better yet, find a restaurant that will let you bring your own wine and charge a "corkage" fee. At $37.95 plus, say, a $5 fee, this will be the best $43 bottle of wine you've ever had at a restaurant.

Wine Notes

Minor-league Bordeaux in a really good year can be a fine bargain. We found that many 1995 Bordeaux wines are very nice to drink now, and some will even improve with age. Here are some we liked. But it's important to go your own way on this one. There are plenty of small, obscure châteaux in Bordeaux that produce excellent wine in a year like 1995. Take a chance on one.

Inexpensive

Clos Magne Figeac
St.-Émilion $12.95

VERY GOOD • *Best of tasting. Very well made and ageworthy. Well-balanced.*

Château Peyraud
Premières Côtes de Blaye $6.95

VERY GOOD • *Best value. Simple, pleasant, and great fun, with some depth of flavor. A classic example of the kind of great deal you can find in a good year.*

Château Carsin
Premières Côtes de Bordeaux $9.49

GOOD/VERY GOOD • *Some real taste here—rich and chewy, with overtones of tar. It's even age-worthy.*

Vieux-Château Landon
Médoc $13.95

GOOD/VERY GOOD • *Lovely to look at. It was hot and a bit hard in youth, should be perfect this minute.*

Château Rozier
St.-Émilion $13.50

GOOD/VERY GOOD • *Delightful. Simple, yet earthy and very much a Bordeaux.*

As we always say, price and value are different things, and many red Bordeaux wines under $40 are great values because they're such memorable experiences. It's important to find a château with a style you like. For instance, we always like Château Gruaud-Larose, which means we can buy it in every vintage with some confidence. All Bordeaux wines have distinctive personalities. Find one you like, and trust yourself.

Mid-Range

Château Léoville-Barton 1993
St.-Julien $37.95

DELICIOUS • *Best of tasting. Classic claret nose. Big, muscular, and memorable. This is an expansive wine, not embarrassed to be like a big piece of chocolate cake.*

Château de Fieuzal 1993
Graves $24.95

DELICIOUS • *Best value. Young and vibrant. Remarkable elegance and yet, at the same time, pleasant and approachable.*

Château Duhart-Milon 1993
Pauillac $33.95

VERY GOOD/DELICIOUS • *Creamy and plump, with a long, rich finish. Sensuous. This is a very serious wine, with character and class.*

Château Gloria 1993
St.-Julien $23.95

VERY GOOD/DELICIOUS • *Filled with sweet fruit, fat, and sassy. Plump, almost flabby in its rich approachability. You can't go wrong with Gloria.*

Château de Sales 1993
Pomerol $19.95
VERY GOOD • *Soft, pleasant, floral. This doesn't have the depth of the others, with all of its taste right on top, but that's also its charm.*

Storing Wine: Relax!

You can make wine storage complicated if you want to. Just ask the police department of Coral Gables, Florida.

When we moved back to Miami in 1984, we bought an "Old Spanish" house built just two months before the Great Hurricane of 1926. With its romantic arches, it was like a fortress, with thick walls that kept the house cool all year long—perfect for storing wine. And it had a maid's quarters in back that had its own bathroom and air conditioning system. There, for six weeks in mid-1984, a handyman named Tom Miranda built us a real wine cellar. It was made of wood, floor to ceiling, and every single bottle we owned had its own space, the 990 spaces individually nailed and glued by Tom. When it was finished, and our collection was swallowed by it, the room looked like a piece of art, with the bottle caps providing a riot of color against the blond wood. The aroma of the fresh wood and the wines we drank in there (and occasionally spilled)—"the angels' share"—combined to smell a little like a winery.

Miami was a pretty rough place in 1984, so we decided we needed a security system. A security man also named Tom knew a mark when he saw one and sold us a gold-plated, state-of-the-art system with all sorts of bells and whistles. When he saw the wine room, his eyes lit up. "You know," he said, "we could put a thermometer in here attached to the alarm system. If it gets too warm in here, we'd be notified, and we'd call you." It sounded like a good idea at the time.

Just a month later, at 2 A.M., we heard beeping downstairs. It sounded like the security system, but if someone had broken in, we were supposed to hear a siren, not a beep. John, naked, crept down the stairs, Dottie close behind. As we walked into the front room, Dottie yelled, "Watch out! Someone's looking inside!" John scampered back behind the wall, and we both peeked around the corner. From windows all around the house, policemen stared back at us.

Coral Gables is a lovely suburb of Miami—charming, old, peaceful. It also has an efficient and generally not-very-busy police force. We had no idea what was going on. John threw on some shorts and opened a window. "Your security company called," the policeman in front told us. "They said your alarm went off." The security system was still beeping. We couldn't turn it off and were afraid to open the doors for fear it would make the alarm really go off. But from the flashing lights on the control panel, John figured out what had happened: It was a warm Miami night, and the wine room had gone above 55 degrees. The wine room had flashed a message to the security company, which had called the police instead of us.

Under those circumstances, what would *you* tell the cops? We told them we were sorry, that the system was new, that there was something wrong with it—and thank you very much for coming. We were horrified. The wine, however, was unharmed.

This needn't ever happen to you, because most people really don't *need* a wine room. Obviously, if you have a large collection of fine wines, it is better to keep them someplace special, like a wine room with a temperature-sensitive alarm. But if you're like most people, and just want to keep a few bottles around, this isn't neces-sary. We fear many people don't keep any wine in the house because they've been convinced it's so precious, so delicate, that it will quickly disintegrate if it's not treated like a hothouse flower. Not true. Wine is tougher than you think. And while, sure, wines kept in sublime conditions age more gracefully, you're not keeping your wines forever, just for a few weeks. Here's all you need to do with that case you just bought:

1. Identify a place, perhaps the bottom of a closet, that has a fairly constant, moderate temperature (not too hot, not too cold), doesn't get much light, and isn't disturbed very often.

2. Carefully put the box of wine on its side so the bottles are hor-izontal, or just lay the bottles on the floor. It's important that they rest on their side, instead of being stood up, so the wine stays in contact with the cork. This prevents the cork from drying out and allowing air in, which is bad for the wine.

3. Take one out when you want to open it.

That's all there is to it, although you'll probably find yourself slowly improving your storage capacity. In our case, we went from one of those little accordionlike devices to 48-bottle metal racks to tall 60-bottle racks to a whole wine room. But relax. Take it one step at a time. What's important first is just to have wine in the house. The rest will come naturally.

The First Growths

He Said, She Said

EVEN IF YOU'RE NOT RICH, even if you never plan to spend $200 on a bottle of wine, you must be at least a little curious about the "first growths" of Bordeaux. Fashions and fads come and go, but Châteaux Lafite-Rothschild, Latour, Mouton-Rothschild, Haut-Brion, and Margaux endure. Year after year, decade after decade, these "clarets" are the standard by which red wine is judged. They're wines that incite an almost sexual passion among wine lovers. Think we're kidding? Consider this, from one of our favorite old books, a 1928 edition of *The Wines of France*, by H. Warner Allen:

> A great Claret is the queen of all natural wines, and in the present writer's opinion the highest perfection of all wines that have ever been made. It is delicate and harmonious beyond all others; the manifold sensations that it produces are of the most exquisite subtlety, and their intensity is so perfectly balanced and their quality so admirably harmonized that there is no clash or predominance, but bouquet, aroma, velvet, body are all blended into an ideal whole. For the thorough appreciation of a Château Margaux or Latour, the wine-lover must be possessed with the acutest sense of *nuances*, of those subtle shades of taste and fragrance, which are delights that belong exclusively to great wines. For this reason Claret makes great demands on the powers of appreciation of the drinker. Its beauties are never obvious, but all the more fascinating for their elusiveness.

Whew! Over the centuries, men have paid much more than $200 for experiences like *that*. But, all kidding aside, there really does come a time in your wine journey when your thoughts will turn to these great wines of Bordeaux. Maybe you're celebrating something, or giving a gift to a close friend, or you've simply gotten to the point in your wine appreciation where you want to taste what the very best is really like.

First, a little background. In 1855, Napoleon III ordered up a list of the best wines of Bordeaux for the Paris Exposition of that year. They were ranked according to their quality and price—especially their price. Ever since then, the Classification of 1855, in which wines were ranked by "growth," has been enormously important as a benchmark of quality. Lafite, Latour, Margaux, and Haut-Brion were *premiers crus*, or "first growths" (Mouton was added in 1973), and others were ranked lower—wines like Pichon-Lalande, for instance, were "second growths."

We remember the first "first growth" we ever had. We bought it at a lovely little wine store in North Miami Beach, long since shuttered, called Le Château. We were in our wine-drinking infancy then, in the mid-1970s. We were both young, working journalists—Dottie earned $170 a week, and John $175 (he earned more because he'd been editor of the *Columbia Daily Spectator*, she was assured, not because he was a man)—and we were learning about wine very much from the bottom up. One day we walked into Le Château and there, sitting on the floor, was a wooden case filled with Château Lafite-Rothschild. And it was only $8 a bottle! What was the catch? It was from the 1968 vintage, roundly declared one of the worst of the century. This was a wine experts would spit out and demand: "You call this *wine?*" Michael Broadbent, in his classic *The Great Vintage Wine Book,* says of the 1968 Lafite: "It is of course arguable (and none of our business) whether a premier grand cru does its reputation—or that of Bordeaux—any good by selling a wine under its own name in a vintage like this. But in the 1971 to 1973 wine boom period, when this and other '68s were put on the market, the ignorant and the gullible would buy anything."

Well, count us among the ignorant and the gullible. We bought two bottles. And you know what? We loved them. We'd never had any wine of real breeding before—we'd been learning on very inexpensive wines from all over the world—and this Lafite was, to us, a whole new world. It had layers of taste. It had obvious hints of wood. It had a little bit of cream. All wine is personal, a function of where you are in your wine journey when you drink it. To us, this was a real eye-opener. It at least gave us hints of what fine wine was all about.

We continued to drink first growths from time to time after that, but it's not something we could afford very often. Once, in 1984, when Dottie was at the *New York Times,* a colleague told her about a great deal on 1959 Latour. It was a really good year and just $80, so she rushed to the store and bought one for John's birthday. We kept that wine for years, and finally opened it with John's brother Jim in 1992. John took these notes:

"Delicious! Nose is massive, chewy, with tobacco and chocolate. Wow! Huge, dry, massive, rich, drying. Still hardish. Not a lot of 'fruit,' as such—I mean, no sweet fruit or charm, just power, like *the essence of wine.* Holy cow. Wow. Massive, incredibly tough and leathery, but with an incredible amount of depth and class. After a half hour, some sweetness at the end is coming through. Tobacco and old cedar. Huge, massive, yet not a hint of the clumsiness in huge California wines. A gorgeous, essence finish—long, sweetish, and very, very masculine. Just about perfect for a big, muscular wine. I think it'll be better, showing more fruit, in ten to fifteen years. Dottie says it's just perfect right now."

And she still can't believe she only bought one bottle.

The "first growths" are primarily made from Cabernet Sauvignon, with some Merlot and Cabernet Franc stirred into the mix. Generally, the more Cabernet Sauvignon in a wine, the "tougher" and more age-worthy it is. Its tight fruit tastes and tannins do that; the more Merlot, the softer the wine. So it's not surprising that Latour, which is known as the biggest of the first growths, has the least Merlot, while Margaux, which is known as the softest, has more. Still, "soft" is a relative term for these wines, especially in good years. The truth is that for the first few years after a good vintage, these wines are extremely difficult to drink. Don't buy one if you're not planning to hold it for a while. But if you do. . . .

Well, if you do, you will have a remarkable experience.

People often ask us if we ever disagree about wines. We do, of course, but generally we come around to some sort of compromise. Dottie has the better palate and taste memory and John has the better memory for vineyards and vintages, so between us we generally come to some sort of understanding. If we can't, well, there's always the sofa bed to sleep on.

Our usual amicable musings hit a snag with our tasting of the first growths from 1995, a terrific year. This tasting cost almost $1,500, and, having not won the lottery, we could do it only because the *Wall Street Journal* pays for our wines. While we usually taste wines blind and against each other, in this case we knew what we were drinking, and we drank just one bottle a night, every night, for five nights. We knew these would be challenging wines, wines that would change with each sip. And we knew we'd have to concentrate to figure out what was really going on in each bottle.

As we expected, especially at this point in their development—they're infants—these wines are more an intellectual exercise than a truly pleasurable experience. The fruit, to varying degrees, is tightly wound and largely unyielding. Each of these wines has layers of wood, tobacco, and vanilla, and some have undertones of menthol. But the layers, at this point, are like the layers of phyllo dough—so thin and compact they're hard to distinguish without a great deal of care and thought. We've been studying wine for twenty-five years, and, for us, deconstructing these young children is part of the fun of drinking them now. We imagine first-grade teachers must have the same kind of fun as they look at each child and try to guess how he or she will grow up.

It was impossible to say which was "best." They were all extra-ordinary in their own way. In fact, we disagreed about these wines so thoroughly that we kept separate notes. These wines are filled with contradictions, especially when they're young. The Mouton-Rothschild was showing more fruit than the Haut-Brion, although John thought and Dorothy hoped that the Haut-Brion had more fruit than it was showing. It's just that the Mouton had plump, "forward" fruit, while the Haut-Brion had intense, tight fruit. It was a Ralph Fiennes kind of wine.

It's better to buy a mature first growth, of course, but who's got that kind of money? So buy a young one, if you can, and put it in the bottom of your closet. There's nothing like having a first growth among your wines. Its very proximity to your other wines makes everything seem more special. You should enjoy its company for a few years, and then, under some special circumstances, drink it slowly and with the respect it deserves. If you do all of this, regardless of what you paid for it, your first growth will be an outstanding value.

Wine Notes

The 1995 First Growths

JOHN'S RATINGS

Château Margaux $325

Best of tasting. Remarkably wonderful when first opened—round, classy, and crisp. It turned green after an hour, indicating there's more depth there than was apparent at first. At its best, velvety, soft, and pretty well perfect. When people talk about great claret, this is what they're talking about.

Château Haut-Brion $245

Purple, young, and grapey, like a barrel sample. An awesome core of ripe fruit that's still so tight it's almost like a fruit pill, or hard candy. It's clear there is layer upon layer of fruit, wood, vanilla, and tobacco here. It's a risky wine, edgy in its intensity. My guess is that twenty years from now, this will turn out to be the best of the five—and yet, for the next few years, the cheapest because it hasn't gotten as much press as the others. Result: Probably the best buy for the next few years.

Château Latour $360

Surprisingly approachable. Packed with explosive, black fruit. The nose is so huge and creamy it can knock you off your chair. It's still tough, but filled with the kind of fruit and earth that give it tremendous character.

Château Lafite-Rothschild $250

Cedar nose, like a cigar humidor. Green and a bit harsh; very dry. Muscular and sinewy, but with a core of blackberry/cassis fruit. It tastes too much like its components, like you can feel the wheels turning. Just a little too obvious.

Château Mouton-Rothschild $250

Rich looking, with a warm, smoky nose. It's chewy and meaty, with notes of cherry, wood, and cream. In general, it's the most generous of the wines, with plumper fruit, but also seems a bit less classy than the others. Obviously a fine bottle, but without the intensity and character of the others.

DOROTHY'S RATINGS

Château Lafite-Rothschild $250

Best of tasting. An incredibly intense experience. A winning, complete, and harmonious balance of fruit, wood, and soil. It's all there, and it's elegant and heady. This wine engages the intellect, sends you reeling with expectations. If it were a demure woman, it might be said to flash just enough throat to make you catch your breath and then sit back, resigned to the wait and certain of the reward that lies ahead when it chooses to reveal itself more fully.

Château Margaux $325

This was, as expected, beautiful and approachable. If any of these could be said to be enjoyable in a couple of years, this would be the one. Although it played a little peek-a-boo through the night and was for a few minutes asleep in the glass, it was mostly soft and sweet and revealing. I wondered whether it had enough stuff to hang in there for several years or if its easy virtues would too soon dissipate.

Château Latour $360

After a few minutes of a strong mineral and prune nose, this became creamy and awesome. The sweetness went down bone dry and fanned out through the chest with a glorious glow. Then, without warning, it would get a little tough, then lovely again. But the fruit makes me think this may be spectacular in several years.

Château Haut-Brion $245

Show me the fruit! Show me the fruit! All right, so it's beautiful to look at and smells wonderful and my better half really likes it. But it was so tight that I almost had to take it on faith that it had fruit. Sure, there were hints, stingy flashes of sweetness. But getting to it was almost like cracking a jawbreaker. And yet . . . who knows in twenty years?

Château Mouton-Rothschild $250

This looked and smelled wonderful, but the fruit, while more apparent, seemed weak, lacking intensity. The least impressive of the lot.

When Do I Open That Bottle?
A Guide to Aging

"I have a bottle of Château Whatever 1945 that I got for graduation. When do I open it?" This is the question we're asked second most (the most asked? See page 125). Truth is, the answer to that question is easy, and we provide it below. But the much broader question—when can you tell when any wine is ready to drink?—is very difficult, and yet one of the great pleasures of wine drinking.

Everybody knows that the great "first growths" of Bordeaux, such as Château Lafite-Rothschild, can age for many years. Everybody also knows that Beaujolais and fresh whites such as Pinot Grigio from Italy are best drunk young. Between those two extremes, however, is a whole world of wine.

It is impossible to say, for sure, how any wine will age. Even two bottles of the exact same wine will age differently, based on a number of factors including, of course, how they're stored. We tend to keep our wines for too long, to tell you the truth, because we grow attached to them as the years go on. Consider this, for instance: Back in 1984, a reporter who worked for John named Joel Achenbach had an assignment in Washington State and came back with a present—a Woodward Canyon 1981 Cabernet Sauvignon, the winery's first release. It cost him $12.60. The wine was so special that we could never bear to open it, even though it said on the label that the wine "should drink very nicely into the late 1980s."

Finally, on August 21, 1998, we opened it. Get this:

"Cherries, blackberries, chocolate on a rich, dark nose. Smells like a Latour. Huge, sweet-fruit nose. Like a young Latour! Massive and rich. Incredible fruit, totally intoxicating." Fully ninety minutes later, we finally finished the bottle and declared it "young 'til the last drop."

On the other hand, around the same time, we had a 1985

Insignia from Joseph Phelps, a famous Cabernet Sauvignon–Merlot–Cabernet Franc blend from a fine year. It should have been perfect, but it was clearly tired and over the hill. Maybe it was just that bottle, what's called bottle variation. But that's the point: You can never tell for sure. So here is some general advice:

~ Next time you're at your local wineshop, see if it's giving away a vintage chart. They're sometimes near the cash register, and they usually give you some idea when various wines should be drunk. All are pretty much the same.

~ Remember that "heavier" wines should age longer than "lighter" wines, and this is just as true of whites as reds. Just as a big, heavy red Rhône is going to age better—that is, longer—than a light Rioja, a heavier Chardonnay, one with plenty of oak, will age better than a lighter Sauvignon Blanc. We find—although this is a source of some controversy in the wine world—that even heavier Champagne gets better, nuttier, and richer, with some age.

~ Trust yourself. If you buy a bottle of Zinfandel and you really like it, but it seems a bit harsh and young, think about buying more and leaving it in the bottom of your closet for a year or two. See what happens. Don't let price be your guide. Some of our greatest experiences were with wines that were inexpensive to begin with, but tasted quite expensive by the time we drank them.

~ Take some risks. It's rare for a wine to go bad unless it is really abused. There is nothing in the world more wonderful than a perfectly aged wine, and it's worth taking some chances to get there. You might think, for instance, that Gewürztraminer is the kind of wine you'd want to drink young and fresh, and it is; but, as we said earlier, we find that a Gewürz with some age on it is a remarkable experience (see page 34). In any event, usually if a wine is a little too old, it still has an elegance and charm that just weren't possible in its youth.

And, finally, about that old bottle you got for graduation, or from Uncle Harry, or for your wedding. Forget all the advice and the vintage charts and the books. We know this wine intimately, and we know *exactly* when it will be absolutely at the peak of its perfection:

This coming Saturday night. That's right: This coming Saturday night. Put the kids to bed, open it up, and drink it. Instead of waiting for a special occasion to open this wine, why not let the wine be the special occasion?

BEAUJOLAIS

*Why French Wines Are Great Bargains
(No, Really)*

WHAT COUNTRY PRODUCES the best bargains in wine? Some people say it's Chile. Chilean reds do have a surprising amount of depth and sophistication for the price. Others point to Italy, which can't be beaten for the sheer amount of delightful, inexpensive red wine it produces. Still others say it's South Africa, which has a long, rich tradition of winemaking and produces classy wines that are still quite reasonable because they were shunned for so many years for political reasons, much like the wines of Chile.

But if you asked us, we would say France. France, home of $500 "first growths"? Well, yes. For our money, there are few white wines that can match a Muscadet dollar for dollar. Ditto for that very accessible red, Beaujolais. It's consistently one of the best-made, most delightful and self-confident wines on the shelves—and it's always available and almost always costs between $5 and $10. What more could you want?

Beaujolais is produced by the ton from the Gamay grape in the Beaujolais region of France. It's fruity, delightful, and meant to be drunk young. There are some wines even nonexperts can identify without a label, and Beaujolais is one of them. Regardless of the vintage or the producer, good Beaujolais has a fruity, lively smell, a grapey, berrylike taste, and a finish we describe as "salty." There's no salt, of course, but that lingering taste is, for us, one of the hallmarks of Beaujolais. That, and its jazzy blue-purple color.

Just as the great "first growths" are used as points of reference—

"It's big, like a Latour"—Beaujolais, for us, is the point of reference on the other end of the scale: "It's fruity, like a Beaujolais." It's so fundamental to a wine vocabulary that you simply can't "talk wine" without knowing Beaujolais. So let's start at the beginning—quite literally at the beginning, with Beaujolais Nouveau.

Even if you don't know much about Beaujolais, you've surely heard of Beaujolais Nouveau because of all the hype that surrounds it. "Nouveau est arrivé!" scream the signs posted everywhere on the third Thursday of November. That's the day that year's Nouveau, just weeks old, arrives in stores and restaurants. We love that day. Yeah, we admit it: This is a commercial event, like National Secretaries' Day, and, yep, Nouveau may be less a wine than an upscale fruit juice. But it doesn't matter. Nouveau is the very first wine that will touch our lips from the current vintage, and that's something to celebrate.

Wine areas all over the world celebrate their new vintages in various ways. We attended a harvest festival at Paumanok Vineyards in Long Island one early October afternoon where, while Media and Zoë took a hayride, Charles and Ursula Massoud served us just-squeezed Riesling that was still fermenting. They poured it from big glass jugs with a hole in the top so the containers wouldn't explode. The wine was cloudy with yeast, still very much a rough agricultural product, and tasted and smelled more like grapefruit juice than wine. And it couldn't have been more wonderful.

Two weeks later, John was in Germany, where, after a blowout German meal, the restaurant's owner brought out a special treat from his own vineyard in Rheinhessen: still-fermenting Riesling! It's called *Federweiss* (feather white) and is the star of the harvest festivals in places like the Mosel region, where our friend Greg Steinmetz, the *Journal's* Berlin bureau chief, says it's classically served with onion cake and cheese. Well, guess what? The new wine in Germany looked and tasted just like the brand-new Riesling we'd had on the North Fork of Long Island, truly making John feel like he was part of some global celebration.

All of this explains why we, who are not big party people, throw a party every year on the third Thursday of November. Nouveau is a great excuse for a party, and this gives us a chance to see all of our very best friends, whom we never get to see often enough during the rest of the year. Just hours before the party, John runs around to wine stores and picks up as many different Nouveaux as he can find. Then we serve all of them to our guests, who swear every year they won't be able to tell the difference between one and another—and every year they can.

Some wine snobs scoff at Nouveau as a kind of grownup Kool-Aid that pretty much all tastes the same, but we don't think that's true. At its worst, Beaujolais can be thin, metallic, harsh, and salty, and all of that is accentuated with Nouveau, which is basically just picked, pressed, fermented, bottled, and shipped. At its best, Beaujolais is fruity, vivacious, and about as much fun as any wine out there—and that, too, is accentuated with Nouveau.

We loved the Nouveau of 1995, hated the '96, and found '97 OK but inconsistent. In general, we'd say the Nouveau of 1998 was like '97: Certainly none of the big negatives—not much saltiness, thank heavens—but few big positives. The wines on the whole were acceptable and pleasant, but nothing special.

One, however, stood out. It's a funny thing: If you get any group of people together, even people who say they don't know anything about wine, it will soon become clear which is their favorite wine. Sometimes it's because everybody starts talking about one wine; sometimes it's just because you notice there are more empty bottles of one kind. At our party, it was clear the overwhelming favorite choice was No. 4, followed by No. 1.

The next night, alone, we put all seven of our Nouveaux in bags and conducted a blind tasting. Once again, there was one clear winner and one clear runner-up. While most of the wines were acceptable, too many were thin or hard—a couple were thin *and* hard, which isn't a good mix. But one was "creamy and nice. Sweet with fruit, drinkable, fun. Very attractive." We were sure this was No. 4, the consensus favorite from the night before. And we were right. It was Beaujolais Nouveau "Les Grandes Coasses" from Pierre and Paul Durdilly. The runner-up was "Domaine des Sables d'Or" from Olivier Ravier.

By tradition, Nouveau should be drunk before January 1. What about the rest of the year? You'd be making a big mistake to drink Beaujolais only around Nouveau time. Regular Beaujolais, the wine that gets more care and is released some time after the Nouveau arrives in stores, is the classic year-round wine. It's perfect in spring with lamb or shad roe; good, especially when chilled, with barbecue in the summer; and often accompanies turkey at Thanksgiving.

If you wanted to make Beaujolais complicated, you could: There is plain Beaujolais, from the Beaujolais region of France. Then there is Beaujolais-Villages, which has to come from specific areas and is supposed to be better than plain Beaujolais. Then there are ten areas within Beaujolais allowed their own "appellations": Fleurie, Morgon, Moulin-à-Vent, Brouilly, Côte de Brouilly, Chénas, Chiroubles, Juliénas, Regnié, and St.-Amour. Each has its own character: For instance, Fleurie is flowery, while Moulin-à-Vent is the heaviest. In a good vintage, some Beaujolais, such as Morgon and Moulin-à-Vent, can keep well for a couple of years. But one of Beaujolais's many charms is that you don't have to know any of that. Just look for the most recent vintage of Beaujolais or Beaujolais-Villages. It will almost certainly cost less than $10. Take it home. A half hour before you plan to drink it, put it in the refrigerator. Open. And gulp.

We conducted two separate tastings of regular Beaujolais to test our theory, one in early 1998, when both the 1996 and 1997 vintages were on the shelves, and one in late 1998, focusing more on the differences in the various villages. The one thing that became absolutely clear was this: Beaujolais is a great buy. Most were well made and exuberantly drinkable. These are wines meant to be gulped at the bistro, not sniffed and debated. In tasting after tasting, the simple Georges Duboeuf Beaujolais-Villages, which only costs around $6 or $7, showed well. Duboeuf has done much to popularize Beaujolais in the U.S., and his wines are widely available.

It was easy to pinpoint the Moulin-à-Vent. It's heavier, richer, more of a serious, "real" wine, but still very much, at heart, a Beaujolais.

Our very best of tasting, which we'd urge you to try, was the Fleurie from Georges Duboeuf. Beaujolais-Villages is soft, winning, simple, and Moulin-à-Vent is somewhat heavy. Fleurie is the perfect middle ground. "'Sweet,' with classy fruit," we wrote. "'Feminine' and just lovely. A combination of charm and power, right in-between. There's a lot of stuff going on in that glass, and none of it's negative." This is a serious Beaujolais—serious about being fun—a party animal kind of wine. Find the most recent vintage of this, chill it slightly, and drink up. We dare you not to smile.

Wine Notes

Beaujolais is one of the most delightful wines on the planet—red, but light, so you can drink it with any food, at any time of year. Buy the most recent vintage you can find and chill it slightly. There are various villages of Beaujolais—Moulin-à-Vent makes the "heaviest" wines, Fleurie is one of our favorites for its fruity femininity—but you don't have to worry about all that. Our first tasting, in early 1998, combined the 1996 and 1997 vintages; the second tasting, on the third Thursday of November, was 1998 Beaujolais Nouveau; and the third tasting, in late 1998, focused on the various villages from the 1997 vintage. For that last tasting, we tried wines from a few well-known producers, but we focused on the various different Beaujolais wines of Georges Duboeuf because his are so widely available. All Beaujolais wines are meant to be drunk young—Nouveau by January 1—so buy the youngest you can find, although the heaviest regular Beaujolais, from Moulin-à-Vent and Morgon, can improve for a few years, especially in good vintages.

1998 Beaujolais Nouveau

Pierre et Paul Durdilly "Les Grandes Coasses"
Beaujolais Nouveau **$8.99**
GOOD/VERY GOOD • *Best of tasting. Plenty of fruit, with full, lively, attractive tastes. Some real body compared to the others.*

Olivier Ravier "Domaine des Sables d'Or"
Beaujolais Nouveau **$8.99**
GOOD • *Nice, rich tastes at the front, but watery at the back. Still, a very pleasant wine.*

Leonard de Saint-Aubin Beaujolais-Villages Nouveau **$6.99**
GOOD • *Loveliest nose of the bunch, but it's a bit thin and metallic.*

Jean-Jacques et Sylvaine Martin Beaujolais-Villages **$6.99**
OK/GOOD • *Interesting. At first, some salt, pepper, and spices, some heft and guts. But in your mouth it quickly gets thin and watery.*

1996 vs. 1997 Beaujolais

Georges Duboeuf 1997 Regnié **$6.95**
VERY GOOD/DELICIOUS • *Best of tasting. Classic tastes, but with an extra oomph.*

Georges Duboeuf 1997 Beaujolais-Villages **$5.99**
VERY GOOD • *What Beaujolais should be. Buy it, chill it, gulp it.*

Olivier Ravier 1996 Beaujolais $6.99

VERY GOOD • *The classic happy wine. Fruity, simple, and so much fun.*

Georges Duboeuf 1996 Beaujolais-Villages $8.99

VERY GOOD • *Light, fruity. Now that is Beaujolais.*

Olivier Ravier 1996 Morgon $8.99

GOOD/VERY GOOD • *Yes, it's Beaujolais, but with a surprising richness and depth.*

1997 Beaujolais

Georges Duboeuf Fleurie $9.95

VERY GOOD • *Best of tasting. "Sweet" with classy fruit and real finesse. A combination of charm and power that's pretty remarkable. No negatives at all. A serious wine that doesn't take itself too seriously.*

Georges Duboeuf Beaujolais-Villages $5.99

VERY GOOD • *Best value. What a great buy: Simply a classic, fun, makes-you-smile Beaujolais. Delightful.*

Georges Duboeuf Moulin-à-Vent $11.49

VERY GOOD • *Deep, rich, and creamy, with character and guts. It would be clear in any tasting that this was the Moulin-à-Vent—it's so big sometimes it doesn't even seem like a Beaujolais.*

Georges Duboeuf Morgon $8.75

VERY GOOD • *Big and rich, more blackberries than raspberries. Pure fruit, with some guts but still easy to gulp.*

Georges Duboeuf St.-Amour $10.95
GOOD/VERY GOOD • *Nice and pleasant, but not quite fruity enough. Some depth.*

Georges Duboeuf Chénas $7.95
GOOD/VERY GOOD • *A little bit of salt and metal, but on the whole quite nice. Chewy and a bit rich, with nice cream.*

RHÔNE

Comfort Wine with Comfort Food

WE THINK OF RED WINES from the Rhône Valley of France as being life-affirming. They're big, rich, and—well, it's impossible not to use the word "hearty." They're a Dan Blocker kind of wine, what he and Pa Cartwright might drink with a big steak at the Ponderosa Ranch in the old *Bonanza* television series. When we say life-affirming, we really mean it. We had a horrible experience in 1992. Doctors told us Dottie had pancreatic cancer and had three to four months to live. And, they added, alcohol would be toxic to her deteriorating pancreas, so she couldn't drink any wine during her last days. Jeez. We always thought doctors said things like: "You've got a year. Maybe two." But three to four *months*? And *no wine*?

Around four months later, doctors at Memorial Sloan-Kettering gave us the good news: Dottie's pancreas had some abnormalities, but it was perfectly healthy. She didn't have cancer, she wasn't going to die, and there was no reason to give up wine. We were ecstatic, of course, but numb from the devastating ordeal. Staggering from the weight of it all, we left the hospital all bundled up against the cold and walked into the first restaurant we saw to collect ourselves, to let all of this begin to sink in, and to celebrate. It was a cute little East Side bistro called Sel et Poivre. Grabbing a window seat and menus, we told the French waitress, "We'd like a glass of a big red wine, please." Moments later, she returned with a huge empty goblet. "This is the biggest we have," she said. Completely at a loss, we told her to go ahead and fill two of them with red wine. It turned out to be just what we needed: some sort of rough Rhône wine, the kind of big, red, walks-to-the-table-and-introduces-itself kind of wine that makes you happy to be alive.

When we think of certain dishes, we immediately think of certain wines. We think of Bordeaux with steak, Chianti with spaghetti. But what do you drink with "comfort food"—beef stew, meat loaf and mashed potatoes, chili?

It's got to be Rhône. Red Rhônes have much in common with meat loaf. They're comforting, too, in an almost inexplicable way. How do you explain meat loaf's appeal? If you were describing it to a Martian, how could you possibly make it seem appetizing? Rhône is like that. Any description of the wine will inevitably include words like "rough" and "raw." Yet there's something about a Rhône—like a meat loaf— that is so thoroughly basic and soulful that it's hard not to like.

But which Rhône?

To start at the beginning, Rhône wines are from the Rhône Valley of France. The Rhône is a long river, and the valley produces an ocean of wine—some white, mostly red—so vast that even some vintage charts include one section for "Northern Rhône" and another for "Southern Rhône." The northern part includes some of France's most distinctive wines, such as Hermitage and Côte-Rôtie. The primary grape there is Syrah, a big, deep, dark, rich red that also makes those awesome Shiraz wines of Australia (and, of course, the Syrah wines of California). If you ever have the opportunity to taste an Hermitage, especially one with some age on it, it's quite an experience. The wine not only looks black, but tastes black, too, with a depth of flavor that's like staring into space on a dark night. At the same time, though, this remarkable wine manages not to be heavy, which makes it sur- prisingly drinkable. The downside: Hermitage is quite expensive, although, sip for sip, probably one of France's better bargains because it doesn't have the cachet of, say, fine Bordeaux.

Southern Rhône is home to the famous Châteauneuf-du-Pape and all sorts of wines simply called Côtes-du-Rhône. These are made from a wide selection of grape varieties, including Grenache, Syrah, and sometimes even some white varieties to even out the roughness of the reds. We once spent a couple of nights in an old castle converted to a hotel in Châteauneuf-du-Pape, and we'll always remember the white, rocky, hard-to-even-walk-on soil in which the grapes were forced to grow. Whenever we taste these big, "hot" wines, we think of the big, white rocks reflecting the intense sun.

Rhône is also home to all sorts of wines you've probably seen from time to time, but never paid much attention to, such as Gigondas, St.-Joseph, and Côtes du Ventoux. These are generally not identified by a specific château or winemaker, but usually by the name of a big producer, who buys grapes from many vineyards (and, in some cases, makes its own wines from its own vineyards). There's Jaboulet, for instance, and Guigal, who ship many different Rhônes in large quantities.

It all seems pretty boggling, doesn't it? Well, our assumption, in a tasting, was that you don't really need to know all of that. We assumed we could just walk into a wine store, stroll over to the Rhône section, spend less than $10, and get just what we were looking for: a rough-hewn, callused-hand, cowboy red that could make a cold night warmer. So we did just that: We picked up dozens of Rhônes, at random, almost all of them below $10 (some were just above, and one Châteauneuf-du-Pape was $17.99), to test our thesis.

We're happy to report we were correct—and that, in fact, our best of tasting was the most easily recognizable and available of the whole bunch.

As we expected, these wines do not aspire to class. As we drank them, we wondered why American winemakers don't make better "rough" wines. Sure, there are American reds that are "rough," but that's because they're cheap and just plain lousy. Most American winemakers who make good, inexpensive reds are trying to make something "smooth," easily drinkable, and inoffensive, and we appreciate that, believe us, we do. Inexpensive Rhônes, on the other hand, are genuinely peasant wines—proud to be a bit rough, yet, in their own way, surprisingly drinkable because they're so comfortable being just what they are: a beverage to have with big, brown food. The nose of our wines was almost uniformly a bit biting, with slight hints of green pepper and a little bit of vines.

Bottle after bottle, the taste was similar, too. Some bottles were better than others, but the average quality was good. The wines had a strong, fruity taste at the front of the mouth that grew into a sharp, earthy mouthful. The finish was generally pretty hot and a bit leathery. These wines would be perfect under the stars with that kettle o' beans Pa Cartwright was cookin' up over the campfire.

We had several favorites. Wines from Jaboulet and Guigal were, as we would have expected, quite nice—nothing special, but solid, drinkable reds. One of the hard things about Côtes-du-Rhône, though, is that there are a million labels out there, and you can never be sure which bottle contains liquid gold. We tried something called Domaine d'Andézon, a Côtes-du-Rhône we'd never seen before, but that said "Mis en bouteille à la Propriété" on the label, which seemed like a good sign. And this wine was special. It had real character and was richer and fruitier than most. And, like most good Rhônes, it was definitely worth hiding in a closet for a few years.

The best of tasting, though, turned to be the most common name of all. Georges Duboeuf, who is famous for his Beaujolais, sells a plain Côtes-du-Rhône he calls Domaine des Moulins for just $5.99, and it was our clear best of tasting. (In fact, we had accidentally bought two bottles, and it was best in both blind "flights" we tasted it in.) This is a Rhône without the usual edges—it was drinkable, light, fruity, and pleasant, but it had the traditional, soul-stirring depth of the best Rhônes. While it lacked some of the usual brawniness of many Rhônes, it's a righteous bottle of wine, and an outstanding introduction to what comfort wine is all about.

Wine Notes

Red wines from the Rhône Valley can be excellent bargains. They tend to be aggressive and raw, which means they're not great for sipping—it would be a mistake to order "a glass of Rhône" at a bar—but they're perfect to pair with beef stew, meat loaf, or other peasant food. Look for simple Côtes-du-Rhône on the label, although Gigondas and St.-Joseph are also names to look for on labels. Châteauneuf-du-Pape is a Rhône, too, but it tends to be more expensive (and classier) than generic Côtes-du-Rhône. These wines get better with age, so buy older ones if you see them, or lay some younger ones down for several years. In any event, getting air to them before you drink them will help smooth out some rough spots. If you want to know more about Rhône wines, look for Wines of the Rhône Valley *by the famous wine writer Robert M. Parker Jr.*

Georges Duboeuf Domaine des Moulins
Côtes-du-Rhône 1996 **$5.99**
GOOD/VERY GOOD • *Best of tasting and best value. Pleasant, creamy, and surprisingly drinkable. Lighter on its feet than most, and simply lovely. A great deal from a well-known name—and it's widely available, too.*

Parallèle "45" Côtes-du-Rhône 1996 (Paul Jaboulet) **$7.99**
GOOD • *Chewy and very much mid-range in its power—not as intense as some, but more serious than others. This will give you an idea of what Rhône is all about, and it's fairly easy to find. "Jaboulet" is a reliable name in Rhône; look for it.*

E. Guigal Côtes-du-Rhône 1995 $9.99

GOOD • *An easy-drinking Rhône from a well-known name. A bit candy-like, which seems odd, but altogether easy to like.*

Domaine Santa Duc Côtes-du-Rhône 1996 $9.99

GOOD • *You want the real thing? This is it. Hard and green, with a real taste of green peppers. Unrepentant Rhône. And yet, after an hour of air, it starts to get a bit sweet and fruity, indicating real potential in the future.*

Domaine d'Andézon Côtes-du-Rhône 1996 $9.99

GOOD • *This one shows the advantage of sometimes taking a chance on an unknown. The label says "Vieilles Vignes" (Old Vines) and "Non Filtré," which looked promising. And indeed, it was richer and fruitier than most, with some real seriousness of purpose. Still young, this is one you could lay down for a long time, then open up and say, "Can you believe I only paid $9.99 for this?"*

Clos du Mont-Olivet Châteauneuf-du-Pape 1996 $17.99

GOOD • *Young and surprisingly light, but lovely in the mouth. Rich, vibrant, and fruity—and yet age-worthy, too. This shows the character and breeding that a few more bucks buys in the Rhône.*

Why Pairing Wine and Food
Is Like Choosing a Tie

Let's say a sartorially inquisitive Martian, newly landed, asked you how exactly you choose a tie to wear with a particular shirt. What would you say? If you're wearing a dark blue shirt, you probably don't want a dark blue tie; if you're wearing stripes you probably don't want polka dots. But how, really—how, exactly—would you explain why one particular tie goes well, or poorly, with one particular shirt?

Choosing wine to go with food is like that. Whole books have been written with awesome lists of "ideal" pairings. But, as with many aspects of wine, we believe the more detailed and specific the advice, the more likely people will roll their eyes, say, "Oh, brother," and pop open a soda. Besides, other people's specifics tend to constrain your creativity and experimentation, which is how you learn what you like. We're not much for dogma, especially with something as subjective and sensuous as food and wine. And being children of the '60s, we're of a mind that if it tastes good, eat it; if you like it, drink it. Who are we to tell you that Chardonnay doesn't go that well with peanut butter and jelly sandwiches? So we've tried to come up with some general themes you might think about when you're trying to pair food and wine, stuff that has worked well for us.

~ **The wine and the food shouldn't be too much alike, but should instead be different enough to bring out the best in each other.** You know how sometimes people say, "It's no wonder those two hate each other—they're so much alike"? It's the same thing with food and wine. In other words, if you're having a big, plump white fish, you wouldn't want a big, plump, white wine like a buttery Chardonnay, because they're too much alike to bring out anything different in each other. It would be better to have a wine with some crispness and acidity, like Muscadet,

Chablis, or Pinot Gris. In general, it has been our experience that acidic wines go well with cream and butter sauces. The wine's acid and fruit cut right through the sauces, which helps the palate sort out the layers of flavors.

Acidic wines also can complement pretty heavy dishes because they can be refreshing and bracing. Think of the sausages, the breaded meats, and pickled vegetables of Germany and that country's delightful, crisp, and floral white wines. Some meals, like a dish of herbed meats, roasted peppers, and garlic potatoes, could stand up to a huge, dry red as well as a huge, crisp white. Then there's that classic combo, oysters and Chablis, where the creamy and briny shellfish and the elegant, flinty white play off one another.

~ **On the other hand, avoid obvious clashes.** You wouldn't have a big red Rhône with a simple fillet of sole. You don't want to overpower and obliterate a dish—or a wine. A big red Rhône, on the other hand, would enliven and enhance the taste of comfort foods like meat loaf.

~ **Think about the character of the food and wine, not their color.** For instance, one of the all-time classic French combinations is a simple roast chicken with a red Burgundy, even though chicken seems like a "white" dish. Why? Consider the taste of the smoke, the crisp skin, the juicy meat. An elegant red wine, with some soul and earth and fruit, brings out the best in all of that, more than some white wines would. A heavier red wine, say a Cabernet, could overwhelm the subtle flavors. But the Cab would go well with red-meat dishes, something with a lively tomato-based sauce, like osso bucco.

~ **Consider the personality of the food and the wine.** Some foods are delicate; some are robust. If you're having a rough-hewn dinner, like ribs, you'd want a robust wine to match it, like a big, young Red Zinfandel. The fruit of the Zin would enhance the ribs' smoky and spicy taste. A chilled Beaujolais would work well, too, with not only the taste of the wine but its temperature contributing to the experience. A delicate dish, like shad roe, would do well with a young, fruity Pinot Noir, the soulful mustiness of the roe balancing nicely with the spirited fruit of the Pinot.

Here, just to give you some examples, are some of the greatest food-wine matches we've had at restaurants.

~ Château Gruaud-Larose 1970, from France, with perfectly aged steak at the Post House in New York, 1981. Good steak always demands Bordeaux, but a great steak—with layers of taste ranging from lean to meaty and plump—deserves an equally well-aged Bordeaux. When both the steak and the wine are just right, there are few greater combinations. The tannins in a Cab play off the meat's essential flatness and cut through some of its butteriness. At the same time, the Cab's dry fruit heightens the taste of the steak's smoky and salty juices.

~ Freemark Abbey Cabernet Sauvignon 1976, from California, with rare prime rib in 1981 at Bally's hotel, Atlantic City. The wine had a delicate complexity—unlike the raw power of many California Cabernets—that paired perfectly with the rich complexity of perfectly done prime rib. Here again, the juices and plump meat played off the wine's dry and fruity tannic tastes.

~ Fisher Vineyards Chardonnay 1980, from California, with sweetbreads in 1982 at Hubert's Restaurant in New York. The greatest white wine combination we've ever tasted: this rich, sensuous Chardonnay paired with perfectly cooked, rich, sensuous—and yet crispy on the outside—sweetbreads. We said in our notes that the Chardonnay was so huge that we had to drink it in small sips—just as you have to eat great sweetbreads in small bites. The woody acids in this full-flavored Chardonnay played off the crunchy sweetbreads' creamy interior and rich Champagne sauce.

~ Sokol Blosser Pinot Noir 1983, from Oregon, with salmon at Chez Panisse, Berkeley, California, in 1987. The waiter suggested this pairing and we were dubious. Red wine with fish? In fact, never has there been a more perfect pairing. Many Oregon Pinot Noirs are light and fresh and not too heavily "red," either in the way they look or the way they taste—just like salmon, when you think about it. Here, the wine's "sweet" and zesty fruit tweaked the fish's subtle flavors.

~ Grande Reserve Naoussa 1992, from Greece, with feta cheese at Periyali, New York, in 1988. We knew little about Greek wines, so we asked the owner for some help. He brought out this wine and some fabulous feta cheese. The soft red wine was totally weightless, like drinking clouds. Paired with light, airy—and yet, at the same time, earthy—feta, it was sublime. It's hard to explain just why this worked, but there was a wonderful interplay between the cheese's sly and slow pungent bite and the wine's soothing, ephemeral taste.

Finally, here's a tip you won't hear anywhere else: If the wine and food you're having don't seem to go well together—but you're stuck with them anyway—change the temperature of the wine. Maybe you're drinking a white too cold, or a red too warm. Take the white out of the ice bucket; put the red into an ice bucket. Wines are different at different temperatures. By manipulating the temperatures you just might transform a so-so food-and-wine pairing into something you'll remember forever.

BAROLO

A Trip to Italy at a Fraction of the Price

BAROLO ISN'T WINE. It's magic. Think we're kidding? Listen to this.

We planned a trip to northern Italy—to the Piedmont region, where the great red wine Barolo is made—based on wine books. Sure, we should have bought maps and guidebooks, but we thought we'd be more interested in what wine writers advised. One of them mentioned in passing a marvelous place he'd visited in the Piedmont region of northern Italy. We made reservations and left Miami after Dorothy memorized a single sentence—"Possiamo assaggiare un po' del Suo vino e forse ne compriamo una bottiglia?"—which means, we were told, "May we taste your wine and perhaps buy a bottle?"

We were looking for an innkeeper named Giorgio Rocce at an inn called the Felicin in a town called Monforte d'Alba. We flew to Milan and drove west toward Alba. Before we'd left, a friend who had lived in Italy gave us two pieces of advice: (1) You have to beg waiters for your check at the end of every meal, and (2) Italians think everyone is Italian at heart, so they will keep speaking to you in Italian on the assumption that, sooner or later, your inner Italian self will understand. We thought of him when we got lost in Alba and asked for directions. As we drove from person to person, asking where Monforte was, all we got was minutes-long explanations, totally in Italian, of which we understood not a single word. We kept driving, heading into the mountains. We had a strange car, no maps, and no clue where we were. Then things got worse.

The great grape of Piedmont, the grape from which Barolo is made, is called *nebbiolo*, which is derived from "fog" in Italian. The fog that rolls in over the vineyards each autumn night helps the grapes reach a perfect acid-fruit balance. It keeps the temperature just so, manipulating the speed and quality of the ripening of the grapes. It has been this way for centuries. Great. But it was not a welcome sight when we were lost on mountain roads, still looking for Giorgio's place. It was almost time to panic. Then the strangest thing happened.

Years before, when we worked at the *Miami Herald,* we'd known a restaurant critic named Harvey Steiman. Harvey was everything you'd want a wine and food expert to be: bearded, charming, erudite, and passionate. He had become one of the top food and wine experts in the world and a top writer at *Wine Spectator* magazine, which we've long considered a reliable source of high-level wine information. There, along an increasingly foggy road, on the top of a mountain, somewhere in Piedmont, we spotted a large man walking along the road. Dottie, feeling a little foolish, said, "You know, that looks a little like Harvey Steiman from the back." We slowed down to a stop. Dottie lowered her window. "Harvey?" she said softly.

"Dorothy!" whooped Harvey. "John!"

Harvey was on assignment for *Wine Spectator.* He was staying at Giorgio's place. He hopped in and we all drove to the hotel. Later, as we were unpacking, Harvey knocked on the door. He was having dinner with the Cerettos, one of the most famous wine families of Italy— and they'd love to have us join them.

Magic. It's in every bottle of Barolo. There is, simply, no other wine like it. Barolo is filled with fruit, yet has a tightness, a restraint, that keeps it from being the kind of "plump" red wine you find in California. It has a raisiny intensity that only years can tame—but, even with age, it remains deep, dense, and remarkably dry. Just about all red wines are dry, of course, which means they don't have any residual sugar, but Barolo doesn't have the kind of sweet, yielding fruit that gives some dry wines their personality. Instead, it has the kind of tannins and bite that make it special.

Beneath all of that, even on the "nose," Barolo is especially notable for its dusty earthiness; you can almost taste those Italian hills as you drink it, and we think that's one reason why Barolo makes us want to rush out and eat earthy foods with it—meats, roasted, herbed, and sauced. Barolo is a wine that demands attention when you drink it—it's complex, powerful, and, at its best, majestic. And Barolo ages beautifully. How beautifully? In Miami, there's a terrific restaurant named La Bussola that allowed us to keep our own wines in its cellar along with its own excellent collection. On January 2, 1987, over dinner there, we opened a 1971 Barolo from Casa Vinacola Dosio. Our notes: "Totally closed up and overwhelming. After ten minutes, hints of fruit. First real taste only after twenty minutes. A little bitterness. Hard and austere. That's clearly how it was made. Muscular. Unyielding. Yet a hint of sweetness. Concentrated. After one hour, delicious. Tough, with a long, hot finish. Lots of fruit and wood. Raisiny. The essence of Italian fruit."

There's something about Barolo that touches you deep in your soul. It's as though its tastes and smells register in your heart, not in your mouth. We know we're babbling a bit here, but this wine can make hardhearted grown men whimper. When we write big feature stories for the *Wall Street Journal,* we like to say readers bring stronger feelings to articles when they're allowed to reach their own conclusions. Barolo is a wine that allows you to reach your own conclusions. And, incredibly, that becomes even more pronounced as the wine ages. Most wines, as they get older, get "rounder," softer and more approachable. Barolo gets tighter as it withdraws into the essence of itself. The sense of the earth becomes even more pronounced. What you get is pure fruit, with the wisdom of the grape.

There are not that many big Barolo producers, so this is one kind of wine you can get to know fairly easily. The top names—Ceretto, Gaja, Aldo Conterno, and some others—can be very expensive. But we thought we would see what we could get for $40 and under. The answer: great stuff. Wine after wine impressed us with its earthy intensity and concentrated fruit. These are challenging wines, but they are also so earthy and *real* that they're fun to drink. Choosing a favorite was quite difficult. In fact, we're happy to say one of our favorites was one of the least expensive (at $21.99), the Tenuta Carretta "Poderi Cannubi" 1991. "Looks old, with lots of gold/yellow," we wrote. "Tastes old and elegant, a wonderful old Barolo. Raisiny and tight, but the nose has cream and perfume." We also liked the Tenuta Carretta "Vigneti in Cannubi" 1993.

The best of tasting was an extraordinary bottle. "Looks and tastes like Barolo, with some red, chocolate, and raspberries. Dries your mouth in the end. Really real. Dry yet big, with real age potential. Not even a little 'plump.' Lean, sinewy, yet fruity. Young and fresh. A little bite. Great nose, with earth and nutmeg and cream." This was Poderi Colla "Dardi Le Rose Bussia," from 1994, which wasn't even much of a year.

After our tasting was over, we thought we'd conduct one last experiment. The next night, we opened an old Barolo—from the 1971 vintage—from our own stash. It was from Poderi e Cantine di Marengo. And here is the amazing thing: If we had opened it as part of our blind tasting, we doubt we would have known it was more than two decades older than the other wines. It was incredible: Tightly wound, very intense, filled with hard-candy fruit. After John took his first sip, he slapped himself in the face. This, like all good Barolos, is a wine for all of the senses, truly one of the greatest experiences in wine drinking.

A postscript: The other great red wine of Piedmont is Barbaresco. In our minds, a great Barbaresco can be even greater than a Barolo because it has an extra complexity that engages the intellect as well as the soul. What we've found, though, is that it's just about impossible to find an affordable Barbaresco in the United States that walks that line between power and finesse. It's worth trying to find a great Barbaresco, but your search may be a difficult one.

Wine Notes

Barolo is the great red wine from the Piedmont region of northern Italy. It is intense and big, especially in its youth, so you need to serve it with lusty food—and be careful, because it tends to be high in alcohol. There are some great producers—Ceretto, Gaja, Aldo Conterno, for instance— but they tend to be expensive. Buy old Barolo if you can, since it ages beautifully. If you buy young Barolo, be sure to pour a couple of glasses, taste a drop, and then let the wine breathe for maybe an hour or so before you plan to drink it. If you see "Riserva" on the label, this means it was aged in barrels for a long time, making it an even more intense experience.

Poderi Colla "Dardi Le Rose Bussia" 1994 $34.95
VERY GOOD/DELICIOUS • *Best of tasting. Great nose, with earth and nutmeg and cream. Looks and tastes like Barolo, with some red, choco- late, and raspberries. Dries your mouth in the end. Really real. Dry yet big, with real aging potential. Not even a little "plump." Lean, sinewy, yet fruity. Sweet with fruit after one hour, still with some bite.*

Tenuta Carretta "Poderi Cannubi" 1991 $21.99
VERY GOOD • *Best value. Looks old, with plenty of gold/yellow. Cream and perfume on the nose. Tastes old and elegant, a wonderful old Barolo, raisiny and tight.*

Molino "Vigna Conca" 1993 $39.99
VERY GOOD • *Rich and serious. Young but wow. Tight, raisiny, and yum. A real Barolo with vibrant youth instead of bigness. Chocolate*

finish, like chocolate-raspberry fondue with a dash of cinnamon. Shocking in its intensity.

Prunotto 1993 $28.99

VERY GOOD • *Lovely. Fabulous, earthy nose; that nose is Barolo. Not majestic, but young, with nice fruit. Not a "serious" wine, but lovely. Slightly watery and green, but still lovely.*

G. D. Vajra 1993 $29.95

GOOD/VERY GOOD • *Pretty color. Smells like earth. Sweet with young fruit. Tight and good. A little too California—plump, not tight— at first, but later it tightens up and becomes raisiny. What an experience!*

Tenuta Carretta "Vigneti in Cannubi" 1993 $21.95

GOOD/VERY GOOD • *Classic nose, with abundant fruit and earth, even tobacco. But just a bit two-dimensional.*

Manzone "Le Gramolere" 1992 $27.99

GOOD • *Some age on the edges. Dust and earth and fruit on the nose. Sensuous, with tight, raisiny fruit. A little bit hot and alcoholic.*

Silvio Grasso "Ciabot Manzoni" 1993 $29.99

GOOD • *Earthy, with real texture. Creamy intensity, with a little age.*

La Rocca e La Pira 1993 $29.99

GOOD • *Tight fruit, but very drinkable. Not big, but restrained and classy, with hints of soil.*

Elio Grasso "Ginestra 'Vigna Casa Maté'" 1993 $29.95

GOOD • *Green. Maybe it's just young but it seems a bit hard. After two hours, though, it's puckery and good. With time …?*

THE CHIANTI CONTRADICTION

Life and Depth

WHEN WAS THE LAST TIME YOU SPENT $25 on a Chianti? Maybe never, and why should you? Chianti is a cheap, fun red wine that's fun to quaff with pizza. It's a one-night stand, not a relationship. Well, all of that's true, up to a point—and we discovered just where that point was in a surprising tasting.

First, let's talk about what Chianti is *not*. For too many years, it suffered the same fate as that wonderful white wine Chablis. Just about every cheap red jug wine in America was called "Chianti." The name became generic for "cheap red wine." Poor real Chianti. What a *horrible* fate. Real Chianti is from Tuscany. The Italians make it primarily from the Sangiovese grape, which gives it a mouth-popping vibrancy. But even among real Chiantis, there are two very distinct styles. One—like the kind we all grew up with, in those straw-covered bottles at that little Italian place on the corner with the red-and-white checkered tablecloths—is fruity, light, and fun. The other is a serious wine capable of developing a marvelously complex combination of depth and sprightliness.

We once had an interesting experience in Chianti that brought home to us how different the "two" Chiantis can be. We were staying at the elegant Villa la Barone in Panzano in Chianti. Driving up and down hills, trying to get our bearings, we had passed a small, rustic restaurant that looked charming. Bruno, the concierge at the villa, made reservations for us, and we soon found ourselves in what was basically a farmhouse, with family-style seating, rough-hewn food, and rougher-hewn waiters who looked like farmers.

Fortuitously, the restaurant was part of a winery, and its various vintages of Chianti were listed in pencil on the menu. We couldn't believe it: They had both 1975, a very good year, and 1971, a classic year. With the waiter who spoke no English looking over our shoulders, we pointed to the 1971. You would've thought we'd made some sort of indecent proposal! Dark eyes flashing and lips a bit tight, he shook his head violently and pointed to the 1975. Taking his rather forceful hint, we ordered the '75. Heck, we were almost afraid not to. And it was delicious: vibrant, fruity, alive, and perfect with our roast pigeon. We enjoyed it so much that we wanted our waiter to try it. He poured himself a glass—the wine was served in plain water glasses—and he clearly was pleased with how beautifully it still tasted in 1986.

But we kept thinking about that '71. It was right there. If the '75 was that fabulous, what must the '71 taste like? We called the waiter back over and, despite his objections—frankly, he could have blown a gasket; nothing was going to stand between us and that wine—we ordered it. It was great: deep, big, rich, chewy, with a vibrating core of fruit. Again, we called the waiter over and offered him a glass. He shook his head. We kept trying. He kept shaking his head.

We never did get him to taste the '71, and we think we know why: It was such a great year, the wine was so deep and rich, that in some ways it didn't taste like Chianti, at least not to us—and, we guessed, apparently not to him either. He just didn't like it.

But we're not in Italy now. And we wondered: Here in the States, if you bought dozens of Chiantis, in all price ranges, what would you find? As with all of our tastings, we weren't looking for the "best" Chianti. There are so many out there, from so many different vintages, that it would be impossible to declare a "best." Our mission was much more basic: We wondered whether it was a good idea for you to go out and buy one—period. The answer: absolutely, but there are a couple of things you should know.

Our Chiantis cost from $6.99 to $32.99. With one exception noted below, it was clear they were all related—kind of like an extended family in which everybody has the same eyes. No matter what other tastes were present in the wines, their core—the Sangiovese grape—was always evident. Sangiovese has a vibrant, light-red taste that wakes up your mouth with fruit flavors.

All of the Chiantis under $14 fell into the "simple" category—except one. They reminded us of Beaujolais—fun to gulp, perfectly fine, often soft and winning, but nothing to write home about. Still, there were some excellent bargains, as Italian wines so often are. One Chianti was simply called Zipolino, from the 1996 vintage, and it was exactly what you want in a gulping Chianti. "It doesn't shoot for complexity," Dorothy said while we were drinking it. "It's just a big mouthful of fruit—and it makes you smile."

One of the less expensive Chiantis was a shocker. "Rich, plump, yet with a core of vibrant Sangiovese," we wrote in our notes. "Lots of soil and sweet with fruit. A very serious and very real Chianti." To our surprise, this turned out to be Viticcio 1996, which cost just $9.99.

The more expensive Chiantis were almost uniformly good. The Castello di Fonterutoli 1995 was dark, rich, beautiful in the glass. The nose was deep red and the taste was plump and round. Remember, though, that all of this richness coexists with that Sangiovese liveliness. Sound contradictory? That's what made it such a good, interesting, and wonderfully balanced wine. And for $14.95, that's a lot of taste. (Back labels often provide important information—or at least something interesting. This one read: "This wine is produced from select grapes of the vineyards within the Castello di Fonterutoli estate, property of the Mazzei family since 1435. The nature of the land, so rocky the wine has frequently been called 'stone wine,' severely limits production, never exceeding 1.6 tons per acre. It is aged for a minimum of two years in small oak casks.")

The Villa Antinori 1995, a wine you can often find in good wineshops, was elegant and classy. The Marchese Antinori 1994 was lovely, too—light on its feet, with serious berry tastes, but also with some real depth. Creamy, rich, and yet lively—once again that wonderful contradiction of tastes. This is a beautifully made wine in which all of the tastes were in perfect balance. Antinori is a famous name in Chianti—and we can understand why.

The Cennatoio 1994 was just remarkable, a terrific wine, but the only one in which we didn't taste that obvious foundation of Sangiovese. It was huge—massive, rich, deep with fruit. If we hadn't known these were all Chiantis, we probably would have guessed it was a fine California Cabernet; that's how big it was. This is a wine we'd never seen before in the U.S., and it's pricey at $29.95. But if you happen to run across it, buy it.

The best of our tasting was Podere il Palazzino Grosso Sanese 1994, another big, rich wine that, in our notes, received two words of high praise: "Voluptuous" and "Wow!" As we've said, wine people sometimes talk about how they can taste soil in some wines. All of the best Chiantis had that taste of earth, which gave the fruity complexity of the Sangiovese a firm foundation. And the Podere il Palazzino had it in spades. What a mouthful of tastes. This wine was even better after the bottle had been open a full day, indicating it's likely to age well. It costs $29.95, but isn't it worth that much to open your eyes to a whole new experience?

Wine Notes

Chianti—the real stuff, which costs some money—is a memorable experience. It has some depth and darkness around its core, but the core itself is vibrant, fruity, alive. It's that combination of life and depth that makes Chianti special. All of the best wines in our tasting were Chianti Classico, which is a specific region, and many of those were riservas, which means they were aged longer. Look for those words on a label. Also, look for these words: Denominazione di Origine Controllata e Garantita, which wine people just refer to as "DOCG." This means, loosely, that the wine in the bottle really does come from the Chianti region of Tuscany;

despite its name, it's no guarantee of quality, but it helps. You should buy the most recent vintage you can find, not because a serious Chianti can't age—it definitely can—but because recent vintages have been excellent. But don't get hung up on vintages! Just go get a more expensive bottle of Chianti than you're used to buying.

Podere il Palazzino Grosso Sanese 1994 $29.95
VERY GOOD/ DELICIOUS • *Best of tasting. Dark, rich, and voluptuous. This is a big wine that's willing to trade a little charm for depth. It's a wow wine, a real taste of the Tuscan soil.*

Viticcio 1996 $9.99
VERY GOOD • *Best value. Amazingly rich and serious for the price. Plenty of soil, fruit, and life, with a nice overlay of richness.*

Castello di Fonterutoli 1995 $14.95
VERY GOOD • *Beautiful to look at and lovely to smell, with a deep, red nose and big, rich taste. Plump and round, with wonderfully balanced flavors.*

Villa Antinori Riserva 1995 $15.99
VERY GOOD • *Elegant and classy, with a nice combination of forward, sweet fruit and real depth. A beautifully made wine at a very good price.*

Cennatoio Riserva 1994 $29.95
VERY GOOD • *Massive, more like a California Cabernet. A serious mouthful of very big red wine. If you see this name, buy it for the experience, even if it doesn't taste like a classic Chianti.*

Marchese Antinori Riserva 1994 $28.95

VERY GOOD • *Characteristic berrylike flavors, but with real depth.*
Beautiful.

Ruffino Riserva Ducale 1995 $19.99

VERY GOOD • *This is the familiar "gold label" that you see everywhere.*
This has the kind of complexity people don't expect to find in a Chianti.
Not as vibrant as some, but a classy bottle of wine.

Ruffino Riserva Ducale 1994 $17.95

GOOD/VERY GOOD • *Not as good as the '95, but still quite good. The*
nose is hotter and spicier than most, but it's pleasant and very drinkable.

Villa Antinori Riserva 1994 $15.95

GOOD/VERY GOOD • *Grapey nose and a little bit of simple richness.*
Interesting in the way it walks the line between lighter and heavier Chi-
antis.

Podere il Palazzino 1995 $15.95

GOOD/VERY GOOD • *Same producer as the best of tasting, so this is*
definitely a label to look for. Sprightly and light, with some real excitement
on the tongue, yet a hint of depth. Plenty of verve. A real Chianti.

Zipolino 1996 $6.99

GOOD • *Pleasant and simple and Beaujolais-like. This would be great*
lightly chilled with some lasagna. It doesn't shoot for complexity. It's just
a big mouthful of happy fruit.

Do Vintages Matter?
Sure, but Should You Care?

After we began writing our column for the *Wall Street Journal*, we started getting tons of mail, and some of it has been sad. One lovely man from Washington, D.C., wrote to say how much he enjoyed our writing and added: "I have been a casual wine drinker for twenty-five years. Sadly, I profess insufficient memory cells to store and retrieve which vintages are special for which wines. As a result, I rarely read what wine critics have to say...."

The emphasis on "good" and "bad" vintages is one of the many things that make drinking wine so intimidating—and why so many people just say, "Forget it," and retreat to other, more user-friendly beverages.

Do vintages matter? Well, of *course* they do. But the question is whether this is something you need to worry about very much. It's exceedingly rare that the difference between two recent vintages is the difference between perfection and vinegar. Instead, in general—and there are always exceptions—the differences tend to be more subtle, between years when the weather was just perfect and the grapes were picked nice and ripe, and years when the weather wasn't so perfect and the grapes were less ripe. But the big question is this: Are you such an aficionado of wine that you would find yourself enjoying a 1995 Barolo but spitting out your 1994 Barolo? We think few people fit into that category.

In any event, there are all sorts of factors that make this even more complex than it already seems. For instance, let's say you decided tonight that you wanted a Barolo and it had to be from the fine 1996 vintage, so you skipped wines from the 1993 vintage and bought a '96. Well, congratulations—but have you bought a better wine for tonight? Maybe not, since the '96s are so massive, concentrated, and young that they need a few years to become truly drinkable, while the '93s—from a year that was fine, but not nearly as good—are more likely to be drinking beautifully much earlier. As you can see from our chapter on Barolo, our best-of-tasting was from the 1994 vintage, not a great year in Piedmont.

Price and availability matter, too. This is a good thing to remember when you're wondering about vintages: Price will usually tell. A wine from a great vintage will cost more than the same wine from a so-so year. Cult status notwithstanding, the market usually rules. But even if the price is no object, there's one thing that you can't finesse. That's availability. In Italy, 1982 was a terrific year for Barolo. But are you likely to see a 1982 Barolo in your local wineshop tonight? Sometimes price and availability combine to thwart your search for a certain vintage. In California, 1994 was a great year for Cabernet, so if you knew your vintages, you'd want to pick up a '94. But they were popular and grabbed up early, so you may not find one, and if you do, it'll likely be expensive. Does that mean you should just skip buying wine tonight? Of course not.

We lead very full lives and so do you. We've got all sorts of stuff in our brains—the date of the next orthodontist appointment, when the dog needs his next rabies shot, that teacher-parent conference in a week, when that employee's evaluation must be done. Not to mention all of the birthdays you can't let slip by. These are important things we *need* to know, things we should not forget. That's why we use daily organizers and calendars.

We don't make a point of committing to memory which vintages were great and which weren't, although naturally, some of that has stuck over the years. There are people who memorize stuff like that and use it to wow people with their knowledge. Hats off to them. Truth is, though, this information is so readily available that you shouldn't worry about it not being in your head when it can be as close to you as in your wallet. We have charts from wine books and we've helped ourselves to free charts that wineshops place near their cash register. Both *Wine Spectator* and the *New York Times* print vintage charts, which we photocopy and keep in our wallets. The beauty of all of these charts is that you can consult them with confidence; they rarely disagree with each other.

As your wine sophistication and interest grow, you'll naturally want to pay more attention to vintages. If you had a Barolo you really liked from 1993, you might want to try a 1995 to taste the difference, which you'll remember. And if you ever become a collector, being familiar with vintages—whether from memory or a chart—will help you decide if you should open a wine right away or cellar it for a few more years. Ultimately, it's more important to know generally whether the kinds of wines you're buying should be drunk young or older. In other words, if you're buying fresh whites from Italy, or Sauvignon Blanc or Pinot Gris, you know you want to buy the youngest you can find. If you're buying big reds, like Barolos, it's better to buy them with some age if you can.

But if you don't know whether 1993 or 1991 was better in Burgundy, don't worry about it. If you really want to know, just consult the chart in your wallet. Don't be embarrassed to look at it, especially if you're considering an expensive purchase. We'll consult ours in a minute if we're curious. We don't need to impress anyone, and neither do you.

DOLCETTO

One of the World's Happiest Wines (But, Shhhh, It's a Secret)

MOST OF THE WINES IN THIS BOOK are integral to a fundamental knowledge of wine—Chardonnay, Merlot, Champagne. But indulge us here while we introduce you to something a little off the beaten track. It's a red wine of charm and life, and it's a great bargain. It's a wine we always try to turn our friends on to, and we always start with this story, which we love to tell:

We were in northern Italy, in Barolo country, on a mission to drink wine, and everyone told us to drive to Dogliani for the weekly market. There, the old town square was bursting alive with carts heavy with food. The fresh fruits, vegetables, and meats that surrounded us, even early in the morning, were intoxicating. We walked from cart to cart, amazed at the bounty. And then, suddenly, there was a palpable buzz in the crowd.

Into the mix drove a beat-up old pickup truck. In the back of the truck was a roast pig. The truck stopped. We fell into a long line. An old man and his wife got out, and the man began to carve the pig—not like a butcher, but like a surgeon, carefully, with love. Quietly, reverentially, the line moved forward. The surgeon took a piece of bread, recovered a chunk of garlic from the pig, slathered the garlic on the bread, then sliced perfect pieces of meat and placed them on the bread. At ten in the morning, we sat on a curb and ate the greatest sandwich we had ever had, or would ever have.

That's when we fell in love with Dogliani, and its best-known wine, Dolcetto. But even if you haven't eaten roast pig in Dogliani, you might find something special in this delightful red from northern Italy. We say "might" advisedly. Some people don't like the in-your-face, berrylike fruit of Dolcetto. And, as we found in a tasting (and, indeed, have found over the years), Dolcetto is remarkably fickle. Far too many are so simple that they aren't worth your time. What's more, the youthful charm of Dolcetto can be ephemeral. It doesn't always travel well; sometimes something's lost in shipping. But when you get one that's just right, with the right balance of fruit, youth, and cream, it's wonderful fun.

One of the great pleasures of wine drinking is the element of risk. Sure, every night you could drink the same wine, or the same kind of wine, that you already like. But you'll never know what else is out there unless you're willing to take a gamble from time to time on something new. And when it's something like Dolcetto, the very idea that you don't know how you'll like it is part of the charm.

Dolcetto (pronounced dol-CHEH-toh) is a kind of grape. It can be grown anywhere, but it reaches nirvana in the Piedmont region of Italy. That's where the greatest wines of Italy come from, Barolo and Barbaresco. But Dolcetto isn't like them. It's not majestic, it's not "serious," it's not a wine for the ages. But when it's good, it's fun. Dolcetto is fruity and yet, at its best, surprisingly rich and deep in your mouth, when you least expect it. Imagine the vibrancy of a Beaujolais with some of the darkness of a Cabernet Sauvignon.

There are different kinds of Dolcettos from different areas—Dolcetto di Dogliani, Dolcetto d'Alba and so on—but we'd be hard-pressed to tell one from another. And we'd be taking this delightful wine much too seriously to even try. (But if you wonder, there are a number of very good books about Italian wine you could consult.)

Few wine stores stock many Dolcettos, but many will have at least one or two. We visited several wineshops so we could put together a tasting, and ultimately found a nice range of ages and prices ($8.99 to $24.99, but mostly around $12).

Here's a tip: At fine Italian restaurants, look for Dolcetto on the wine list. The finer restaurants tend to get the small production of better Dolcettos, and, because they're fresh and well kept, they sometimes will taste better than those purchased at wine stores. And they tend to be good buys, even in restaurants, because they aren't really well known.

In our tasting, the first thing we found, not surprisingly, was this: Buy 'em young. Some Dolcettos are better after a year or two, but, in general, they're better younger. The 1996 Dolcettos—the youngest we found—were on the whole better than anything older, with one big exception. At the same time, there were some 1996s that would be better if you put them in the bottom of your closet for a year.

Our favorite, to our surprise, was a '95: Dolcetto di Diano d'Alba from Alario Claudio e Matteo. It has some firmness along with its sweet fruit, which added a special dimension. Another one we liked, to our complete surprise, was a ringer. Hanging around New York City wineshops, we happened to see something called Scotland Craig Dolcetto 1995, from California. We'd never had an American Dolcetto, so we picked it up. It was remarkably good: deep and rich, with massive, sweet fruit. It seems unlikely you will see this wine in your local wineshop—they made only three hundred cases—but it's a good indication of what U.S. winemakers can do with this grape.

Most of the 1996s were just lovely. The Sorì San Martino 1996 from Dogliani was a winner. Rich, fruity, and fun, it was pretty well perfect, but we would've liked a little bit more of a creamy taste in the "finish." We found that later in an outstanding wine, the Vajra 1996. It was terrific: fruity and plump and very much a Dolcetto, but with a little bit of cream that made us think this must have gotten some extra barrel aging that gave it real character.

Dolcetto, at its best, is a happy wine. Buy the youngest you can find, spend about $12, take it home, maybe refrigerate it for fifteen minutes, and pop it open with some spaghetti. Or maybe with some roast pork.

Wine Notes

Dolcetto is a vibrant red wine you can almost feel jumping around in your mouth. But for some reason, it's terribly inconsistent. No one makes very much Dolcetto, and not much gets to this country, so don't worry if you can't find these specific bottles; just buy the youngest you can find, spend about $12—and enjoy it. Most will improve with a few minutes in the refrigerator. The Scotland Craig, below, is from the U.S. More and more American winemakers are making wine from Italian grapes, such as Sangiovese, and these are experiments worth trying if you see them, though they tend to be more expensive than the real thing from Italy.

**Alario Claudio e Matteo Dolcetto di Diano d'Alba 1995
(Costa Fiore)** $11.99

VERY GOOD/DELICIOUS • *Best of tasting. Firm, rich, has everything: fruit, soil, even tobacco.*

G. D. Vajra Dolcetto d'Alba 1996 $11.95

VERY GOOD • *Best value. Classic Dolcetto. Blackberry cream pie. Yum.*

Scotland Craig 1995 (Napa Valley) $22.50

VERY GOOD/DELICIOUS • *A shocker from the U.S. Aggressive, sweet fruit, with plenty of soil.*

**Sorì San Martino 1996 Dolcetto di Dogliani,
Francesco Boschis** $14.99

VERY GOOD • *Rich, fruity, and fun.*

Elio Altare 1996 Dolcetto d'Alba $16.99

GOOD/VERY GOOD • *Classic blackberry fruit, with some soil. Not as fruity as some.*

Fratelli Revello 1996 Dolcetto d'Alba $12.99

GOOD/VERY GOOD • *Soft, creamy, rich, and yummy. Classy and beautifully made.*

SHIRAZ
The Next Big Thing (Trust Us)

WE HAVEN'T SPENT MUCH TIME alone together since we had kids, more than ten years ago. But in early 1996, we asked our nanny to stay with Media and Zoë for a week so we could have a romantic getaway and do what an old married couple like us loves best: eat, drink wine, and sleep without interruption.

We checked into the romantic Mayflower Inn in Washington, Connecticut, which had a fireplace in our room that breathed flames at the flip of a switch, a mattress that was about six feet high, snow on its rolling hills, and an elegant little restaurant. There on the wine list was something extraordinary and rare: a 1986 Penfolds Grange Hermitage, Australia's most famous red wine. It was $100, which was actually a bargain. On some lists, it can cost several times as much. We didn't order the wine the first night, but on the second day, we told the innkeepers to plan our whole evening around it.

First, at six, with Dottie resplendent in a green crushed velvet gown, we sat by a fireplace in a cozy sitting room and drank the first sips of the wine. Holy cow! It was huge and mouthfilling, but with a brawny elegance that made it unique. After an hour, we moved into the dining room, where for hours we continued to sip—and we do mean sip; this is a wine that, like a martini, cannot be gulped. The wine was delicious throughout, and never lost that massive, fruity, blackberry intensity. By the fire, at an elegant inn, in the middle of winter, with snow on the ground, alone together—well, a big red wine just doesn't get much better than that.

Grange is made from a grape you should keep your eye on: Shiraz. The wines of Australia tend to be powerful and big, a little like the wines of California in the 1970s. Even the Chardonnays live large. We've never had a shy Australian wine; in fact, they seem to announce their presence in your mouth IN CAPITAL LETTERS.

The wines of Australia are well made, plentiful, and generally good values. We think Shiraz is the best and most interesting of them, and it's only a matter of time before it develops a big following in the U.S. And why shouldn't it? It's widely available in a range of prices, has a name that's easy to pronounce (just like it looks), is almost always good, and has extra cachet because it's from an unusual locale.

If Shiraz sounds like Syrah, that's no coincidence. It's the Australian name for Syrah, the grape that makes those kick-ass Rhône Valley wines of France (see page 169). Syrah makes a deep, dark, heavy wine that evokes fireplaces, winter, and peasant food. It can be elegant, but that usually takes many years.

More and more California wineries are making Syrah-based wines, too, and while we haven't had one yet that knocked our socks off, the appearance of these new California wines is an indication that this grape's coming on strong. Here's another: John had to fly to Chicago to visit the *Wall Street Journal* bureau there and figured he'd drop in (anonymously, of course) on Charlie Trotter's, the restaurant famous for both its food and its wine. He asked the waiter to pair each course with a different glass of wine—always a good idea at fancy restaurants—and the sommelier brought out some treasures from France: a grand cru Chablis, an old Meursault-Genevrières, a Vosne-Romanée from Burgundy. He also brought out an Elderton "Command" Shiraz 1994, from Australia, and you know what? It was John's best of tasting. Even without the inn, the fireplace, the snow—and, alas, Dottie, who was minding the kids back home—the rich, ripe, forward tastes of the Shiraz, especially with an outstanding fall dinner, were simply delicious.

How to describe Shiraz? At its best, it's peppery, huge, and deep red, with a hot-fruit finish, almost like a Cognac. There are hints of basil and other herbs. In fact, it tastes a bit like it should be dark green. Shiraz is intense with tight fruit, maybe with a little hint of salt, and some menthol at the finish. It's a challenging wine—and as Dottie puts it, "it can be lethal" because it's high in alcohol.

We know none of this sounds particularly attractive. We've talked about that quite a bit. It's difficult to describe Shiraz in a way that would make someone go out and buy it. So this is something you'll have to take on faith: It's a remarkable experience—and sometimes a fabulous one. But which Shiraz to buy? We tasted dozens that cost from $7.49 to $60. The most inexpensive and widely available Shirazes didn't have the power and remarkable varietal character of the real thing. The two most expensive wines weren't the best, but both were memorable, for different reasons. The E&E Barossa Valley Estates Black Pepper Shiraz 1994, at $60, was like a kick in the stomach. Back in the '70s, California winemakers experimented with late-harvest Zinfandel. It was overwhelming, alcoholic, and sometimes finished a little sweet. Few were great, but they were always an amazing experience. The E&E reminded us of those days—massive, unyielding, proud to be utterly outsized. Like many Shirazes, it will be better in a few years. In fact, we have a bottle of the E&E in our personal cellar and we've written on it, "Open when Zoë graduates from Harvard." Zoë is nine.

We were disappointed at first with the Hardys Eileen Hardy 1994, a special bottling that cost $47. We found it pungent and plain, and compared it to Manischewitz. Ouch! When we opened the bag and saw its price, we were shocked. However, we left the half-empty bottle on the counter and came back to it a full week later. It still wasn't great, but it was much better and just beginning to show layers of complexity and taste. In other words, a decade from now, this could be a very good wine.

But what should you drink tonight? Several of the wines were really quite good. We were sure the best of our tasting would be the Pikes 1996, which we had had in one of the first flights of this blind tasting. It had the deep, dark fruit of a Shiraz, but the class and complexity of a fine Bordeaux. What a combination! It was delicious, and good right now. But the Pikes turned out not to be the best.

As we keep saying, value and price are two different things. Some wines that cost $10 are bad values. Some wines that cost $40 are good values. The best was one of the latter: the 1993 Wynns Michael Shiraz. It's huge, fruity, and dark. But at the same time, remarkably crisp and clean. As we said in our notes: "Huge but not heavy. Beautifully made. Everything you'd want in a wine. Minerals, fruit, restraint. It's beautiful."

In a quarter-century of wine drinking together, only seventy-nine wines had earned our highest rating, Delicious! This was number eighty.

But here's the bad news: Most truly remarkable Australian wine experiences require a great deal of patience. Back in the mid-'70s, when we'd barely heard of Australian wines, we ran across a 1970 Cabernet Sauvignon with a label that simply said, "Mildara Wines Limited, Coonawarra." It was such a keepsake—a 1970 Cab from Australia!—that we couldn't stand to open it until June 22, 1996. Here's what we wrote about this twenty-six-year-old wine:

"Delicious! Wow! Thick, rich, and fiery. *Classic.* Lots of Cab character with classy age and no hint of decay. A real mouthful. Like a classic old claret. Long, lush finish. Lush, velvety, and sensuous in mouth."

This is what the wines from Down Under can be. Australian wine, and especially Shiraz, is different from anything else. You should get to know it.

Wine Notes

Shiraz is the Australian version of Syrah, from the Rhône Valley, and it's BIG. It's a wine that needs age or, if you must drink it young, plenty of air before you drink it. This is sometimes better drunk a full day after you open the bottle. Be sure to drink it with a big, heavy meal, like beef stew—or, on a cold night, drink it out on the balcony like Port. The Barossa Valley of Australia is increasingly known as the hotbed of fine Shiraz.

Wynns Michael Coonawarra 1993 $40.00

DELICIOUS! • *Best of tasting. Dark and rich, with a great nose. Ripe fruit on the nose, like a late-harvest Zin. Intense, clean, and crisp, yet huge—what a combination: huge but not heavy. Minerals, fruit, and restraint. Beautifully made. Everything you'd want in a wine. Simply beautiful.*

Pikes Clare Valley 1996 $22.00

DELICIOUS • *Best value. Dark, rich, and classy, with a long, sweet finish that lasts forever. Tastes fabulously expensive.*

Leasingham Clare Valley 1995 $13.99

VERY GOOD/DELICIOUS • *Bright red color—looks just-made. Red, rich, and chewy. Quite young, but it's got everything going for it: blackberry sweetness, taste of the earth, and a long, plump finish.*

Ebenezer Barossa Valley 1994 $28.00

VERY GOOD/DELICIOUS • *Dark, rich, sweet with fruit. More forward fruit than some, not as deep. Still, it's better after it has been open for three hours.*

Tyrell's 1993 $30.00

VERY GOOD • *This will get your engines going. Huge, rich, grapey, with a big, hot finish. Powerful and young. Fruitier and more fun as it airs.*

Frankland Estate Isolation Ridge 1995 $19.99

VERY GOOD • *Not as powerful as some others, but classier, with more complexity. There's some real elegance here. Dottie described it as "a little black dress."*

E&E Barossa Valley Black Pepper 1994 $60.00

GOOD • *Holy cow! What a wine! Massive, overpowering, remarkable. This is a wine that will blow your head off—and is proud of it. Portlike and simply massive. Have it, in small sips, on a cold night.*

Yalumba Barossa 1995 $13.99

GOOD • *Simple and grapey. The Merlot of Shirazes—cuddly, friendly. This is one to drink tonight, without thinking about it too much.*

Penfolds 1994 Bin 128 $19.99

GOOD • *Dark, rich, blackberry wine. Sweet, huge fruit. Almost primitive tastes.*

Hardys Eileen Hardy 1994 $47.00

OK/GOOD • *Pungent and plain. After a full week open, it shows some complexity. Lay down for several years.*

How to Remember That
Wine You Liked

People are always saying to us, "I had a wine I really loved at a restaurant, but when I woke up the next day I couldn't remember what it was." Wine merchants tell us, in fact, that they're constantly frustrated by people who come in and say, "I had a really good wine last night. It was a white wine, with a green label. Do you have it?"

So here's an easy way to remember your wines: Save labels. It's easier than you think.

Readers often ask us how in the world we remember that the 1976 Firestone cost $5.99 and was "dark and pretty." The answer is that, for almost twenty-five years, we've been taking notes and saving labels. Now, if we heard that someone did that, we'd probably say, "Whoa! Those people are much more organized and prissy than I would ever be." But the fact is, our lives are a mess. Our desks are a mess, our house is a mess, our finances are a mess. But for some odd reason, way back in the '70s, we started saving labels of wines that we enjoyed. Even labels from some wines we didn't enjoy that much. We don't know why we did this except that every wine, for us, was paired with a memory, and by saving labels we were saving our past together.

We caught another break at Christmas 1979—the year we got married—when John's parents gave us *The Cellar Key Wine Diary & Catalog*, a loose-leaf binder for keeping notes about wine. We have no idea why they gave us this; we can't imagine that they thought we would ever be organized enough to keep notes. But we did. Our first entry: Christian Brothers Cabernet Sauvignon 1974, bought at Wine Warehouse in Miami for $7.59. We drank that bottle on May 12, 1996, on Mother's Day. It was the first time John made a brisket in Grandma Helen's heavy, cast-iron pot. John's beloved Grandma Helen was the first person who believed in his writing, and her pot was the only thing John wanted from his own mother's estate when she died in early 1996.

See what we mean about memories?

(By the way, the wine, then twenty-two years ago, was "very good. Big, rich, chewy. Deep and dark. A bit old, but still lovely and fruity with lots of '74 Cab character that walks to the table. Lots of fruit/oak taste.")

You might never keep notes on wines. But at least you can keep labels. Here's how:

~ When you have a good wine at a restaurant, just say, "This was so good, I'd like to take the bottle home. I save labels." Don't be embarrassed. The restaurant will be flattered that you liked the wine so much. Chances are the restaurant will offer to take the label off for you. If the restaurant doesn't offer, and sometimes this is a blessing because some kitchens aren't competent at this, at least they'll give you a nice bag for your wine so you don't have to walk around carrying a wine bottle.

~ Once you get the bottle home, fill your sink with hot water and submerge the bottle in the water. In a few minutes, see if the label is coming off. If it's not, put the empty bottle on its side on a towel and, starting with a corner, work a knife under the label. Sometimes after a couple of edges are lifted, the rest of the label comes off easily. This is how Dottie does it. John's method is as follows: Boil a pot of water and gently lower the bottle into it for a few minutes. The label will probably float off. If not, take the bottle out—very carefully because it's hot—and start lifting it off with a fingernail or a knife. If that doesn't work, call Dottie.

~ Place some plastic wrap on a flat surface and put the label on the plastic wrap until it dries.

~ Get a simple photo album, the kind with loose-leaf transparent pages that lift off and then stick back down. Put the labels into the album.

Recently, someone introduced a label-removal system that is essentially a big strip of very strong adhesive. You press the adhesive strip onto the wine label and then lift off. It took us some practice—and this is certainly more expensive than soaking—but these work well with difficult-to-remove labels.

All of this is much easier than it sounds. In our case, we just put empty bottles on the windowsill until we have a dozen or so, then plop them all into water. We now have labels organized by year going back a quarter-century. We can tell our whole life story through those labels. We've affixed little notes reminding us of where we had the wine, but you don't have to get that complex. All you're trying to do is save labels so you can have the same wine again. But before you know it, you'll have a diary of some of your best times.

ROSÉ
WINE

WHITE ZINFANDEL
. . . and the Ex-Firefighter

IT'S A FUNNY THING. *Nobody* drinks White Zinfandel anymore. It was a fad for a time, and then it disappeared, gone from the face of the earth. Except . . .

White Zinfandel continues to be the second most popular varietal wine in America, after Chardonnay. California wineries shipped more than 19.2 million cases of it in 1997. That is almost a bottle for every man, woman, and child in America. Frightening.

Truth is, White Zinfandel continues to be enormously popular as a simple wine you can drink and not have to think about. The old saw in the wine industry is that "Americans talk dry but drink sweet," and most "White Zin" tends to be slightly sweet, simple, and refreshing. So if you're going to drink White Zin anyway, whether you admit it or not, you might as well drink the best one—and there really is a single best one.

Let's start at the beginning of the phenomenon. We were there—by accident, as usual.

In the '70s, during a visit to Napa Valley, we were stopping at one winery after another, and we dropped into a quiet little place called Sutter Home. There was no one else there, just us and the man behind the counter. "This is our latest thing, and it's getting really popular," said the man. "It's White Zinfandel." With that, another man burst in, almost shouting, "Can I get two cases of your White Zinfandel?" The man behind the counter looked at us, smiled, and said: "I swear to you I didn't set that up."

Unknowingly, we had stumbled onto ground zero of one of America's great wine fads. Sutter Home was the winery that put White Zin on the map. We were skeptical when we first tasted it. To us, God meant for Zinfandel to be red, bold, and distinctive. But any wine can be made "white." All grapes are white inside. Contact with the grape-skins gives wine its color. That's how Champagne can be made from Pinot Noir grapes, which are purple. If you take away the skins imme-diately, you get a white wine; leave the wine on the skins for a short time and you get a pink, or rosé, wine. Leave the wine on its skins for a longer time and you get red wine.

Truth be told, the Sutter Home White Zin that day was pretty good. It was crisp and steely, with nice backbone—an inexpensive, fun drink that had a lot going for it. On its Web page, Sutter Home recounts the history of White Zinfandel:

In 1972, Sutter Home winemaker Bob Trinchero was experimenting with ways to make his acclaimed Amador County Reserve Zinfandel more robust. Finally, he drained some free-run juice from the skins before fermentation to increase the ratio of skins to juice. (The skins give red wine its color and body.) Emulating the French rosés he so admired, Bob fermented the juice to dryness and barrel-aged it before bottling the pale pink elixir as a curiosity item for his tasting-room clientele.

Although Bob's customers liked this novel "blanc de noir" table wine, many felt it was too dry. So Bob began leaving a small amount of residual sugar in his "white" Zinfandel—an adjustment which pleased not only the palates of his tasting-room customers, but, as it turned out, millions of American wine consumers. During the 1980s, Sutter Home White Zinfandel was the single most popular premium wine in the United States, with sales growing exponentially from 25,000 cases in 1981 to three million in 1990.

We were living in steamy Miami at the time, and so we became fans of White Zin—and quickly got our hearts broken. Winery after winery began turning out oceans of simple, sweet, yucky White Zin. The more people drank, the worse the wine became. Sutter Home's Web page might explain why: "This unprecedented sales success spawned an army of emulative 'blush' wines, many of which became the salvations of the financially-strapped small wineries producing them. (The ultimate cash-flow wine, White Zinfandel is easy to produce, requires very little aging, and begins returning revenue a few scant months after the harvest.)"

Nevertheless, we kept trying and were briefly rewarded. One day in early 1981, we picked up a 1979 White Zin from De Loach Vineyards for $5.79, which was quite a bit for a White Zin then. Our notes: "Delicious, the best ever. Orange. Lots of crisp, steely character, but red tannins for backbone. Smooth yet assertive." It was so good we wrote a fan letter to the owner. We got a nice letter back from Cecil De Loach, who invited us to visit when we were in the area, and we did. He told us he worked as a firefighter in San Francisco for sixteen years, and grew and sold grapes while building his winery. He said White Zin was a wonderful cash cow, and he could sell all the White Zin he could make, except he didn't want to. There were other wines he was excited about making.

Cecil De Loach went on to become a well-known winemaker. White Zin didn't fare so well. It long ago ceased to be an "in" wine. In fact, it's one of those things that seem to be rarely discussed anymore in polite company. But after years of not drinking a White Zin, we wondered: How are they now? We know some "serious" wine people consider "good White Zin" an oxymoron, but, hey, America celebrates those who dare to take a courageous stand.

Our first surprise was how difficult it was to find young White Zinfandels in "sophisticated" New York City. Our experience at a very good wine store called 67 Wine & Spirits was typical. After browsing through hundreds of wines, we finally had to ask if they had any White Zinfandel. They pointed us to an area in the back, off in a corner where the really cheap stuff was hidden away. We felt as if we had asked for the sex-toys department at Wal-Mart.

Alas, our tasting, and a followup tasting a few months later to confirm our view, showed caution is indeed warranted. Many of these wines had nothing to them. They were simple, sugary sweet, and watery. Our daughters, Media and Zoë, drink a lot of Kool-Aid, and some of these wines—including, we're sad to say, the Sutter Home—tasted as though they had been concocted from a powder. At the same time, some would be just fine, deeply chilled, by the pool or at the beach—and the fact that their alcohol content is generally 9 to 10 percent, compared with about 12 percent for more serious wines, is a plus in the hot sun.

The Corbett Canyon was soft and approachable, with all kinds of fruit flavors. "It tastes real," Dorothy said, which in this tasting was high praise. Similarly, the R. H. Phillips was real wine, with some real character. "It's not embarrassed to have some taste," we said in our notes. It left our tongue coated with melon tastes that were quite pleasant.

We were surprised by Weinstock, a kosher wine we had never seen before. It had a little bit of toughness that gave it some character, and it had real fruit tastes. This was the first wine we ever had, though, that said on the label that it is "redolent of cotton candy aroma notes." Another kosher wine, Baron Herzog, was also good—not as obviously sweet as most, with tastes that were crisp, pleasant, and restrained. This is a well-made wine.

We're delighted to say that, even all these years later, the best of tasting was De Loach. It's a real wine, with some backbone and fruit. It has a touch of sweetness, but in general tastes like a delightful white wine with some blush, as opposed to a pink wine. It's more difficult to find than some—a lot of it goes to restaurants—and it still costs a little more: $8.99.

After all these years, we called Cecil De Loach to ask why his White Zin is better—and why he doesn't make more, and why it costs more than others. He said he uses good, ripe, hand-picked grapes that are processed in small lots using small presses. "It's not a mass-produced item," he said. He makes around 20,000 cases, 70 percent of which goes to restaurants, where diners are used to paying more for their wine. His White Zin costs more than most White Zins in wine stores, he says, "because we don't have the economies of scale, we don't make a million or two million cases." And he doesn't make more because he's discovered that the market appears to be stable at 20,000 cases at the price he charges. In other words, he says, "I can only sell so much at that price, no matter how good it is—and I think it's really good."

We think it's really good, too.

We don't know how much good press has to do with the quality of wines, but Mr. De Loach says that in the late '80s many wine writers stopped reviewing White Zin. Maybe that removed the incentive for some winemakers to make a good wine. "They said it wasn't a serious wine. A serious wine!" De Loach said, still incredulous. "Why does a wine have to be serious? It's just something you drink." And those other wines he wanted to make? He now makes a wide variety of wines, including seven single-vineyard Red Zinfandels from vines planted between 1895 and 1934. Meantime, his property has grown from fifty acres at the time of our first visit to about seven hundred acres today.

One of the great pleasures of wine drinking is coming back to wines you haven't had in a while. When you think of White Zin, admit it, a little smile comes across your face, right? It was part of a happy time of experimentation and discovery. Pick one up, throw it on ice, and enjoy.

Wine Notes

White Zinfandel from California isn't so much a wine as a reminder of how quickly wine fads come and go. But real winemakers once made some good, steely White Zins, and, years later, we wondered if this might still be a good under-the-sun drink. Be sure to buy the most recent vintage you can find, and chill very well.

De Loach Vineyards 1997 $8.99
GOOD • *Best of tasting. Great fun, highly drinkable, perfect with bar-becue.*

Weinstock Cellars   1997 $6.99
GOOD • *Spritzy and pink, but pleasant, with a little backbone and some real fruit.*

R. H. Phillips Vineyard Night Harvest 1997 $5.99
GOOD • *There's some real character here, with caramel, cream, and a little spritz. It's unusual, but it coats your tongue with taste, and that's good.*

Baron Herzog Wine Cellars 1997 $6.99
GOOD • *A real nose, like a crisp white wine. Pleasant and less obviously sweet than most. Very agreeable with food.*

Corbett Canyon Vineyards 1997 $3.99
OK/GOOD • *Too sweet and punchlike, but it's real wine, with some nice fruit flavors.*

Beringer Vineyards 1997   **$5.49**

OK/GOOD • *Cranberry nose and the taste of pleasant wine underneath the sweetness.*

Turning Leaf 1996   **$5.99**

OK/GOOD • *Nice, fresh melon nose, nutty. A little sweet and simple. Pleasant.*

ROSÉ WINES

From France . . . by Popular Demand

AFTER WE BEGAN writing our wine column for the *Wall Street Journal,* many people we knew suggested topics based on their own passions. How about great wines under $10? How about Alsatian Gewürztraminers? But the most curious thing was the number of people who would walk up to us, stand really close, look around furtively, and whisper, "Could you write something about rosés?"

Apparently, rosés are a popular guilty pleasure. A lot of people enjoy them as their everyday summer wine. And why not? A good rosé is special—not red, not white, but something wholly different. As we've said, grape juice is white; the skin gives a wine its color. For a rosé, the juice gets just a little bit of contact with the skin, which gives the wine not only some color but also some extra body. The result is a wine that, at best, has more character than a simple white but isn't as heavy as a light red.

We haven't had that many rosés over the years, and we're not sure why. We never really thought about it until all of those people asked us to write a rosé column. Whenever we felt like a white, we had a white, and whenever we felt like a red, we had a red. Beyond that, though, we never had that Great Experience with a rosé, or an American "pink" or "blush" wine, that set us off on a quest to broaden our experience with them.

In general, the readers who urged us to write a rosé column recommended French rosés such as Anjou from the Loire region, as well as Bandol and other wines from the Provence region. But rosé wines are made all over the world, so we thought we'd scour wineshops and just pick up every pink wine we could find, from everywhere. (We excluded White Zinfandel from this tasting because we wrote about it separately.)

What did we learn? First, if you're used to drinking American "pink" wines, you owe it to yourself to try a real rosé from somewhere else. We found American pinks—with one exception—simple, sweet, and one-dimensional, with no real soul compared to the others. We tend to be generous with wines, but too many of the U.S. wines elicited comments like this: "tastes artificial," "harsh and a little herbaceous," "pretty foul," and "yechy, with a fertilizer nose." This doesn't mean there are no good American rosés. But our experience suggests your chances of getting one with character aren't good.

And our reader-writers were right: There is something special about a French rosé. In our blind tastings, the favorites were from France, in some cases from places we knew little about. If you walk into wine stores and sometimes think many of the wines are from another planet, it's important for you to know: It's a big world out there, and hardly anybody really knows what all those wines are, although a lot of people fake it really well.

Our favorite was Château Grande Cassagne 1997 from Costières de Nîmes. This is from the easternmost edges of the Languedoc region in southern France, which has always produced boatloads of so-so wine, but which lately has been making the wine world sit up and take note. We've recently tried some reds from Languedoc that were quite good, and excellent bargains. This rosé was both. The wine looks burnt orange and smells like roses. It tastes like a very light red wine—and yet it's dry and crisp like a white. White taste, red body, lovely acids for balance—sounds like a winner, right? Most important, underneath all of that is a hint of soil that gives the wine a firm foundation. And that, more than anything, is what gave all of the French wines a special quality:

~ Château Bellevue-la-Forêt 1997, Côtes du Frontonnais: "Dark and pretty. Melon nose, lots of fruit. Burnt orange color. Plenty of fruit, yet dry and steely."

~ Mas de Gourgonnier 1997 les Baux de Provence: "Dark and rich looking. Taste is crispy and steely, dry, but not fruity or sweet. Pleasant, but like cold steel."

~ Barton & Guestier Rosé d'Anjou 1996. "Pink and pink *tasting*. Very, very pleasant."

~ Château Pradeaux Bandol 1997: "Refreshing and dry."

The rosés from France had a special depth that indicated a wine with purpose. These are not simply cash cows, turned out to support the more "serious" wines that are a winemaker's real passion; these wines *are* these winemakers' passion, and it shows. In the U.S., winemakers base their reputations on great Chardonnays, Cabernet Sauvignons, or Pinot Noirs. They might make some pink wine, too, because it can be produced and sold quickly from whatever grapes happen to be around. But pink wine is not what their winery is about.

To some extent, it was the same seriousness of purpose that gave a handful of wines from other countries their class in our tasting. We were surprised and pleased that two of our favorites were from Italy—1997 Regaleali Tasca d'Almerita from Sicily and 1996 Castello di Ama Rosato Toscana from Tuscany. They lacked the depth of the better French wines, but they were delightful—the kind of wines made for gulping at the beach.

Rosés are meant to be drunk young and fresh. On the very first hot day of the year, run out, pick up a rosé, and drink up.

Wine Notes

When it's hot outside, a well-chilled rosé will hit the spot. While many American wineries make rosés, we found that French rosés have a special spirit and taste of the earth that make them more than just a cold drink. These are all meant to be drunk young, so buy the youngest you can find and drink it up. Don't hesitate to put a bottle in the refrigerator today so it will be ready when you need it on a hot day sometime soon. In any case, be sure to serve these well chilled.

Château Grande Cassagne 1997,
Costières de Nîmes, France   **$9.99**
GOOD/VERY GOOD • *Best of tasting. Dark orange, pretty. Smells like roses, tastes like melons, with a real, earthy backbone. This is real wine.*

Barton & Guestier Rosé d'Anjou 1996, Anjou, France   **$5.99**
GOOD • *Best value. Pure pink. Even tastes pink.*

Château Bellevue-la-Forêt 1997,
Côtes du Frontonnais, France   **$8.99**
GOOD/VERY GOOD • *Dark and pretty, with a melon nose. Lots of fruit, yet still dry and steely.*

Château Pradeaux 1997, Bandol, France   **$17.99**
GOOD/VERY GOOD • *Crisp and steely, refreshingly dry. Lots of acid, lots of earth. Nice food wine.*

Mas de Gourgonnier 1997, les Baux de Provence, France   **$11.99**
GOOD • *Crisp, dry, with more steel than fruit. Crackles with freshness.*

Regaleali 1997 Tasca d'Almerita, Rosato Sicilia, Italy $9.99
GOOD • *Salmon-colored. Simple and slightly sweet but totally winning.*

Sokol Blosser 1997 Vin Gris of Pinot Noir,
Willamette Valley, Oregon $9.99
GOOD • *A bit like a good White Zin, simple and spritzy. But clean, pleasant, and fun.*

Castello di Ama 1996, Rosato Toscana, Italy $9.99
GOOD • *So very easy to drink, so very nice. Pleasant as can be.*

Domaine Tempier 1997, Bandol, France $23.99
GOOD • *Smells like oranges, with real weight. Pleasant, but slightly harsh.*

Visiting Wineries
Twelve Steps to a Good Time

Visit a winery this weekend.

"Me? Visit a winery?" you may be thinking. "But I live in Missouri"—or Texas or Florida or Georgia. Truth is, there are wineries all over the country, and they're dying to greet you. How do you find them? Look in the Yellow Pages under "Wineries." You'll be surprised how many are listed.

Some people think wineries are intimidating, the kind of place where John Beresford Tipton, the stuffy gent in the '50s TV series *The Millionaire*, greets you with a bow tie, a vest, and an attitude. But we've visited hundreds of wineries—the last decade with kids in tow—and we've almost always had a great time. You wouldn't be nervous about visiting a pumpkin farm, right? Well, just think of a winery as a grape farm—and a grape farm that usually gives away free samples of its products, at that.

Here are twelve tips to make your visit more enjoyable:

1. Go early. It might seem odd to start drinking wine before noon, but the real point of your visit is to talk to the folks who make the stuff. That might not be possible later in the day when the place gets crowded.

2. Plan a picnic. Many wineries now have picnic tables. Having lunch surrounded by vines that produced the wine you've just bought is marvelous. (Wines, especially light whites, never taste better than they do straight from the cellar of the winery. Buy it, open it to have with your sandwiches, and—we guarantee this— the wine will be great.)

3. Don't be shy. If you drive up and there's no one else there, that's not a problem—it's an opportunity. You'll have a much better time. Many wineries have special bottles under the counter they don't pour for everybody; if it's crowded, they stay under the counter. If you're there all alone, you may get a sip.

4. Avoid crowds. If the parking lot is crowded or there's a bus outside, go to another winery nearby if you can. A crowded tasting room is no fun, trust us. On the North Fork of Long Island, there's a delightful little winery called Pugliese, where Pat Pugliese runs the tasting room and her husband, Ralph, makes the wine and often hangs out in the tasting room, too. Most days, we can sit for hours and talk with them. But on weekends, it's all they can do to count out change. When it's crowded, you'll never hear the story of why a bolt of lightning—literally, a bolt of lightning— convinced Ralph to plant Sangiovese.

5. Keep an open mind. Too many people walk into wineries and say, "I'd like to try your sweet wine," or "I only like Chardonnay." Relax. Experiment. When the person at the counter asks, "What would you like to try?" ask, "What do you recommend?" The person doing the pouring will likely suggest starting with dry whites and moving to reds, or say, "We're particularly proud of our..."

6. Do comparative tastings. You don't want to drink too much, of course, especially if you're driving. But this is a terrific opportunity to taste wines against each other. Tasting rooms often have, say, the regular Chardonnay and a special-reserve Chardonnay (usually the first is simpler, the second more complex because of more care and barrel aging). If there are two of you, ask to try a glass of each, and take a sip of each other's. You'll enjoy discovering the difference.

7. Be respectful. You wouldn't walk into an artist's studio and say, "I don't like that painting." Think of a winery as an artist's studio. The person behind the counter could well be the winemaker, the owner, or a member of the owner's family. If you don't like a wine, just pour it discreetly into the bucket on the counter. It's OK— that's what it's there for. But you should still be able to find something nice to say about at least one of the wines.

8. Show interest. Listen to what the pourer is saying and ask questions. If a wine smells like melons to you, say, "This has a really interesting melon nose." There's no right or wrong here. Just the fact that you smell or taste something interesting will likely be enough to get the pourer's attention, which might lead to a taste of that wine under the counter. Ask commonsense questions like the ones you would ask a strawberry farmer: "Where are you in the production cycle?" or "How many acres do you have?"

9. Don't pretend you're an expert. There are few things more obnoxious in a tasting room—in fact, anywhere—than a wine showoff. You're there to learn and have fun. If you do know something about wine, it will be clear from your enthusiasm.

10. Ask about wines sold only at the winery. Sometimes wineries make small amounts of special stuff they sell only in their tasting room. It'll be all the more special when you open it because it'll remind you of your visit.

11. Buy a bottle. You don't have to; we have left wineries without buying and have never gotten a dirty look. But it's a sweet gesture. And if you've had a nice talk with the winemaker or owner, ask him or her to sign the bottle. Signed bottles always taste especially good.

12. Finally, about kids: You really should think about taking your kids along, especially if the alternative is not to go at all. Children love farms, and wineries are grape farms. In all of our years, we've only run across one winery that said kids weren't welcome, and its wines weren't anything to write home about. Many more are smart enough to keep toys, books, or candy around, figuring that parents will stay longer—and buy more—if the kids are happy. But keep a close eye on your children. Farms can be dangerous places, and wineries are filled with breakables.

SPARKLING
WINE

AMERICAN SPARKLING WINES
Making Life a Celebration

CHAMPAGNE IS FOR CELEBRATIONS. But many people get it ass-backwards. They think that when they have some sort of celebration, they should drink Champagne. It's just the opposite: They should drink Champagne to *make* a celebration. And it doesn't have to be Champagne with a capital *C*, either—and we mean that quite literally. In fact, if you asked us about the best sparkling wines we've ever had, we'd tell you about some of the greatest wines of France (see page 245), but we'd also tell you this:

We always wanted to live in New York, and we finally got our chance in 1980. We lived in a one-bedroom off Central Park West and Seventy-second Street, with a little balcony overlooking the spot where John Lennon was shot. Columbus Avenue was the center of our universe. We were young, with no kids, and we would sit at outdoor cafés for hours watching beautiful Manhattanites go by. Back then, there was a restaurant on Columbus called the Rocking Horse that served huge portions of heavy, stick-to-your-ribs Mexican food and an even heavier, delicious sangria. One beautiful spring night, we sat at the Rocking Horse for hours, drinking sangria and generally feeling very lucky to be together in Manhattan. Across the street was—and still is—a little wine and liquor shop. That night it had a big sign in the window: "André Champagne. 2 for $3.99!" All night, we talked, we watched—and we saw that sign. So when we finally left the Rocking Horse, we couldn't resist: We bought a bottle of André, chilled.

Sparkling wine can be made in many ways, from very inexpensive to time-consuming, special handling for the very precious. Real Champagne is made with a great deal of attention to each bottle, with the second fermentation—the one that makes the bubbles—taking place inside the bottle under tremendous pressure. This is called "méthode champenoise." There's another way sparkling wine can be made. It's called the Charmat bulk process (named for its inventor, Eugene Charmat), and it's just what it sounds like: fermenting in great big tanks. This is why sparkling wines like André can be so inexpensive—cheap, bulk grapes made into cheap, bulk wine. However, on that perfect spring night, we took our bottle of André back to our apartment. There, on our balcony, seven stories up, we popped it open and drank it, watching the world go by. The wine was cold and fresh after the heavy Mexican food; the bubbles, forceful as they were, were comforting going down, and the weather was perfect. That night, no sparkling wine could possibly have been more delicious.

That's what we mean about champagne making a celebration. You can make that kind of celebration any night and you don't have to spend a fortune or settle for André. Here's why. Until about twenty-five years ago, there were generally two kinds of sparkling wine: cheap stuff from the U.S. and expensive stuff from France. When we were growing up, there was Korbel, of course, but it wasn't that fine. Schramsberg has been making fine sparkling wine since 1966, but not in large enough quantities that it was widely distributed. Aficionados prized it, but most of us were clueless about Schramsberg until Richard Nixon took it with him to China in 1972 and made Schramsberg famous.

In 1973 the Moët & Chandon people changed the world of American bubbly by opening Domaine Chandon in California. They began producing massive quantities of outstanding sparkling wine for a reasonable price—still usually between $12 and $16. Like a flash, others jumped in, from France and Spain, and homegrown wineries joined the rush. Now, you can find several excellent sparkling wines from

California without much searching and most will cost you about what you'd pay for a decent bottle of Chardonnay or Merlot.

Let's get this out of the way, OK? There is no American Champagne. Real Champagne is made only in the Champagne region of France and it's special for many reasons, including tradition and soil. All of the other stuff, from wherever, is sparkling wine. But look, although this really miffs the French, it isn't something you should lose any sleep over; life is too short. Can you imagine coming home and saying, "Honey, I got a promotion! Let's open a bottle of sparkling wine?" Of course not.

In any event, many of the best American "champagnes" have much in common with the real thing. Good American sparkling wine is made much the same way as Champagne: It's produced from Pinot Noir, Pinot Meunier, Chardonnay grapes, or a combination of them, and each bottle is carefully turned, tilted in a special contraption for weeks or months as the impurities flow toward the cork, to be popped out before final corking. "Brut" means dry and "extra dry" means a little sweeter (the same way a "medium" soft drink at a fast-food joint is actually the smallest).

One thing that often separates Champagne from champagne is the bubbles. In real Champagne, the bubbles and the taste are inextricably bound; Champagne wouldn't be the same as a still wine. But most American sparklers seem to have a taste aside from the bubbles. The bubbles are lovely to have, but they aren't as much a part of the wine's soul as they are in the real thing.

That said, though, America is producing some really fine stuff, in large quantities and at great prices. A blind tasting, in which we drank most of the widely available American sparklers under $20, proved our point. The overall quality is high. The wines were well made, fun, and tremendously drinkable. And later, tasted alone, not head-to-head, each was enjoyable. This is a wonderful time to be alive.

When we took off the bags, the best of tasting made us smile. One of the greatest pleasures of New York is Bobby Short, the elegant pianist who has entertained for years at the Cafe Carlyle. We first went to see Bobby Short in 1983 and the occasion seemed to call for bubbly. On the wine list was something we had never seen before: a Scharffenberger Brut 1981, from California. It was $30 and we still remember it as having class, charm, and real body.

It turns out it wasn't just the mood talking. The best of our blind tasting was a Scharffenberger, the 1991 Blanc de Blancs. The real surprise came next. Another bottle was a close second. "Nice, classy bubbles. Nutty, like the real thing. Some chalk, a little lemon on the finish. A glass of class. There's a real winemaker here." When we unveiled that bottle it was the regular bottling of Scharffenberger, which cost just $13.99.

Perhaps the bad news here—it's always impossible to tell—is that Scharffenberger has since been sold (it is now called Pacific Echo). In California and in France, wineries seem to change hands often. Sometimes new owners make wineries better; sometimes they don't. It's clear the new owners have a treasure to work with here.

But what about Chandon? It has been our house bubbly for years. We usually buy it on sale for $10.99 and always have a bottle in the fridge. We give them away to our doormen. We hand them to friends—just because. We love it so that when we tasted that outstanding Scharffenberger blind, our first notes were: "Clearly Chandon." But in fact, in our tasting, the Chandon was simply good, not one of the best. We were surprised, but such lessons are part of the journey.

The bottom line: Buy an American sparkler today, put it in the refrigerator tonight, and sometime soon, for no reason at all, open it up. It will make a bad day better and a good day a celebration. For just $15, that's a heck of a deal.

Wine Notes

American wineries are making mass quantities of fine sparkling wines for very reasonable prices. While regions all over the U.S. make sparkling wine, we've found that the best, dollar for dollar, are from California. Most of these are available everywhere. (Scharffenberger is now known as Pacific Echo.) Chill well and be very careful opening them (see page 235).

Scharffenberger Cellars 1991 Blanc de Blancs $17.49

VERY GOOD • *Best of tasting. Classy, clean, and festive, pretty much everything you want in a bubbly. The bubbles are too big and it's a tiny bit clumsy, but it's so alive in your mouth.*

Piper Sonoma Cellars Brut NV $9.99

GOOD/VERY GOOD • *Best value. Lovely nose, like real Champagne. Very fine bubbles. Flowery and lovely.*

Scharffenberger Cellars Brut NV $13.99

GOOD/VERY GOOD • *Elegant little bubbles in a nutty, classy sparkler. Some chalk and lemon. A glass of class.*

Domaine Carneros Brut 1992 $13.99

GOOD • *Simple, lemony, very bubbly—just plain fun.*

Mumm Cuvée Napa Brut Prestige NV $13.99

GOOD • *The bubbles are as big as beach balls, but the wine is citrusy and refreshing. It's well made, pleasant, and there's a lemony brightness that's hard to resist.*

Chandon (Anniversary Cuvée) NV $15.99

GOOD • *Pleasant and nutty, but a bit clumsy, with too much of every-thing. It even tastes slightly sweet.*

How to Open Champagne Without Killing Anybody

Opening a bottle of Champagne the right way is an art. Sure, it might be fun to pop it open and let the Champagne spray everywhere. This is especially fun if you've just won the World Series. But experts say that's a bad idea for the wine. It lets carbonation escape, they say, leaving you with a flatter wine. That may be true, but we think it's a bad idea for another reason: We're sure the cork will smack one of us in the eye and blind us.

In any event, we saw a movie once in which one of those very suave '40s characters in a tuxedo—probably William Holden—was explaining how to open a bottle of bubbly. "It shouldn't pop," he explained. "It should cough, apologetically." Always remember that: It should cough, apologetically.

This is how we do it. It might not be as elegant as some methods, but it always works and it's safe:

~ Take off the foil wrapping. This is just decorative, so there is nothing to be concerned about.

~ Get a kitchen towel, maybe one that's especially pretty, like Dottie's antique linens.

~ Drape the towel over the top of the bottle.

~ Put your hand under the towel and unscrew that metal retainer that holds down the cork. Lift it off. Be careful! This is when the cork could pop out on its own. This is why you have the towel draped over the bottle: The cork has nowhere to go.

~ If the cork hasn't popped out, take your hand out of the towel and grab the cork through the towel. Hold the cork firmly and slowly turn the bottle. Keep holding the cork down, with steady pressure. Remember that you don't want it to pop out.

~ When you start to feel the cork giving, let up the pressure just slightly to allow the cork to slowly push its way out. When you feel the cork just about ready to come out altogether, tilt it sideways slightly.

Right then, it will cough, apologetically. All of the bubbles will be saved, as will your eyes. And you can pretend you're William Holden.

How to Travel by Train

(This Is the Champagne Chapter)

PEOPLE SAY THE ROMANCE of the rails is dead. They're wrong. You can still have a remarkably romantic little vacation aboard an Amtrak train, although, as with all true romance, it's your responsibility to make the magic—and to bring the Champagne. We honeymooned on a train in 1979 with Taittinger Champagne and have been second-honeymooning on trains ever since. While many people think of trains, in principle, as romantic—remember Cary Grant and Eva Marie Saint in *North by Northwest*? (we would rank that steamy scene a Delicious!)—many people are convinced they need to pay a fortune for an Orient Express–type experience to travel back to the good old days of train travel. They don't.

We're not rough-it types, and we're here to tell you how to have a romantic getaway on Amtrak, in nine easy steps:

1. Get a route map. Don't let anyone plan your trip for you; travel agents generally don't know much about trains. Ditto for Amtrak's own agents. Besides, looking through the route map and deciphering the timetables, which are still wonderfully old-fashioned, is fun.

2. Decide where you want to go—not where you need to be. If you need to go to a wedding or to a business conference, take a plane. Trains can be unreliable; if you're going to worry about a schedule, this won't work for you. Part of the romance is that you don't have to be anywhere at any particular time. Best advice: Choose a route, not a destination. If this is your first time on a long-distance train, find a route that will keep you—allll aboarddd—for at least twenty-four hours, but not too much longer.

3. Get a deluxe bedroom—and get it well in advance. Make sure you ask for "deluxe bedroom," and do not settle for anything less, when you make reservations. Sleepers go fast, so nail down your reservation a.s.a.p.

4. Take four parcels on board with you. One should be a large suitcase filled with items that will be unnecessary aboard the train, like clothes. Store this in your room. The second bag should be a small suitcase with necessities: Champagne, glasses, two table settings, toiletries, and night clothes modest enough to be seen in by the porter, whom you'll tip when he brings you ice. Take 50 percent more Champagne than you can possibly imagine drinking. The third thing you must bring is an ice bucket, already packed with a bottle of Champagne on ice so that as soon as the train gets under way, you'll be ready. And the fourth—and this is critical—should be the greatest picnic you can arrange.

Finally, you're ready to board the train.

5. Tell the porter to put down the lower bed and leave it down throughout the trip. Your room will be small, but it has the essentials: Two beds (upper and lower), a toilet with a shower, a sink, and, in some newer trains, a video screen that shows current movies continuously.

6. Close the door. Put on your night clothes. Sit on the bed and gaze out the large window that runs the length of your compartment. Get your glasses. Open the Champagne. Drink it. Think about the fact that, from this moment until the trip is over, you *never have to get out of* *bed.* You have your Champagne, your ice bucket (the porter will bring more ice when you ring), and you already have your first meal. And, if you ask and tip nicely, the porter will usually bring to your bedroom all of your meals.

7. Don't worry about delays or other glitches on the trains. Just look out the window. Sitting there, glass in hand, consider some important questions: Is the trip nicer during the day, when you can see America spread out before you, or after dark, when the most humble home seems warm with its windows golden and bright?

8. Drift off to sleep together in the lower bed. The beds are about the size of a twin. Normally, that would be too small for two people, but the clickety-clack of the rails—honest, the train really goes clickety-clack—is hypnotic. Let the room get a little bit cold, bundle up, and watch things go by. Sunrise aboard a train is a wondrous event you don't really have to wake up to enjoy; just try to open your eyes long enough to see it. Then go back to sleep.

9. Don't let the porter put up the bed. He'll likely want to do that in the morning. Don't let him. About a half hour before you reach your destination, it'll be time to get dressed.

All of this, of course, begs the big question: What Champagne do you take with you? We decided to conduct a tasting to see what we would recommend.

In the previous chapter, we talked about "everyday" American sparklers. In the next chapter, we discuss those once-a-year, very expensive Champagnes. For a train trip, we would recommend the classic in-between bubbly: the widely available French nonvintage brut, like Moët, Mumm, and Piper-Heidsieck, that usually cost around $18 to $30.

Ultimately, your favorite Champagne may have everything to do with the memories associated with it, and less to do with how it actually tastes. Taittinger is "our" Champagne because we served it at our wedding and drank it on our honeymoon train. Nothing will ever change that. Maybe Moët is "your" Champagne. But, if you put our Taittinger and your Moët and all of the other well-known Champagne names against each other, what would you find?

For starters, Champagnes, like all wines, have their own style. Some are heavy, some are light, and some are in between. This is a function of the winemaker's taste, the blend (or "cuvée") of grapes selected (is there more Chardonnay, Pinot Noir, or Pinot Meunier in the blend?), and how long the wine sits on its sediment or "lees" before it is "disgorged." Disgorging is the process by which the sediment is removed and the bottle is topped off with a sugary mixture called the "dosage," then finally sealed for sale. The amount of sugar in the dosage determines the Champagne's sweetness or dryness. Champagnes with no sugar added in the dosage are rare and expensive; you will sometimes see them called something like "Brut Nature."

Nonvintage Champagne is blended year after year to ensure a consistent style. So any opinion about which is the "best" Champagne is inevitably also a statement about the style you prefer. But there are some more or less objective benchmarks: tiny bubbles and many of them; a complete bond between the taste of the bubbles and the taste of the wine (it shouldn't taste like a still wine with bubbles added later); enough acidity to make the wine come alive; and at least a little taste of chalky soil.

OK, so how were they?

One of the fun things about tasting wines in groups or "flights" of several bottles is that both flaws and perfection are more obvious in comparative tastings. These are all fine wines, but we were surprised that some of our longtime favorites seemed clunky and simple in a blind tasting. Our beloved Taittinger rated just OK/Good. "Very simple. Not a lot there. Pleasant, but seems inexpensive," we wrote, even though, going back to our point, we're sure that if we tasted this by itself, we would have liked it more.

Some of the best-known names went the way of the Taittinger. But many were much better and memorable, including our three favorites—a threesome that provided a bizarre footnote to our tasting.

About our third favorite, we wrote: "Lots of class, lots of taste. Cream, nuts, and yeast. Lovely and very much a winemaker's wine. For those who like 'heavier' Champagne." This tasted very expensive to us. We were shocked to discover it was plain old Piper-Heidsieck, available everywhere, and just $19.99 at that. This is a great deal.

But were we ever surprised when we took the bags off our co-favorites. Both were classy and excellent, but very different. One was bold and approachable, with a great deal of fruit and depth. It had an element of weight that made it feel good in our mouths. The other was the most beautiful to look at—perfect pale straw color, perfect bubbles, classy. The taste was restrained, austere, and chalky, the essence of what you think of when you think of really good Champagne.

One approachable and rich, the other austere and classy. Both wonderful. What were they? Incredibly, the first was Charles Heidsieck. The second turned out to be Heidsieck & Co. Monopole Blue Top. That's right: Our top three all had Heidsieck in the name. We told you the outcome was bizarre.

We looked up these wines and this is what we found: Florenz-Louis Heidsieck founded a great Champagne house, Heidsieck & Co., in Reims in 1785, with three nephews. After Florenz's death, one nephew stayed with the company; the other two nephews started their own separate Heidsieck houses. Today, Remy-Cointreau owns Piper-Heidsieck and Charles Heidsieck, which share a winemaker; and Vranken Monopole owns the original company, now called Heidsieck & Co. Monopole.

Does any of this mean we'll give up on our Taittinger? No way. It is still "our" Champagne. If we took a train trip tomorrow, we'd have the Taittinger first because—well, just because. And that's the best reason of all.

Wine Notes

Nonvintage Champagne—the real stuff, from the Champagne district of France—is widely available at prices from $18 to $30. Most of the names are well known, like Mumm and Moët, and it's hard to go wrong. "Brut" means dry, while "extra dry" means a little sweeter. All Champagnes should be well chilled. Champagne prices vary widely. When you see Champagnes on sale, it's a good idea to buy them since prices tend to rise when demand is high, like around holidays. Champagne keeps well, so buy a few extra bottles and put them in the bottom of your closet.

Heidsieck & Co. Monopole Blue Top Brut $23.99
VERY GOOD/DELICIOUS • *Best of tasting (tie). Absolutely gorgeous. Austere, chalky, and classy. Plenty of lemon and yeast and a real hint of age, which gives it some bearing.*

Charles Heidsieck Brut Réserve $21.99
VERY GOOD/DELICIOUS • *Best of tasting (tie). Lemony fruit, yeasty taste. A bigger, more approachable style than Heidsieck & Co., but just as classy. This is the real thing—and it tastes incredibly expensive.*

Piper-Heidsieck Brut $19.99
VERY GOOD • *Best value. Yeast and nuttiness on the nose, like a classy, expensive Champagne. Cream, nuts, and yeast combine into a big mouthful of bubbly. Big taste, for those who prefer a bigger-style sparkler.*

Laurent-Perrier Brut L.P. $29.99
VERY GOOD • *On the lighter side. Lovely and flowery, like a big bouquet of very fresh roses.*

Lanson Black Label Brut $18.99
VERY GOOD • *A very complex wine, with plenty going on in the glass: nuts, yeast, and flowers. This got better as it was open, making it all the more interesting. A lot of wine for the price.*

A. Charbaut et Fils Brut $17.99
GOOD/VERY GOOD • *Much simpler than those above, without much taste of soil, chalk, or yeast, but so clean and crisp that it made us smile.*

Perrier-Jouët Brut $22.99
GOOD • *Huge bubbles don't look very elegant. There's plenty of nice flavor, but the bubbles are just way too forceful, which makes this seem less classy than most.*

Moët et Chandon Brut $26.99
GOOD • *Not much nose at all, except for a tiny bit of lemon zest. Simple, without much there, but pleasant enough.*

Jacquesson Brut $21.99
GOOD • *Pleasant and flowery, but not special.*

Bollinger Brut $27.99
GOOD • *Nutty, classy, and rich on the nose. Very pretty. A pleasant, balanced taste, but on the simple side.*

Nicolas Feuillate Brut $19.99
GOOD • *Nice bubbles and many of them. But it's a bit too lemony and clumsy.*

Mumm's Cordon Rouge Brut   **$23.99**

GOOD • *Smells American—huge and citrusy. Light. Pleasant but not very classy.*

A. Drappier Brut   **$23.99**

GOOD • *Sweet and yeasty. Pleasant, but the bubbles are so forceful it's like it's been pumped up.*

FANCY CHAMPAGNE
Celebrate the New Millennium

A HUNDRED DOLLARS is a lot of money for a bottle of Champagne. But it's not that much money for an experience you'll remember forever. When you celebrate something truly special—a new millennium, say, or a new job—it's time to live out loud, and that's what "super-premium" Champagne is all about.

When Dorothy was very pregnant with our first daughter, some people told us about an old French custom that they thought we might want to emulate. To wish the newborn a happy life, they said, the French touch Champagne to the baby's lips as it emerges into the world. Now, we have no idea if this is truly an old French custom, but it sounded like a lovely, romantic gesture. And, hey, we're always, always game for those. So we dropped into Crown Liquors to visit our old friend Chip Cassidy—a painful place for Dottie to be, since she hadn't touched wine in months. We told Chip why we needed a special bottle of Champagne and he said, "Wait a minute." When he reappeared from a back room, he was holding a bottle of Salon le Mesnil 1979, a Champagne so precious that the entire state of Florida had been allocated just a few bottles. It cost a fortune, but we were going to buy it when Chip said, "It's my gift."

Just days later, at 4:00 A.M., Dottie went into labor five weeks before her due date. In a panic, we forgot to take her socks, her robe, and the back massager. But we remembered the Salon. After ten hours of labor, our child emerged into the world and, as she did, John dipped his finger into the Salon and touched the Champagne to her lips. "Hello, Media," we both said through our tears.

How much was that wine worth?

There are several very expensive Champagnes out there, many in only limited supply. The most famous, of course, is Dom Pérignon, named after the monk who was involved in early Champagne making. Perrier-Jouët's flower bottle and Cristal are popular, too. We decided it would be fun—and maybe even useful—to taste all of the best-known, special Champagnes against each other. So we bought eleven, all Brut (no rosé) and all expensive. The average price was $99.99. All of the wines were vintage except the Krug, whose best and most famous wine is its nonvintage "Grande Cuvée." Because Americans equate vintage-dating with excellence, Krug also offers vintage-dated Champagne, but connoisseurs all over the world know that the Grande Cuvée is truly special. When we had dinner in Piedmont with the Ceretto family, one of the great winemaking families of Italy, we were surprised they began the meal with Krug Grand Cuvée. "French?" we asked. Marcello Ceretto looked at us, furrowed his brow, and simply said, "Of course."

Remember, all of these wines are terrific, and most of them are special to us in their own way. There's not only the Salon that touched Media's lips, but the Taittinger that touched Zoë's, the Cristal John proposed over, the Dom with which we celebrated the twenty-fifth anniversary of the day we met. About the cost: These wines are expensive for a reason. In today's world, where so many things are expensive because of their cachet, these Champagnes are expensive because they cost a fortune to make. They're crafted from great grapes (Pinot Noir, Chardonnay, and/or Pinot Meunier) in a specific region (Champagne) and only in the best years. Each bottle requires years of personal attention. These are, after all, the prestige wines of great Champagne houses; it's important they be outstanding, and they are.

Our tasting was so special that we invited our friends Joanne Lipman and Tom Distler, and we all got dressed up. John and Tom even wore tuxedos. We bought pâté and caviar at Zabar's and, instead of our usual brown-paper bags, put each wine in a festive foil bag. The tasting was on.

One thing to keep in mind with all of these super-premium Champagnes is that each has its own style. Vintages change, but Champagne houses have distinctive styles. Some are light and even fruity, others are heavy. The winemakers can control the taste and heft of these special wines in many ways. They could decide to use more of one grape in a blend than another or keep the wine sitting on its sediment for a longer time before it's "disgorged."

Bollinger R.D. has always been one of the most interesting of the high-end stuff. The "R.D." stands for "recently disgorged," which means the wine was kept on its sediment for many years, longer than most Champagnes. This gives the Bollinger a heavy, very serious taste that's like a drum roll. We consider it a connoisseur's wine, something that engages the intellect. We immediately guessed No. 7 was the R.D.: "Lots of yeasty taste. Expensive. Classy. Heavy. Acid and lemon. Good with food."

But Joanne, who's not an experienced wine taster, had this to say about it: "It's a depressing kind of Champagne." At first, we were shocked by this, but we soon understood what she meant: While most people think of wine as a celebratory beverage, this is heavy and serious—and meant to be. Dottie recalled it was the wedding Champagne for Prince Charles and Princess Di. Hmmmm ...

In the long run, after tasting and retasting—gee, this was tough duty—the best of tasting finally emerged. Our difficulty at agreeing on which was best proved how very good each of these Champagnes was. There was not much separating them. But of our favorite we wrote: "Great, nutty nose. Classy Champagne. Just the right amount of acid, cream, and vanilla. Light, not heavy." This was the perfect wine for a celebration. As Tom said, it was "serious" enough for a special occasion—rich, creamy, nutty, and fine—and yet, at the same time, light enough to drink all the way past midnight. It turned out to be Pol Roger Cuvée Sir Winston Churchill 1986, which cost $89.99. It's a comparative bargain, probably because it isn't as well known as some others.

Because these special Champagnes are sometimes given as gifts, people often ask us if they can age. This is a matter of great debate in the wine community. Champagne makers will tell you their wines aren't meant to age, that they're released when they're ready to drink. And most experts will tell you flatly that Champagne doesn't get better with age. But we trust our palates, and we believe Champagne does get richer, nuttier, and fuller with time. We've found that even reasonably priced American sparklers seem to calm down and get a bit more flavorful with some cellaring. That said, there's no better time than tonight to open that special bottle that you have, and here's why:

Because we opened eleven bottles of great Champagne for only four people to drink in our special tasting, we obviously had gallons left over. And unlike other wines in our blind tastings, this wine was *not* going down the drain. So we gave the Louis Roederer Cristal to Joanne and Tom, put corks into the rest and put them in our refrigerator. Now, we're not advocating keeping bottles of fine Champagne in the refrigerator after you've opened them, but the fact is that each one of these was delicious for more than a week after we opened them. Sure, they lost some of their fizz, but they kept some; and sure, they weren't as fine, but they were mighty fine. Joanne discovered this, too.

One night, a full week after our tasting, Joanne and Tom and their two young children came home exhausted from a weekend away. Too tired to cook, Joanne ordered some spareribs from the takeout place around the corner. When they looked for something to drink with it, they discovered the Cristal, which they'd put in the back of the refrigerator and forgotten. Figuring it had long since gone flat, they decided they might as well drink it like 7-Up with the ribs. Their first surprise was that the cork popped; the wine was still sparkling! Then they tasted it. On its own, not going head to head with others, even a week later, it was remarkably delicious. "It was awesome," Joanne said later. "The Cristal seemed to have lost almost none of its fizz, and that Champagne was so damn good, the noisy kids and takeout food just didn't matter. The best greasy ribs we ever ate—and romantic, too. We actually lingered over dinner!"

How much is that worth?

Wine Notes

Behind the counter of your local wineshop are some very expensive Champagnes. They're expensive for a reason: Each required years of personal attention to some of the world's most precious grapes. Individually, all of the following Champagnes would be terrific, and almost every one is, in its own way, special to us. Don't worry too much about vintages. These wines aren't even produced in bad years, so it's hard to go wrong. They should be chilled well to bring all of their tastes into focus.

Pol Roger Cuvée Sir Winston Churchill 1986   **$89.99**

DELICIOUS • *Best of tasting and best value. Great, nutty nose. Classy, with just the right balance of acid and cream, and real hints of vanilla. This is a Champagne you could celebrate with all through the night.*

Veuve Clicquot Ponsardin La Grande Dame 1989   **$96.99**

VERY GOOD/DELICIOUS • *Fragrant and flowery, with enough chalk and yeast to give it some depth. Light, fruity, and completely winning. This may not be the "finest" Champagne, but it's hard to find one that's more charming.*

Moët et Chandon Cuvée Dom Pérignon 1990   **$108.99**

VERY GOOD/DELICIOUS • *Simply beautiful, and so very elegant. Dry, delicate, flowery, and fruity. Maybe not as easy to drink as the first two because there's more going on in the glass. Still, as Joanne Lipman said, it's "very Manhattan penthouse."*

Perrier-Jouët Fleur de Champagne 1990 — $69.99

GOOD/VERY GOOD · *Flowery nose and big bubbles. But elegant, restrained, and fine taste, with a hint of soil. Starker and more austere than others, truly fine, and even a little bit edgy.*

Krug Grande Cuvée NV — $105.99

GOOD · *Yeasty, creamy, and rich, but big and not very refined. This has just a little bit too much taste, making it seem a tad clumsy.*

Louis Roederer Cristal 1990 — $145.99

GOOD · *Looks more like Sprite than Champagne because it's so pale. A great deal of taste, with a long lemon/Chardonnay finish.*

Bollinger R.D. 1985 — $124.99

GOOD · *Yeasty and clearly expensive. A heavy wine that would be good with food. Joanne calls it "a depressing kind of Champagne" because it's so very serious. But that's also what makes it different and special.*

Billecart-Salmon Blanc de Blancs 1988 — $61.99

OK/GOOD · *Smells great, with sweet yeast. Clean, lemony, crisp, and nutty. But it's a bit watery, diminishing the tastes.*

Salon le Mesnil 1988 — $129.99

OK/GOOD · *Citrus tastes and more than enough acid. Overwhelming nose and taste of grapefruit.*

Taittinger Comtes de Champagne 1989   **$89.99**

OK • *This tasted sour, simple, and just OK, a big surprise for one of our favorites.*

How to Choose
the Perfect Glass for Wine

The experts will tell you that the traditional "Champagne glass" with the flat, wide bowl is all wrong for Champagne. The bubbles dissipate too quickly, the nose of the wine is hard to pick up, and the subtle tastes can get jumbled. A narrow flute is better, they say. Well, yeah, that's probably true. However...

On April 14, 1943, John's aunt gave his parents six Champagne glasses for a wedding present. They were traditional Champagne glasses with the big bowl that's supposedly shaped like Marie Antoinette's breasts, but they were more: light as air, elegant, delicately etched, with hollow stems. Incredibly, in the after-wedding hysteria at 915 West End Avenue in New York, they were thrown down the garbage chute with all of the wedding paper and gift boxes. John's parents spent their wedding night sorting through the garbage in the basement looking for them. Miraculously, only one of the six glasses had broken.

God, how John loved those glasses. Once a year, on Thanksgiving or New Year's, his father would fill them with the best bubbly he could afford, usually Korbel, from California. In those glasses, any wine was magical. As John's father poured, all three Brecher boys would put their chins on the table, their eyes fixed on the bottom of those thin, hollow tubes. There, like magic, bubbles would simply appear, from nowhere. Tiny as pinpoints, they would start—very slowly—wending their way up through the stem. Faster and faster they'd rise, until they exploded at the top. If you looked very closely, you could see little liquid fireworks all across the bowl of the glass. The exploding bubbles in the tiny space above the bowl could not have been more celebratory, like the Fourth of July.

By January 3, 1979, we'd already been living together for five years. Our parents knew it, although they would have preferred our not living in sin. For four years when we visited our parents, they put us in separate bedrooms. John's mother shocked us in the fifth year when she broke with that tradition, quietly hauling Dottie's luggage from the guest room into John's bedroom. John's parents loved Dorothy like the daughter they never had. John was the Gaiters' son. All in all, it didn't seem as though marriage could possibly improve things. But at home for Christmas, John finally decided that maybe if the wedding was very quiet and understated, it wouldn't ruin a wonderful relationship. "Mom and Dad," John said to his father in the recliner watching TV, his mother cooking a brisket, "I think I'm going to marry Dottie." Silence. Dad kept watching TV. Mom kept cooking the brisket. Finally, John said: "Well?" His mother said: "It's about time, don't you think?"

The next day, John's mother gave him those glasses to propose over. And he did. Now, once a year, we take out those glasses and tell our daughters the story about their grandparents' wedding night.

Forget the experts: There is not a more perfect Champagne glass in the world than those. All wineglasses have that capacity. The glass that makes the wine most special to you is the best glass. That said, there are some general guidelines we've found to be true about wineglasses:

~ The glasses need to have a stem—long, narrow, and delicate if possible. This allows you to hold the glass without warming the wine.

~ For red wines, the bigger the better, to a point. The glass should hold at least sixteen ounces and should taper in toward the top, to hold the nose in. (Of course, you don't want to put more than about *four* ounces in the glass. You want to give the wine—red or white—plenty of room to breathe.)

~ For white wines, a rounder bowl, wider at the bottom, which also tapers in at the top, is best. With whites, too, bigger is better than smaller, though white-wine glasses are often a bit smaller than red-wine glasses. The way a wine smells is an important part of how you experience it. A stingy, small bowl just doesn't allow enough of the nose to come through. A bowl that's too wide allows too much of the aroma to escape.

~ Forget fancy. Simple, uncolored glass is best.

~ Lighter, more delicate, thinner glasses help the wine show you its best. You taste wine, not glass.

~ Forget expensive. Wineglasses should be comfortable; they are, after all, just the vessel. If you spend too much on glasses, you'll worry about breaking them. Chances are, you then won't use them. What's the point? Buy glasses that are simple and inexpensive so that you can use them every day without worry.

~ And finally, yes, it is better to use a Champagne glass that's thin and elegant, without a big bowl. It captures the bubbles better and makes the bubbles explode into your mouth and onto your nose and tongue. But if a traditional "Champagne glass" like John's parents' makes the mood more celebratory, you can't get a better glass than that.

DESSERT
WINE

DESSERT WINES
Wait, Do NOT Turn the Page!

TIF YOU WERE AT OUR HOUSE for dinner tonight, this is what we'd do: After dinner was over and we'd moved to the living room, we'd pour everyone a small glass of dessert wine and bring it out, probably with some cashews (Squire's Choice, unsalted). "This is a dessert wine we like," we'd say, and if you're like most people, you'd say, "Thanks, but I don't like dessert wine." "Just try it," we'd say. Then, if you're like most of our guests, you'd take a sip and say something like, "Hey, this is pretty good"—and a few minutes later you'd be helping yourself to more.

We realize most people think they don't like dessert wine, and they offer plenty of reasons: (1) they're expensive; (2) they're so sweet they make my teeth hurt; (3) I don't have time to savor a wine after dinner—hell, I don't even have time to savor dinner; and (4) I can only drink a tiny bit of sweet wine and then what am I supposed to do with the rest of the bottle?

But stick with us here and we'll try to convince you to at least *try* a dessert wine, because (1) they don't have to be expensive; (2) good dessert wines can be light even though they're sweet; (3) a special dessert wine will make you feel you're savoring life even while doing the dishes; and (4) you can have a little glass every night for days, and the wine will keep just fine. In the long run, though, we believe one taste of a good dessert wine will do more to convince you than any number of reasoned arguments.

Verbatim, from our after-dinner notes, November 1983:

"At the American Harvest Restaurant during our weekend at the Vista Hotel in the World Trade Center, New York, we ordered the 1979 Raymond Cab ($22 and

too young to drink). Cellarmaster came over and we asked if he had anything special around. He talked about a few bottles, then said he'd tasted a Mondavi Sauvignon Blanc botrytis-affected wine at the winery, mentioned it months later to a winery person who asked, 'Would you like 12 bottles? This is made only for Robert Mondavi. It's never sold.' The cellarmaster said the botrytized Sauvignon Blanc had cost him $16 a bottle and he'd sell it to us for $32. If we wanted it, he said, we should tell him right away because he'd have to get a security guard to get it from a locked area and chill it.

"It was a half bottle, 1978, and it was spectacular. Nose was pure nectar, with every imaginable fruit. Bright gold. So incredibly rich that we took very small sips, then let it linger for several minutes; the half-bottle lasted forever. The amazing thing is that it was not thick at all; it smelled thick and from the nectarlike description you'd expect it, but it was clean and no less crisp than a fine wine that wasn't for dessert. Unbelievably clean; seemed to coat mouth with pure taste, not so much with thickness."

One problem, of course, is that any sweet wine can be called a "dessert wine" (not even to mention other fine things, like Port and Sherry). Some are made from super-ripe grapes, while others are "fortified" with sugar or spirits. Some are made from Sauvignon Blanc grapes, others Chenin Blanc or (at least in part) Sémillon. And they are made all over the world. For years, our house dessert wine was Muscat de Beaumes-de-Venise, Muscat des Papes, from France, which was nonvintage and cost about $8 for a full-size, strangely shaped bottle. This is the bottle we'd usually serve to our skeptical guests after dinner—and which they'd drain. We haven't seen that particular Muscat de Beaumes-de-Venise, which is from the Rhône Valley, in years, but there are many others.

We were staying at the New Otani Hotel in Los Angeles in 1986 and walked a few blocks to check out a Japanese market. There, just sitting on the shelf, was a remarkable bottle of California wine we'd never even heard of: Chateau St. Jean Sauvignon d'Or 1982, Select Late Harvest. It said on the label that it was 59 percent Sauvignon Blanc and 41 percent Sémillon, that the grapes were picked at 35.3 percent sugar and the wine was bottled with 12.8 percent residual sugar. It was bot-

tle No. 112. And it was just $14.98. What a deal! We schlepped it all the way home on Amtrak.

Over the years, we desperately tried to find out something, anything, about this wine. We dropped into Chateau St. Jean once, where they told us we'd confused this with a simple Sauvignon Blanc and we should drink it up. We even once met the winemaker whose signature was on the label, the famous Richard Arrowood, at a tasting in Miami, and he told us we couldn't possibly have a bottle of 1982 Sauvignon d'Or. And through it all, the wine, which started out golden in a clear bottle, got darker and darker, just like a Château d'Yquem, the greatest sweet wine in the world. Several times a year, we would take it out and just stare at it as the wine got deeper, darker, more concentrated.

We finally opened it. We are drinking it now, as we write this. Oh, God. It is deep brown, with a nose like burnt sugar. The taste is indescribable, like sugar cane syrup and peaches, still surrounded by dark, fertile soil—yet with no real mouthfeel and no real weight. It's just pure, sweet taste. A little like prune juice in the intensity of its mineral tastes, layered with flavors you would get from the juices of stewed peaches and plums. Smoky, frothy nectars. Nirvana.

The great sweet wines of Sauternes and Barsac, in France, are in a special category, and in their own chapter, which follows this. But they tend to be expensive and special. We wondered what would happen if we weren't choosy—if we simply cast our net wide and drank some dessert wines from all over the world. What would we recommend to you? To find out, we bought wines from all over the globe—from California, Canada, France, Italy, New York, even Hungary. Some were inexpensive, some were very expensive. Some were naturally sweet because the grapes were very ripe when picked. Keep this in mind: When grapes are picked, the sugar breaks down about half and half into alcohol (55 to 60 percent) and carbon dioxide (40 to 45 percent). So—and this is very simplified—if you pick a grape at about 24 percent sugar and ferment the wine until it's dry, you'll get a dry wine of maybe 12 percent alcohol. But if you want a sweeter wine that still has real alcohol, you must wait until the grapes get sweeter. This is fraught with risk,

though, because the longer you wait to pick your grapes, the greater
chance they'll be destroyed by insects or birds, who know a good thing
when they see it, or a freeze.

Under certain, very special conditions, grapes are attacked by a
naturally occurring fortuitous mold called *Botrytis cinerea*, or noble rot,
that shrivels the grapes, making them truly ugly, but concentrating
their sugar. From this concentrated juice, a small amount of luscious,
rich wine is made. Some of the wines we tried were made this way. Still
others were "ice wine," made from frozen grapes from which a tiny
amount of sweet juice escapes. And some of the wines were fortified,
which usually means they were blended with brandy to pump up the
taste and the alcohol content.

What did we learn? Well, we generally preferred the unadul-
terated wines, the natural ones. The taste was honest grape, sweet
fruit. The fortified wines were sometimes harsh and over-the-
top sweet, as though camouflaging the wine's inadequacies. Too
many tasted like sugar, not like sweet fruit—and there's a big
difference.

In general, we liked many of these wines, but they fell into three
categories:

1. Light and pleasant. The Moscato d'Asti wines from northern Italy, like La Spinetta Vigneto Biancospino Moscato d'Asti 1997
(Rivetti) and the Saracco Moscato d'Asti 1996, were spritzy, sunny, and
delightful. Sometimes low in alcohol, these are wines you could almost
gulp, but then you'd miss the playful way the wine bursts in your
mouth. They made us smile. They lacked the body we associate with
dessert wines, although their acids suggested they could stand up to
most fruits and cheeses. For our tastes, we liked these better as an
apéritif. They were welcoming and flirtatious, beckoning toward wonderful things to follow. Moscato d'Asti wines are generally very, very
pleasant and not expensive. If you see one—and it must be young—
grab it.

2. Mid-range and lovely. A good place to start a dessert-wine education is with the Muscat-based wines of Robert Pecota Winery in California. Muscat is a lovely, fragrant grape that tastes of orange blossoms. It can sometimes be used to make a heavy wine—such as the Muscat de Beaumes-de-Venise from France, none of which showed well in this tasting—and sometimes can be just great. The Pecota Muscats—the outstanding Moscato d'Andrea and the slightly heavier and sweeter Sweet Andrea—were excellent. These wines had everything going for them that the lighter wines had, but they also had a certain weight that was most satisfying. Not only did the color, the nose, and the taste please, but these wines felt good in our mouths. Seductive. They commanded attention. Don't ever say you don't like dessert wines again until you've tried one of these.

3. Heavier, like dessert. With each progression of weight, the wines became darker and richer. These are the wines we think of as classic "dessert wines," with the weight and stature to end a fine meal on a perfect note. Monbazillac from southwest France tastes much like Sauternes, but is cheaper because it's not as well known. The Seigneurs du Périgord Monbazillac we tried was creamy and rich, but a little on the young side. It was not quite in harmony with the alcohol in it, but it hinted of great potential with some age. The biggest eye-opener of the tasting was Tokaji Aszú, 6 Puttonyos 1993, Disznókö, from Hungary. Wow! It was full-throated and confident. Everything was accentuated—the nectar nose, the earth and spice, even the artful restraint that kept it from going over the top. You know how good chocolate dissipates in your mouth? This was like that. A creamy fullness that finished dry and lingering.

What in the world does "6 puttonyos" mean? The great wine writer Hugh Johnson, in his *Modern Encyclopedia of Wine,* says Tokaji (pronounced toh-KYE) is made by adding botrytis-affected or raisined grapes to the already fermented base wine. The mixture is then refermented, incorporating the shriveled grapes' sweetness. The amount of raisined grapes added to each barrel, and therefore the sweetness, "is conventionally measured in puttonyos—a puttonyo being a grape-carrying hod containing 20 to 25 kilograms. Three-, 4- and 5-puttonyos wines are the most usual; 6 is exceptional." Pretty cool, huh? Wine experts are increasingly excited about the great Tokaji wines coming out of Hungary. They are expensive, but worth every penny—and more. It's only a matter of time before they regain their long-ago fame, when they were a favorite of kings and czars. Move fast!

Some dessert wines are legendary for their long lives. The Moulin Touchais Anjou, a famous sweet wine made from Chenin Blanc grapes in the Loire Valley of France, is said to last forever. We remembered that when we saw the 1964 in a wine store in Dallas during a visit there in 1986. We paid $15 for it and let it sit for years. As it happened, we concluded this dessert wine tasting the night before the 1999 Super Bowl. Why not drink the Moulin Touchais all day Sunday while all manner of football stuff filled the airwaves? Our notes on this wine, then thirty-five years old, two years older than the Super Bowl itself:

"Brown, gold, red, looks like Scotch. Sherrylike on the nose, with earth and alcohol. Rich, earthy, hot on the finish, with sweetness yet lightness. Easy to drink. Baked peaches. So pretty and clean and crisp. Still vibrant, with many years ahead of it. The sugar is fundamental to the taste, like bubbles in Champagne. No harshness. Looks like liquid gold, the perfect weight and the nicest finish. A perfect mouthful. Delicious."

Wine Notes

Don't say you don't like dessert wines until you've tried some good ones. They should taste like sweet fruit, not like sugar. What follows is a list of suggestions from all over the world. If you see something on the label about the sugar, or "Brix," at harvest, that's usually a good sign, because the winery is telling you this is a wine made from superrich, sweet grapes. The label might also say something about "residual sugar." Buy lighter dessert wines, such as the Robert Pecota Muscats, as young as possible, but heavier dessert wines can last for many, many years. Chill all of these well. And don't worry about drinking one glass and leaving the rest corked in the refrigerator—the wine will be fine. For years, our house dessert wine was Muscat de Beaumes-de-Venise, from France, and while we didn't find any in this tasting that we'd recommend, it's still something you should try sometime to see for yourself. Many dessert wines come in half bottles.

Tokaji Aszú, 6 Puttonyos 1993,
Disznókö, Hungary   **$34.95 (500 ml. bottle)**
DELICIOUS • *Smells like nectar. Thick and spicy, sweet yet a bit light, with plenty going on—earth and oranges, apples, and pears. Long, sweet-earth finish makes everything come together.*

Robert Pecota Winery Moscato d'Andrea
Napa Valley Muscat Canelli 1997, California   **$11.00 (half bottle)**
DELICIOUS • *Lovely nose, like flowers and honey. Taste is light and a little spritzy, like just-picked grapes. So easy to drink, almost ephemeral. More of an apéritif. Drink young.*

Robert Pecota Winery, Sweet Andrea
Napa Valley Muscat Canelli 1997, California   **$16.00 (half bottle)**
VERY GOOD • *Heavier, a bit sweeter than the Moscato d'Andrea, with more of a peach taste. More of a classic dessert wine. This can age.*

Herzog Wine Cellars Johannisberg Riesling, Late Harvest, Monterey County 1994, California $9.99 (half bottle)

VERY GOOD • *Peaches and apricots and "sweet dirt" that finishes clean, light, refreshing, and happy. This is a real bargain.*

Seigneurs du Périgord 1996 Monbazillac, France $11.49

GOOD/VERY GOOD • *Young and pleasant, but with some real seriousness of purpose. This will be better in a few years, when it will get creamy and rich. Delightful now, with real potential for the future.*

Saracco Moscato d'Asti 1996, Italy $14.99

GOOD/VERY GOOD • *Bubbly and pleasant, with good acids and oomph. Vibrant, alive, and fun. Totally charming, but better as an apéritif.*

La Spinetta Vigneto Biancospino Moscato d'Asti 1997, Rivetti, Italy $9.99 (half bottle)

GOOD • *Bubbly, light, and very pleasant. Almost like fruit-flavored beer. Low alcohol (5.5 percent). More like an apéritif.*

Joseph Phelps Vineyards Eisrébe 1995, California $25.00 (half bottle)

GOOD • *Sweet, with a clean, fresh finish. Toasted almonds and burnt sugar. A little shy on fruit tastes, but pleasant.*

Inniskillin Wines Ice Wine (Vidal), Niagara Peninsula 1996, Canada $45.00 (half bottle)

GOOD • *One of Canada's most famous wines. Huge, spiced-peach nose. Big taste (Vidal grapes)—almost takes your breath away. A little spritzy. Loads of character, with some bite.*

**Muscat de St.-Jean-de-Minervois, Petit Grain, Les Vignerons
du val d'Orbieu (nonvintage), France**   **$12.00 (half bottle)**
GOOD • *Light, with peaches and earth. Soil leavens the sweetness. A
happy wine.*

How the Internet
Will Change the Wine World

We're certainly not the savviest high-tech couple around, and we're real rookies when it comes to the Internet. Our nine-year-old, Zoë, is much more competent than we are in this realm. But it's clear, even to us, that the Web is going to have a major impact on wine in the years to come. Consider this experience:

The only problem with a great wine list is that there's never enough time to study it so you can find the real hidden treasures. Our editor on this book, Harriet Bell, told us about a restaurant in Manhattan called Veritas that has a great wine list—and suggested we check out its website (http://www.veritas-nyc.com). There on the Web site was its entire, extensive wine list. We made reservations for that evening and then spent the afternoon studying the list (which made our afternoon at work much more pleasant). We ultimately decided on two almost-impossible-to-find wines: a unique Austrian white called Nigl Veltliner-Privat 1996 ($24) and a remarkable California "meritage" red wine, Moraga Bel Air 1993 ($95). We tried both of them—and more, since, at this restaurant, everyone was up and about, sharing wine with folks at other tables. It seemed natural, then, for us to trade glasses of wine with the Internet entrepreneur at the next table.

Now, consider for a minute what would happen if more and more restaurants put their wine lists online. People could compare lists—and, most beneficially, prices. There's power in information. Why does one restaurant have Sonoma-Cutrer for $58 when another has the same wine for $38? Is every wine considerably higher at that restaurant? Why might that be? You already know some restaurant wine lists are ripoffs. This way, you could tell, before wasting your money, which restaurants offered good values—and which did not. You also could scout rare wines that are rationed to restaurants and the few lucky souls on wineries' mailing lists—wines you would never find in stores. So before you took that trip to Chicago in two weeks, you could use what you've gleaned from lists on the Web to help you plan your meals. Some restaurants let you call ahead and reserve the wine, along with the table. Be sure to confirm the wine's availability the day before.

Similarly, more and more big wine stores are putting their entire inventory online, and are shipping to people who order on the Net where state laws allow that. Those lucky shoppers can cruise the Net looking for the best prices for that Flowers Chardonnay. Even if your state doesn't allow you to buy wines from out of state, though, imagine how neat it will be when you can see what wine stores all over the country charge for that 1995 Burgess Cabernet Sauvignon. Maybe you got a bargain. That's always good to know.

Again, we're not experts at the Internet. But here are some sites we've discovered that are fun, informative—and give you some sense of how the Internet will change wine buying.

~ www.winespectator.com. This is the Web site of *Wine Spectator* magazine. It includes all sorts of easy-to-access information, and it's free. There's even a database of thousands of wines—so next time you buy a bottle of wine, you can see what *Wine Spectator*'s tasters thought of it. (For an annual charge, you can access an even broader database.)

~ www.klwines.com. We have never ordered from K&L Wine Merchants, but we love looking at its extensive list of wines. It gives us an idea of what's available out there and how much it costs.

~ www.beringer.com. More and more wineries have information on the Web. When we wondered, for instance, about that great Beringer Sauvignon Blanc listed on page 20, we dialed up the Beringer site and discovered that after vinification was complete, the winemaker blended in some Sémillon. That was fascinating to know and confirmed what we thought we had tasted. (Another site, www.purplepages.com/wineries.htm, has a long list of winery links.)

~ www.WineToday.com. This is an awesome Web site run by the Santa Rosa, California, *Press Democrat,* which is owned by the New York Times Company. It has news, information, tasting notes—you name it—and it's free. It's also a good first stop on the Web, because you can link from there to just about anywhere, it seems.

~ www.virtualvin.com. Virtual Vineyards is a one-stop-shopping source for food, wine, wine reviews—and, again, checking how prices compare.

~ www.intowine.com. This is a fun site filled with wine information—and links to many wineries and wine publications.

~ www.aa.com. This is really cool. At the American Airlines site, you can see what kind of wine American is serving on its various flights, with reviews of the wines. Its *Vineyards in the Sky* also has links to many other wine sites, so it's a good place to check.

Again, there are thousands of sites out there. We don't know nearly enough of them to tell you which we think are the best. But these are a start. In the long run, we believe they're the leading edge of a whole new world of wine buying and discovery.

SAUTERNES
Because—Well, Because You Only Live Once

THIS IS NOT ONLY the last chapter of this book. It is also the chapter we researched and wrote last. What could we possibly drink to celebrate our last chapter? We thought long and hard about that, and we finally made the tough call: It was time to open the 1971 Château d'Yquem.

Château d'Yquem is the most remarkable wine in the world. In the famous Bordeaux Classification of 1855, d'Yquem was listed *above* the "first growths," as the only wine, either red or white, accorded status as "grand premier cru." There's a reason for this. Made from very carefully selected botrytis-affected grapes, and only in good years, this is as close as mortals get to a divine elixir. When we decided to have a baby, after being together for more than twelve years, we drank a bottle of Château d'Yquem 1970 to bless our first attempt. It didn't help—it took us five years, many good bottles of wine, and significant medical and truly divine intervention before we made Media—but the Yquem, our first, was in itself a miraculous experience.

We'd had dessert wines before then, of course, but never a fine, well-aged Sauternes. It was a revelation. The wine was rich, brown, and gorgeous. It was sweet and mouth-coating—and yet it had real backbone, a significant taste of earth and an actual lightness. As we wrote in our notes (which, yes, we wrote the next morning): "More like *wine* than *sweet* wine." We had never imagined it could have that kind of complexity: sweet yet light, rich yet restrained, bursting with ripe juice and yet full of earth.

This is what Sauternes is all about. Sauternes and Barsac, which are neighbors, make spectacular dessert wines, like no other wine on earth. In fact, earth—the clay and gravelly soil of the region—is key. Here the soil presents itself not so much in mineral tastes, but in leavening and infusing the fruity sweetness with a firm structure. Think of toasted almonds bathed in an intensely flavored but light nectar. These wines are not sweet and flabby, with flavors spilling all over the place. The earthy core and abundant alcohol—at least 13 percent—give these sweet flavors a certain discipline and lightness that translates, in marvelous years, as perfect-pitch delicious in your mouth.

Centuries of winemaking knowhow also show here in the careful management of the Sauvignon Blanc and Sémillon grapes that have been attacked by botrytis, or noble rot. An awesome amount of personal care, and a great deal of risk, goes into every bottle. The progression of the rot through the vineyard requires several harvesting trips as the grapes reach their optimum shriveled state at different times. The longer the grapes remain on the vines, the more vulnerable they are to destructive, nasty weather and hungry birds. We've read that it takes the grapes of an entire vine to produce just one glass of Yquem. Given all that expensive care, and the inherent difficulties of fermenting sweet wines, it's a wonder Sauternes don't cost even more. What's more, these are also the only wines that, though very expensive, are worth the money even if you never open them.

What do we mean by that? Well, consider that 1971 Château d'Yquem. We bought it in 1978 for just $30. Even in average years, Yquem can age gracefully just about forever, but in a fine year like 1971, it could last forever. So we just let it sit in our wine closet. Every couple of months, year after year, we would take it out and look at it. At first, the wine, which comes in a clear bottle, was bright yellow-gold. With each passing year, it got darker, richer, more gorgeous, more special. We tasted that wine hundreds of times—in our heads. Finally, to toast the beginning of this chapter, we took it to one of our favorite restaurants, Tabla, where they said we'd be welcome to linger over the bottle all night.

Let's start with the color. Imagine a big brick of solid gold sitting on a California beach as the sun sets over the Pacific. Imagine the interplay of the sunlight, the sand, and the gold. That's what the color was like. Gold, but with fiery red-orange highlights. The nose was earthy, like sweet, damp earth. Here are our notes on the taste:

"Taste is sweet yet ephemeral. A bit creamy, with nice fluffy mouthfeel. It's perfect. Peaches, plums, almonds. Finish is so pure, so clean. There's nothing like age. Burnt oranges, stewed peaches and plums. But it's not 'sweet' the way we usually think of it. It's *very* serious. It's majestic—truly the most majestic white wine we've ever tasted. Wow. It sort of dissolves into your flesh. It evaporates and leaves the essence of itself behind. You taste fruit, not sugar."

We tasted the wine before our dinner, then put it on ice. An hour later, we came back to it—and it had not lost anything, which indicates that, indeed, this wine has years and years ahead of it. We took home enough for one last glass each and waited three days to drink it, just wondering what we'd find. It was remarkable, one of the most incredible tastes of wine we've ever had: It was as if fresh, dark, sweet, rich soil itself had somehow been fermented into wine. We cannot imagine ever again in our lifetimes experiencing such a taste.

Once in your lifetime, you should try a Yquem. But, heaven knows, you don't have to start at the top. There are a number of fine Sauternes out there, often in half bottles. Where would be a good place to start? We conducted a tasting to find out. We bought dozens of Sauternes off the shelves of New York wineshops and tasted them over several nights. We found several from the great vintage of 1989, and many more that were much younger. Some came in half bottles and some in full bottles. All cost real money, but remember: You're not only paying for a great experience, but you can drink any of these wines over several nights, which should make the cost seem more reasonable.

Some of the wines were surprisingly harsh, especially in the finish. Our guess is that those—even some from the great vintage of 1989—

are just too young to drink. On the whole, though, they were out-standing, with a taste of soil, sweet-fruit flavors instead of sugar, and a clean, memorable finish that coated our mouths and throats. Some were flat-out voluptuous, like the Château Roumieu-Lacoste 1996. "Rich, creamy, and sensuous," we wrote. "Very nice, with some nut-meg, cream, and spice. It tastes like a very rich simmering spice!" Or the Château Rayne Vigneau 1990: "Creamy, rich, and fluffy—like egg whites." Others had more edge. And some just had it all. It was a tough choice, but our favorite turned out to be Château Doisy-Védrines 1995, which would be a perfect place to start your discovery of Sauternes. It was light and restrained, with pure peach and pear fla-vors, like a light nectar. It was a wine that, quite simply, no one could dislike. It cost $32.99 for a full bottle, which—trust us—is a huge bar-gain for what you get.

Take a chance. Run out and get a Sauternes. Put it in the refriger-ator and open it up after dinner—or take two glasses to bed.

Wine Notes

Sauternes is the great sweet wine from the Sauternes area of Bordeaux, in France. There aren't that many châteaux, so you won't be overwhelmed with choices. If you see "Grand Cru Classé in 1855" or "1ᵉʳ Cru," that's a good sign but, as always, no guarantee. The wines come in clear glass so you can see how beautiful they are—and so you can watch them slowly turn more deeply golden as they age. Sauternes just gets better and better as it gets older, so if you see an older bottle, grab it. But younger Sauternes has its charm, too, so don't worry too much about it. Some peo-ple pair Sauternes with very rich food like foie gras, but, personally, we prefer to drink it alone, or maybe with some very special cashew nuts. Feel free to drink a little, then cork the bottle and put it back in the refrigera-tor. It'll be fine. Our guess, though, is that you'll save less than you think you will.

Château Doisy-Védrines 1995   **$32.99**

DELICIOUS • *Best of tasting. Restrained and elegant, with all sorts of fruit flavors. Charming, clean, and lovely, with pure, sweet fruit tastes.*

Château Lafaurie-Peyraguey 1995   **$29.95**

DELICIOUS • *Best value. A shy, charming wine with hints of earth, alfalfa, white raisins, vanilla, and spice. There was a very gentle, masterful hand at work here.*

Château Roumieu-Lacoste 1996   **$19.99 (half bottle)**

VERY GOOD/DELICIOUS • *Rich, creamy, and sensuous, with some nutmeg, cream, and spice. Sweet with fruit. Wow.*

Château Rayne Vigneau 1990   **$45.00**

VERY GOOD/DELICIOUS • *Green-gold color with plenty of nose. This is a voluptuous wine, the one to drink by the fireplace with someone you love. It's creamy, rich, and fluffy, like egg whites.*

Château Coutet 1995   **$27.00 (half bottle)**

VERY GOOD • *It tastes like peaches and candy, but with some real backbone. Long, sweet-fruit—yet light—finish.*

Château Bastor-Lamontagne 1994   **$14.99 (half bottle)**

VERY GOOD • *Burnt sugar and pine needles—yet a lovely, dry finish that leaves hints of earth and grass. Beautifully made.*

Château Guiraud 1989   **$52.95**

VERY GOOD • *Luscious, with the taste of very ripe melons. Big and edgy. Real intensity, real taste—real class.*

Château Suduiraut 1989   **$27.95 (half bottle)**

GOOD • *It tastes golden, with all sorts of hints of peaches and pears. But it's a bit harsh at the end. Probably too young.*

Château Rieussec 1995   **$49.95**

GOOD • *This seems to have obvious acids, which make it knifelike. Not as charming as some, but better with food than most. We've liked this wine better in previous years.*

Château Rabaud-Promis 1989   **$30.00 (half bottle)**

GOOD • *Very sweet, without a hint of age. Plenty of sugar and fruit, but it's not showing a lot—yet.*

Want to Know More?
There Are Plenty of Good Books

A mystery book started us on our journey of wine discovery. No, not a book about a mystery. A mystery book. Just before John graduated from Columbia, a little envelope appeared in his mailbox, addressed to him, with a thin book inside: *The Signet Book of Wine: A Complete Introduction*, by Alexis Bespaloff. Since we'd grown up in homes without wine, John found this book a revelation. The first page said:

> Millions of people the world over drink wine as casually as
> we drink coffee or soda. Yet many Americans still assume that
> wine drinking is a complicated ritual, requiring specialized
> knowledge and elaborate equipment. Since all the equipment
> you really need is a corkscrew and a glass, serving wine at
> dinner should be as simple as pouring a glass of beer—and
> it's a lot more fun.

When Dottie met John just a few weeks later, he was already fascinated with wine, thanks to that book. But he hadn't actually had any. The actual going-out-and-buying-a-bottle-and-drinking-it came after we met, and this book served as our bible during those first years of experimenting. Still, for more than a decade, we had no idea how that book had come to land in John's mailbox until, at John's house one Christmas, his mother asked how we'd become interested in wine. When we told the story of that book, John's brother Jim burst out: "Didn't I ever tell you I sent you that book?" It turns out the book was some sort of gift Jim had gotten with a book order. Having no interest in wine, he'd sent the book to John and had always assumed a gift card had been sent along with it.

Since then, we've gone through dozens of books, some new and some old. We have some wonderful antique wine books, such as a 1928 edition of *The Wines of France* that talks about the vintage of 1858 as if it were only yesterday. But there are a few books we keep coming back to again and again. As we said in the introduction to this book, there are many books out there that go much deeper into every possible aspect of wine. There are books devoted exclusively to Burgundy, or to Italian wines, or to Bordeaux; books whose every page is about visiting California wineries. There's even an entire book about the Bordeaux Classification of 1855. If our book has whetted your appetite for greater and deeper knowledge, you'll enjoy buying more books. Here is a very short list of the books we keep coming back to. Some are out of print and hard to find, and there are surely equally good books out there we just haven't become familiar with. In addition, there are some other excellent books we've mentioned in earlier chapters. But these are "our" books, and we recommend them to you.

~ ***The Wines of America,*** by Leon D. Adams. This is a must-read for anyone serious about American wines. The information about "current" wineries is way out of date by now, but the significance of this book is how it traces the history of winemaking in America. This is where we learned, for instance, that the first American wines were made between 1562 and 1564 near the site of John's hometown of Jacksonville, Florida. McGraw-Hill says this is out of print after four editions, but some retailers might be able to find it for you. (Also, for this book and the others listed here, you might try Amazon.com and Barnesandnoble.com.)

~ ***Frank Schoonmaker's Encyclopedia of Wine.*** This is the classic alphabetical explanation of the world of wine. Once again, much of what's in it isn't current, but it is elegantly written, simply presented, and very useful. It even has pronunciations ("Pauillac. Paw-yack"). The most recent version, ***The New Frank Schoonmaker Encyclopedia of Wine,*** was updated in 1988 by Alexis Bespaloff.

(Mr. Schoonmaker died in 1976.) William Morrow & Co. says the 1988 edition is in print and lists at $25.

~ *The World Atlas of Wine,* by Hugh Johnson. We love this book. In fact, we've used it so much that it literally has fallen apart. It's fun to buy a bottle and run back to Johnson to see exactly where it came from. ("Look! It's right next to Latour!") The maps and easy-to-follow text present a concise world view of wine that gives every bottle a home and makes it seem more special. *Hugh Johnson's Modern Encyclopedia of Wine,* at $40, is also good. (List price for the recently updated edition of *The World Atlas of Wine* is $50, Simon & Schuster.)

~ *The Great Vintage Wine Book,* by Michael Broadbent. There are many books that rank long lists of wines by vintage. But those lists get dated quickly and they're certainly not much fun to read. What makes Broadbent special is the language. He writes about his own tasting experiences, year by year, with a wit and poetry that are fun to read even if you'll never see the wine he's writing about. Here's an expert on wine who actually enjoys drinking it. Every wine lover should own Mr. Broadbent's book, if only to know how a real wine lover "talks wine." The latest update is called *The New Great Vintage Wine Book.* List price is $45. Knopf says it no longer has this book in stock, but retailers may have it.

~ *The Simon & Schuster Pocket Guide to Champagne and Sparkling Wines,* by Jane MacQuitty, $7.95; *The Simon & Schuster Pocket Guide to Italian Wines,* by Burton Anderson, $11.95; and *The Simon & Schuster Pocket Guide to the Wines of Bordeaux,* by David Peppercorn, $7.95. It's amazing, but these tiny little books, with tiny little type, pack an awesome amount of information. No muss, no fuss, just straightforward, useful information on producers, vintages, and regions. We planned an entire trip to Italy based on the Anderson book. All three of these are out of print, the publisher says, but all of the authors have written more recent wine books that might be worth a look.

~ **The Connoisseurs' Handbook of the Wines of California and the Pacific Northwest,** by Norman S. Roby and Charles E. Olken. It's hard to find tough, objective criticism of American wineries. That's why we always turn to this book. It's concise, credible, and comprehensive. This remains an essential source of information for us, and it was recently updated. It's a paperback from Knopf for $19.95.

ACKNOWLEDGMENTS

Over the years, many people have helped us learn about wine. A number of them are mentioned throughout this book. But there are a few people without whom this book, quite literally, never would have happened:

~ Paul Steiger, the managing editor of the *Wall Street Journal*, the best boss anyone could hope to have, who has been consistently supportive of our careers, our column, and this book;

~ Joanne Lipman, the editor of *Weekend Journal*, who asked us to write a wine column and then beat us to a pulp until we got it just right;

~ Bill Shinker, who as president and publisher of Broadway Books, saw the potential for a book long before we did;

~ Amanda Urban, our agent at IMC, who made us believe we could do this;

~ Harriet Bell, our editor at Broadway Books, whose combination of maternal care and editorial rigor made the book work;

~ Our daughters, Media and Zoë, who have always been patient with us, and never more so than during the production of this book;

~ And our parents, Worrell and Dorothy E. Gaiter, and Ben and Ruth Brecher, who taught us nothing about wine, but everything about love and passion and, by example, what marriage is all about.

INDEX